Lecture Notes in Computer Science 7061

Commenced Publication in 1973
Founding and Former Series Editors:
Gerhard Goos, Juris Hartmanis, and Jan van Leeuwen

Editorial Board

Bruce Christianson   James Malcolm (Eds.)

Security
Protocols XVIII

18th International Workshop
Cambridge, UK, March 24-26, 2010
Revised Selected Papers

 Springer

Volume Editors

Bruce Christianson
James Malcolm
University of Hertfordshire
Hatfield, Hertfordshire, AL10 9AB, UK
E-mail: {b.christianson, j.a.malcolm}@herts.ac.uk

ISSN 0302-9743   e-ISSN 1611-3349
ISBN 978-3-662-45920-1   e-ISBN 978-3-662-45921-8
DOI 10.1007/978-3-662-45921-8
Springer Heidelberg New York Dordrecht London

Library of Congress Control Number: 2014956746

LNCS Sublibrary: SL 4 – Security and Cryptology

Typesetting: Camera-ready by author, data conversion by Scientific Publishing Services, Chennai, India

Printed on acid-free paper

Springer is part of Springer Science+Business Media (www.springer.com)

Preface

Welcome to the proceedings of the 18th International Security Protocols Workshop (that's XVIII in Roman numerals). Our theme this year was "Virtually Perfect Security" where we attempted to weave together several different strands; you can judge how the tapestry has turned out.

We hope you find the discussions thought-provoking. Perhaps you may spot a loose end which will inspire your own research and lead to a submission to a future protocols workshop. To be invited to the Security Protocols Workshop, your preliminary submission must be assessed as "interesting." If you wish to be considered for invitation to a future workshop, please contact the editors.

As usual, our thanks to Sidney Sussex College for the use of their facilities, to Lori Klimaszewska of the University of Cambridge Computing Service for making the initial transcription of the audio tapes, and to Michael Roe, Vashek Matyas, and Frank Stajano for acting as members of the Program Committee.

November 2014

Bruce Christianson
James Malcolm

Previous Proceedings in This Series

The proceedings of previous International Workshops on Security Protocols have also been published by Springer as *Lecture Notes in Computer Science*, and are occasionally referred to in the text:

17th Workshop (2009), LNCS 7028, ISBN 978-3-642-36212-5
16th Workshop (2008), LNCS 6615, ISBN 978-3-642-22136-1
15th Workshop (2007), LNCS 5964, ISBN 978-3-642-17772-9
14th Workshop (2006), LNCS 5087, ISBN 978-3-642-04903-3
13th Workshop (2005), LNCS 4631, ISBN 3-540-77155-7
12th Workshop (2004), LNCS 3957, ISBN 3-540-40925-4
11th Workshop (2003), LNCS 3364, ISBN 3-540-28389-7
10th Workshop (2002), LNCS 2845, ISBN 3-540-20830-5
9th Workshop (2001), LNCS 2467, ISBN 3-540-44263-4
8th Workshop (2000), LNCS 2133, ISBN 3-540-42566-7
7th Workshop (1999), LNCS 1796, ISBN 3-540-67381-4
6th Workshop (1998), LNCS 1550, ISBN 3-540-65663-4
5th Workshop (1997), LNCS 1361, ISBN 3-540-64040-1
4th Workshop (1996), LNCS 1189, ISBN 3-540-63494-5

Table of Contents

Introduction: Virtually Perfect Security (Transcript of Discussion) . . . . .　1
　Bruce Christianson

Caught in the Maze of Security Standards. . . . .　3
　Jan Meier and Dieter Gollmann

Caught in the Maze of Security Standards (Transcript of Discussion) . . .　4
　Dieter Gollmann

Blood in the Water: Are There Honeymoon Effects Outside
Software? . . . .　12
　Sandy Clark, Matt Blaze, and Jonathan Smith

Blood in the Water (Transcript of Discussion) . . . .　18
　Sandy Clark

Digital Immolation: New Directions for Online Protest. . . . .　25
　Joseph Bonneau

Digital Immolation (Transcript of Discussion) . . . .　34
　Joseph Bonneau

Relay-Proof Channels Using UWB Lasers . . . .　45
　Bruce Christianson, Alex Shafarenko, Frank Stajano,
　and Ford Long Wong

Relay-Proof Channels Using UWB Lasers (Transcript of Discussion). . . .　47
　Alex Shafarenko

Using Dust Clouds to Enhance Anonymous Communication . . . .　54
　Richard Mortier, Anil Madhavapeddy, Theodore Hong,
　Derek Murray, and Malte Schwarzkopf

Using Dust Clouds to Enhance Anonymous Communication
(Transcript of Discussion) . . . .　60
　Malte Schwarzkopf

Generating Channel Ids in Virtual World Operating Systems
(Extended Abstract) . . . .　71
　Michael Roe

Generating Channel Ids in Virtual World Operating Systems
(Transcript of Discussion) 74
  George Danezis

Censorship-Resilient Communications through Information
Scattering 82
  Stefano Ortolani, Mauro Conti, and Bruno Crispo

Censorship-Resilient Communications through Information Scattering
(Transcript of Discussion) 90
  Mauro Conti

On Storing Private Keys in the Cloud 98
  Jonathan Anderson and Frank Stajano

On Storing Private Keys in the Cloud (Transcript of Discussion) 107
  Jonathan Anderson

More Security or Less Insecurity 115
  Partha Das Chowdhury and Bruce Christianson

More Security or Less Insecurity (Transcript of Discussion) 120
  Bruce Christianson

It's the Anthropology, Stupid! 127
  Ross Anderson and Frank Stajano

It's the Anthropology, Stupid! (Transcript of Discussion) 131
  Ross Anderson

Security Design in Human Computation Games 142
  Su-Yang Yu and Jeff Yan

Security Design in Human Computation Games
(Transcript of Discussion) 154
  Jeff Yan

Virtually Perfect Democracy 161
  Giampaolo Bella, Peter Y.A. Ryan, and Vanessa Teague

Virtually Perfect Democracy (Transcript of Discussion) 167
  Peter Y.A. Ryan

Security Protocols for Secret Santa 175
  Sjouke Mauw, Saša Radomirović, and Peter Y.A. Ryan

Security Protocols for Secret Santa (Transcript of Discussion) 185
  Sjouke Mauw

Censorship of eBooks (Extended Abstract) 191
  Michael Roe

Censorship of eBooks (Transcript of Discussion) 200
    Michael Roe

On the Value of Hybrid Security Testing 207
    Saad Aloteibi and Frank Stajano

On the Value of Hybrid Security Testing (Transcript of Discussion)..... 214
    Saad Aloteibi

Security Made, Not Perfect, But Automatic 217
    Paulo Verissimo

Security Made, Not Perfect, But Automatic
(Transcript of Discussion) 224
    Paulo Verissimo

Security Limitations of Virtualization and How to Overcome Them..... 233
    Virgil Gligor

Security Limitations of Virtualization and How to Overcome Them
(Transcript of Discussion) 252
    Virgil Gligor

Recapitulation 266
    Bruce Christianson

Author Index 267

Introduction: Virtually Perfect Security
(Transcript of Discussion)

Bruce Christianson

University of Hertfordshire

Hello everyone, and welcome to the 18th Security Protocols Workshop. Our theme this year is "Virtually Perfect Security", which is an attempt to tie together three slightly different interlocking strands. The first is the fact that although we talk about security as if it were some sort of metaphysical property (so that a system is either secure or isn't), we all know that really whether a system is secure or not depends on the context which you put it, and you can move a system to a different context and change whether it's secure or not. In practice, we also usually prove security relative to a particular abstraction, and the danger is that we have a system that "really" is secure, and then we discover that the attacker is using a different abstraction. Our attempt to find abstractions which the attacker can't fool with this trick with has pushed us into talking about security using abstractions that are further and further away from anything that a user might think of as comprehensible or convenient.

This brings me to the second strand. We're very used to pieces of hardware or software not providing us with the abstraction we want. The basic service provided by a micro-processor is pretty useless to an application programmer, the service provided by a low level network interface is not very useful to anybody doing systems programming, and the solution that we use is usually the same: we build up a series of virtual machines. So long as you keep one eye on the price/performance ratio, you're generally OK. I've said on many occasions in the past that you can think of computer science as a branch of pure mathematics in which the homomorphisms cost money. As soon as we try to use this approach in security protocols we discover that they don't layer well at all, but we keep trying to do it largely because it's the only trick we have. So we build an authentication protocol, and we try to build other security services on top of that, and then somebody else comes along and puts some middle-ware in, and we have to go back and do it all again. It seems there's something about the nature of the abstractions that we're using for security that we really don't understand (or that we're just not allowing for) when we try to layer.

The third strand is that there still seems to be some hope of knowing whether we've got it right or not when all the endpoints have at least one foot in the real world. But increasingly we have situations where one of the parties in the protocol exists entirely in cyberspace. Second Life is an obvious example of this kind of situation, but a potentially more worrying one is applications like e-Science, where you're doing an experiment, the experiment is entirely in cyberspace, and the reason you're doing it is because you don't know what the correct outcome ought to be. Thinking about the potential security implications of projects like this is really quite unsettling.

B. Christianson and J. Malcolm (Eds.): Security Protocols 2010, LNCS 7061, pp. 1–2, 2014.

There has been some work in the past looking at the extent to which an attacker (or a legitimate participant) can find out which virtual machine they're running on. Attackers, for instance, would quite like to know whether or not they have been sand-boxed. David Deutsch has made a very good argument in one of his books[1] that says that the universe is in fact a simulation running on an anonymous computer, and he has an experimental programme that he believes will prove this; there's a counter-argument in some of the early works of Hilary Putnam[2] but personally I regard the last word on the subject as the second of the "Ghost in the Shell" movies[3]. The question is, does having a presence in the real world give the attacker an advantage, or is it actually a handicap?

The intention as always is that this should be a workshop and not a conference, so expect to be interrupted. Conversely if you are interrupted, feel free to depart from whatever it is you planned to stay when you stood up, and if the interruption gives the urge to go off on a tangent, please do so. In the interests of spontaneity and unexpectedness, we've already changed the programme, so please make sure you pick up the new running order.

---

[1] David Deutsch, "The Fabric of Reality", Penguin, 1997.
[2] Hilary Putnam, "Brains in a a Vat", pp 1–21 in "Reason, truth and history", Cambridge University Press, Cambridge, 1981.
[3] See http://en.wikipedia.org/wiki/Ghost_in_the_Shell_2:_Innocence

Caught in the Maze of Security Standards

Jan Meier and Dieter Gollmann

Hamburg University of Technology
Harburger Schloßstr. 20 (HS20), 1st floor, room 123
Hamburg, 21079 Germany
diego@tu-harburg.de

Abstract. We analyze the interactions between several national and international standards for smart card based applications, noting deficiencies in those standards, or at least deficiencies in the documentation of their dependencies. We show that currently smart card protocols are specified in a way that standard compliant protocol implementations may be vulnerable to attacks. We further show that attempts to upgrade security by increasing the length of cryptographic keys may fail when message formats in protocols are not re-examined at the same time[1].

---

[1] A full version of this paper appears in LNCS 6345 — ESORICS 2010, pages 441–454.

B. Christianson and J. Malcolm (Eds.): Security Protocols 2010, LNCS 7061, p. 3, 2014.
© Springer-Verlag Berlin Heidelberg 2014

Caught in the Maze of Security Standards
(Transcript of Discussion)

Dieter Gollmann

Hamburg University of Technology

In the spirit of the workshop, this will be a talk on work in progress, or maybe more precisely, work that has started, and we have yet to see where it is going to take us to.

It will be a talk about security protocols, but not a talk about why the design of security protocols is difficult; that's rubbish, it's not difficult, it's fairly easy if you know what to do[1]. If you insist to do it when you don't know what you're doing, then you might see the customary mistakes.

The talk will also be about standards, and it's again true that you will find standards bodies that adopt protocols that contain no flaws, but it is sometimes the case that people who don't know about security are urged to do it anyway.

So this talk will contain observations about what we did for a German e-Card project. In terms of the workshop agenda, and the general research agenda in security, it is about the interaction between the various standards that come up in a project like that. All e-Card projects, be it electronic identity cards, electronic passwords, electronic camera cards, are linked in a politically charged environment. So the excuse: it's not really an attack, it's a certification weakness, doesn't count. The people who want to fight projects like that will be very happy if they can build even on bad foundations, if they want to discredit some particular scheme.

I have followed the Orange Book in using the terms accreditation, certification and evaluation. With such an e-Card project, or even with bank cards, somebody has to make a decision, we will go and play. This is an executive decision, it is a political decision, it is a management decision, so we can safely assume it will be a decision by people who won't understand a lot of the technical argument, or understand even security proofs in some model. In these applications, in particular these Smart-card based applications, there is a market for different measures, therefore there ought to be a process whereby there can be official statements saying, this card can be used for this application, it meets the stated requirements including the stated security requirements. In the Orange Book world this state is called certification. And then there is a technical analysis of the project, of the product, and that would be evaluation. The question is, I'm still looking for answers, how are these three steps, these processes, coordinated. And if you look at the way security requirements are specified you will find that they're using the same words; authentication is one of my favourites because it means different things to different people.

---

[1] But see Mauw, these proceedings.

B. Christianson and J. Malcolm (Eds.): Security Protocols 2010, LNCS 7061, pp. 4–11, 2014.

So how can we be sure that when people working on these different steps talk about security they're talking about the same thing? Again it goes into different levels of abstraction, and different views of the system. And my case study is security protocols, as it's a protocols workshop I assume everybody knows what I'm talking about. One point I should mention is that RSA will disappear from the NSA list of recommended algorithms, the key length is simply getting too large, they will move to Elliptic Curve cryptography. So algorithms, recommendations key length, there has to be a process that keeps updating these recommendations.

The simplified view of the world we found, here is my e-Card application space. There exist common criteria protection protocols. I would guess double figures if you go into the common criteria protection, some in English, some in German. It's a government project so the government insists the German version is sufficient. In the context of the German security scene, BSI[2] are the official crypto experts that tell you which key length, which algorithms, are permissible in those applications.

Audience: Just a question about the timing of this, so if I follow these recommendations and I build a Smart-card, I deploy it to millions of users, and five years pass and the recommendations change, whose responsibility is it to figure out how to evolve the long tail of deployed technology?

Reply: I think that is fortunately one of the easier answers. You have an ordered migration process, and I guess the banks will tell you they have experience with this, and I would grant that they have experience with this roll-over too.

Audience: That is so for replacement, but we had this problem in Xen where it's embedded very deeply in systems, so you never see the stuff again right, so there's no alternative, you've got to push that secure responsibility all the way to somebody who doesn't care about security.

Reply: Remind me to mention this again when I get to my slide on protection protocols.

George Danezis: A lot of security management standards are really about management, and it would be really surprising if they don't actually include components about how you update the technical things. Do you have experience with those as well, because I don't see the usual security management standards on the board.

Reply: In the security analysis we looked at one small part of the overall IT infrastructure. There was a different group that looked at the management standards, and it's something that does not exist yet. Whether this really will work in an application that involves this kind of context; it's a lot of small enterprises, not banks with branches and hierarchical structure, but very independent small enterprises, who prize their independence and don't want to be told by anybody what they ought to do, so they're the experts in their fields. You get the interesting issue that you certainly tell them, you're not security managers, you're assumed to do all this fancy roll-over stuff in your systems.

---

[2] Bundesamt für Sicherheit in der Informationstechnik.

The technical guidance document for the project is a catalogue of crypto-graphic algorithms, required key lengths, regularly updated. It does not specify protocols; they are pure cryptographers. They do not specify security require-ments on protocols. What they do is they place pointers to other documents — you can go to the website of BSI and get the technical guidance documents, some even in English.

Then there is the next standard. It's the Smart-card standard. And when we were talking to people involved in the project, they were using true functional specifications. What they meant was by and large interface specification to a Smart-card, which commands it should accept, how it should react to certain commands. The argument why there is such a strong focus on interface speci-fication, different vendors might want to do things differently internally in the company, which is a valid argument. Given that it's an interface standard, you have to explain how a message will track, you have to explain how long keys are, you have to explain which cryptographic algorithms you support. On occasion you will find internal checks, but by and large internal checks that should be performed with a card are not within the scope of this community, they don't like it for a good reason, it's not something that they built, that's left to the card designer. This is the ISO standard for Smart-cards which defines also the interfaces, technical communications protocols, and all of the command sets you can send to a Smart-card. I have not found any precise security requirements for protocols. This is a mutual authentication protocol, but what do we expect from a mutual authentication protocol, they will not tell you.

Then there is ISO 9798 entity authentication protocols. I know a lot of the people on this committee, they are academics to a large extent, they give me very nice explanations about the security properties, and if one follows this direction further you will get into cryptography with key extension and key transport, key agreement, key confirmation, and . . . so I thought long and hard about the different aspects of the implementation. How do they define protocols as a generic flow of messages? What they will tell you is, which feeds there should be in it, they will not tell you how long the key is, they will not tell you which algorithm to use, that is part of our developments. There was useful advice on when should certain option feeds be used. And finally there are common criteria protection protocols. Within this they define security requirements for certain application classes. I've mentioned quite a number of profiles for e-Cards. When we look at the security requirements there we want confidentiality and integrity. You can't be more specific. And again, I have looked at some of those profiles, I did not find precise security requirements on authentication protocols, that could relate to what I've just told you about ISO 9798.

Now on the one hand it's a very reasonable approach, the application experts do not invent their own security, their own cryptography, they pick protocols from standards. And it's also in principle reasonable, we shout this all the time, don't invent your own crypto algorithms, don't invent your own security proto-cols, don't implement these algorithm protocols yourself, you will get it wrong if you don't know what you're doing. So if they follow this route, they do what we tell them, but where does it lead?

Questions we were left looking at after this analysis, and it was in the context of this evaluation fairly difficult to define where the security requirements or the application were actually specified. Everybody knew security was important. You would find remarks about confidentiality, integrity, viability, authenticity, but you would not find more precise, more concrete specifications that would allow you to link these. And this question will be very important in the context of the stories I am now going to tell.

The first example is the simple two pass challenge response authentication protocol from ISO 9798, based on symmetric cryptography encryption. You have B sending a random challenge to A, A encrypts it with the shared secret key and sends it back, and there are lots of options you might or might not deduce. And there is in particular this remark about why B is identified to detect certain attacks. So if you come from that angle, you know about reflection attacks, you know if this is an issue to look out for. First of the issues we ran into. In one of the Smart-card protocols used in this project, the technical recommendation says use triple DES. The protocol from a different standard says, this is a 64-bit challenge, which is reasonable, and the standard also says, use triple DES, CBC mode, fixed initial vector. To break this protocol with brute force if you permit all these optional things, you have to get this 64 bit block right. So we have an encrypted 64 bit block. So the fact that you can push to use triple DES, that's fortunate. Who is in charge of picking this up? There's nothing wrong with the recommendation, but the recommendation doesn't talk about the protocol. There's nothing wrong with this protocol, because the protocol doesn't say anything about a crypto algorithm. We know in our community, security, composability, oh... difficult, doesn't work; it's another example.

Next simple challenge response protocol. There is the card reader, here is the Smart-card, but you're now in this particular world, if the Smart-card wants to authenticate the reader it cannot start itself, a Smart-card must be told to do something, it will not become active on its own. So it starts with a get data command serial number of the card being sent back, get challenge command, get a challenge with a parameter and number of bytes, then random numbers being sent back, and then this ring is constructed, random number of the reader, zero number of the reader, random number of the card, zero number of the card, everything encrypted, matched, sent back, decrypted with the shared secret key, checked, another message being created and sent back. It is in essence a standard, nothing wrong directly if you look at this protocol, follows standard advice. Problem: there is a get challenge command parameter, you are supposed to say, get challenge 8, but why should a malicious party say, get challenge 8? As far as we can tell the lowest number it can go is get challenge 1, then instead of having enough bytes the attacker has only an 8 bit challenge, when it has to guess the right eight bits.

We've now jumped into the role of software security. We've jumped into a world where we have to ask, OK, what will the card do when it gets this? Will it have a programme to say, I don't like this, I'm supposed to run with an 8 byte challenge, I'll ignore this rubbish. Will it faithfully implement this command from the ISO standard 7816, and return a 1 byte challenge? I'll take it back to the poor guy equating the system. The poor guy equating the system now has to find out what all the potential Smart-card vendors will do about this issue. I have happened to talk to one of the Smart-card industries recently and about common criteria for Smart-cards, and it was quite an interesting experience because they live in a world where they say, if we have a common criteria certificate and a program that is 1 or 2 years old, it is no longer good enough, we need a new common criteria certificate for our programme. And we have a process of continuously updating certification, we have a working group that captures current state of the art on side-channel analysis, tamper resistance of Smart-card, and so on. We also had a group on software. We are still very weak in this area.

So, a variation of the previous protocol, the reader starts by sending its zero number, its random number, its the same process as before, starts again, and the bad guy gets this from the card and sends it back, reflection attack, and it is a reflection attack that will work if the two random numbers are the same, and if they are random numbers there is a chance in 1 to the 2 to the 64, and the Smart-card people will tell you, that's the relevant certification weakness, but it exists, and there are simple defences against it. But in the current standard as specified in this application, they check a lot of things, but they don't check whether they get a message back they've sent themselves, which they could do easily. Yes, the trick here was the card reader pretends to be the card. That's something the card could easily change. It would be a natural check for people who have the need to defend against reflection attacks, but do we know that the people in this world know about this.

There is a further twist to the story. These feeds K, ICCKFD, 32 byte random values used for key generation, for security are XORed, which is general is a clever idea because if you don't trust the randomness contributed by your correspondent, you XOR your own 32 byte of randomness, and it will be truly random. So in this attack the attacker doesn't know any of the two values, but because of the signature the attacker knows the XOR of the two values, and therefore the attacker knows the key. Who is in charge of the result? In this world of different standards, will it be the evaluation people doing a common criteria evaluation of the cards?

There was this story last November, SSLB broken, and what turned up was that people doing user authentication, web servers that use SSL user authentication and have now used a nice connection of the back servers having the first SSL session server authenticated, and then they want to know the user that's triggered a session with negotiation, and in the session re-negotiation they ask for client certification of a client authentication. And they were assuming that if you re-negotiate then you extend the previous session. I've looked at the RFC, and I have found no remark to that effect whatsoever. What re-negotiation does, it creates a new session. I see a lot of use case specifications now in the world of web services, web application security. And what happens is that people take the plausible assumption about a plausible use case and assume that is what the protocol always does. And to fix the problem you change the protocol so that it does what these users think that it ought to do. Whether that's ultimately the most clever idea, we can discuss.

George Danezis: You said the users, but it's not the users.

Reply: I should not say things like that, it was their application developers.

George Danezis: The people from Open SSL are a bit wrong, they were abstracting the field at the TCP strings, and effectively not closing the TCP connection, and pretending to open a new one, and they were just pumping the data that was coming through. So this is a very interesting one here because if the people who implement the actual security mechanism get it wrong the developers just use the abstractions provided, and you know, this is really I think a specification fraud, it basically encourages people to implement the library that everybody in the Open Source world uses, get it wrong, it means there's something really wrong in the protocol.

Reply: Essentially if something is wrong the question is, where did it go wrong?

Anil Madhavapeddy: OpenSSL is well known as having one of the worst programming APIs possible for security protocols, it's just torture to work with it, so what about the other SSL implementations, were they essentially immune to this because they provided a simpler, perhaps a higher level of abstraction. Now it wouldn't necessarily make it dominant in the space, none of the other implementations are used, but there are some embedded that drop from the other embedded version of SSL, so it sounds like the blame can be placed fairly easily in this situation: SSL, all of the other implementations were in fact immune. I don't like the word immune because this is a big misunderstanding of immunity, but they simplified their theory guide to make it possible, so is it just a case of just re-engineering it, or a little bit more specific?

Sandy Clark: An argument that's always given is that's an implementation detail. We don't have to worry about that, but we know that the main idea is secure, it just helps implement it.

Bruce Christianson: In other words, the problem is at a lower layer.

George Danezis: But in this particular case it is not clear, because the API was not supporting a secure use of this. If you have a stream, half of which is not authenticated and the other half is authenticated, you want to know which bits are which, so I am on the non-authenticated and now I'm on the authenticated side, but such an API wasn't offered. So a security engineer might say, well obviously then you have to interrupt the streams and create a new one.

Anil Madhavapeddy: SSH doesn't have this problem, because it doesn't expose a program interface beyond channels, and all the re-negotiation communication is taken care of by the abstraction, so it's never an issue. OpenSSL actually exposes the fact that you sometimes block a reading when a writing is expected, and it's just incredibly complicated. So it just seems like it's a bad composition more than anything else, but we're stuck with it in some cases.

Bruce Christianson: It's an issue where a lower level server actually allows more than the client wants to use, and in the normal kind of networking environment, that's not a problem, but in this kind of context it's a very big problem because you've got to make another model, you don't want the application to see what should be invisible, and then you start getting all these requirements about managing state.

Reply: Which is the reason why I thought this is something to look at. You have the level of http requests together, and as George was pointing out, you will have below this SSM TCP sessions, and you have in-between the logical SSL channels, which is my fundamental question, who is in charge of coordinating all of this? In line with your introduction, you have one layer that seems to be sent an abstraction, and the people further up try to use this abstraction, and then the people lower down implement something different. And maybe this particular case, because it's a single protocol, you have intentional degrees of freedom and implementation. Sorry, George, for what I say next. We were talking to the people and asked them, about one of these certification weaknesses of the protocols. They are not new attacks, they are patterns we have seen for ages, we can defend against those quite easily, the people from the Smart-card world then give you an answer, we know about this, this is a business discriminator. New entrants to the market might not be as well trained in terms of security, so they might get it wrong so we are better off. What this means to the accreditation process is completely different, because if in the accreditation processes, a card that meets this certification is OK, and then for different reasons the vendor is told, no, you're not good enough, you're meeting all our requirements but you still can't compete in this market, they will have a very good reason to go to court and complain that they are discriminated against.

George Danezis: I would like to compare the situation you presented when you come to do smart-card security engineering with what we have if we were to build a bridge. So you'd have to ask, where do we get the requirements, how do we know how to effectively take the different standards, and put them together in a way that is secure and effective, and all that stuff. Engineers that build bridges have a similar set of problems. They'd have some requirements that they need to work out, and this is part of actually their engineering process, they don't expect to effectively standardise what the requirement is about the bridge. And then they also have all the standards about the thickness of the metal bars, and all that stuff, that they have to compose in a way that their training has given them. So they will not go and look for a standard to tell them what the specification of the bridge is going to be, that's going to be part of the design process.

My argument here is that the ultimate responsibility for designing security systems rests with the engineer that is in charge, the architect in an implemented system, not with the standards. And the fact is that of course when it comes to accreditation, this cannot be taken into account, and effectively, let's say, if a government or if a company wishes to devise a sensitive product, they cannot discriminate on the basis of the quality that the different provider gives them.

That's a separate problem, in the same way as if you had an engineering firm that builds bridges effectively and systematically.

Jonathan Anderson: But the difference is that in civil engineering, for instance, or mechanical engineering, each layer of abstraction comes with a strong guarantee. So if the engineer signs off and said, this bolt will survive this sheer stress, or whatever, and he's wrong and the bridge collapses, then the guy at the top is not responsible, it's the guy at the bottom who said, this bolt is OK. And so at every level you've got a very strong guarantee with your abstraction, which is not something that we do in software.

Joseph Bonneau: The main bridge in San Francisco was serviced for a week, I think, earlier in the year, which was this huge multi-million dollar issue, and there were at least three different people who all blamed each other and said, there was a problem with their standard. I think we tend to assume that other fields don't have the same problems when they largely do.

Reply: Who builds the bridge? You will have one organisation ultimately in charge of the processes. With this e-Card project, it's the government, but they don't want to really feature, they don't really have the security expertise. So they started an organisation that is in charge of it. They have a very interesting remit. As much as possible of the infrastructure should be created by commercial entities, but if commercial entities refuse to do certain things, then they have to do it. So you have an organisation that by now might be five, six years old[3], they do not have institutional experience in creating IT infrastructures with e-Cards. They have some people who know something about security, we have in our group quite constructive conversations with them, and it's also is quite nice to tell, we had two workshops with them, and the second workshop they said, at the first workshop what you were asking seemed really strange, now at this second workshop I see your point, in the future I will ask different questions when people come to me and talk to me about security. So, that's why I go back to accreditation. There is this process where there is in some corners of the body political a wish to have this infrastructure, and they have decided to go ahead with building such an infrastructure. They don't have the expertise, they would like to rely on the expertise of standards, then smart companies assemble this IT infrastructure in a secure way. And of course the answer to my initial question, who is in charge — the easy answer is, we put someone in charge, a security expert, who is allowed to hire the appropriate team of high powered experts, and they will look at this and create a solution. But that's not what people dream of, they want to get it much cheaper.

---

[3] Now older.

Blood in the Water
Are there Honeymoon Effects Outside Software?

Sandy Clark, Matt Blaze, and Jonathan Smith

University of Pennsylvania

1 Honeymoons

In a previous paper at this workshop (and in a forthcoming full paper), we observed that software systems enjoy a security "honeymoon period" in the early stages of their life-cycles. Attackers take considerably longer to make their first discoveries of exploitable flaws in software systems than they do to discover flaws as systems mature. This is true even though the first flaws, presumably, actually represent the easiest bugs to find and even though the more mature systems tend to be more intrinsically robust.

The software honeymoon effect is surprisingly pronounced and pervasive, occurring in virtually every kind of widely used software system, whether open or closed source and whether an operating system, word processor, graphical rendering system, or web browser. While the length of the honeymoon varies, far more often than not, the time between the discovery of the first zero day attack and the second will be considerably shorter than between the initial release and the first.

In a forthcoming paper, we will examine various factors that appear to influence the honeymoon, but the central observation is this: honeymoons occur because, at the early stages of a software system's life, the attacker's (lack of) familiarity with the system matters far more than the system's intrinsic security properties. As the first flaws are discovered, the community of attackers develops more expertise and becomes more efficient at discovering flaws, even after the "low hanging fruit" bugs are patched and eliminated (when, we would otherwise expect, flaws should become harder to find).

This leads us to wonder whether there are security honeymoons in other aspects of system security besides software itself. In particular, are there honeymoon effects in basic security protocols? Cryptographic algorithms? Security architectures? A cursory initial analysis suggests that the answer may be an emphatic "yes".

In the rest of this position paper, we examine representative examples in security protocols (Needham-Schroeder), crypto algorithms (hash functions), and security architecture (virtual machines), where an analysis of inter-arrival times of published papers discussing attacks suggests that honeymoons are enjoyed across a wide range of computer security defenses.

2 Protocols

On the surface at least, security and cryptographic protocols would seem to have very different properties from software. Security protocols, while complex

B. Christianson and J. Malcolm (Eds.): Security Protocols 2010, LNCS 7061, pp. 12–17, 2014.
© Springer-Verlag Berlin Heidelberg 2014

to analyze, have far few steps than software systems have lines of code, they are almost always open source (or at least those discussed in the research community are), and the adversary is historically other members of the research community who have a strong incentive to publish their attacks.

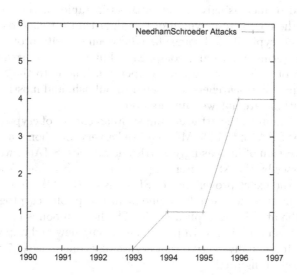

Fig. 1. Numbers of attacks on the Needham-Schroeder family of protocols by year

Consider the rate of vulnerability discovery in the original Needham Schroeder public-key protocol (and its patched successors). Its life-cycle appears to follow almost the same honeymoon curve as we found in a software systems. The protocol enjoyed a long honeymoon period, followed by a trickle of attacks and then a deluge of attacks against it. See Figure 1. For example, in 1994 Paul Syverson [6] outlined a taxonomy that replay and man-in-the-middle attacks would follow and indeed, the next year, Lowe published an attack on the protocol that followed the taxonomy. This was followed the next year by four new attacks and then by four more the year after [1,4] (see figure 1).

One major difference between the this attack life-cycle and the "classic" software system life-cycle is that the "midlife" phase (the post-honeymoon phase) of the cycle here was much shorter, with the attack papers coming in a rapid burst. We suggest that this might be due to a fundamental characteristic of security protocols that isn't present in software systems: a security protocol is typically designed to perform only one main function (key exchange) and is not subject to "feature creep" (we do not, after all, release *Security Protocol 2.0 – Now with More GUI*). When a flaw in a security protocol is found, either a fix is proposed, or the protocol is considered hopelessly broken and abandoned (or the problem ignored). It isn't subject to the same endless patch-revision, feature-addition, re-attack cycle as typical commercial software.

3   Security Architectures and Crypto Algorithms

Basic cryptographic algorithms, too, appear to exhibit a honeymoon, in which a relatively long period may pass before any structural cryptanalytic weaknesses are noticed. But once a first "chink in the armor" is found, this is often followed by a flood of increasingly serious attacks in rapid succession, sometimes culminating in the complete downfall of the algorithm (or class of algorithms). Crypto algorithms typically fall somewhere between security protocols and software systems in terms of size and complexity, but they share several things in common with protocols: they are mostly openly available to the attackers, the attackers are typically researchers motivated to publish, and mostly the tools for analyzing algorithms are not well understood.

Consider, for example, the attacks against broad classes of cryptographic hash functions such as SHA and MD5. MD5 enjoyed a very long honeymoon, followed by a recent succession of increasingly worrisome attacks. SHA(0) was discovered to have weaknesses by the NSA after its public release (we don't know how long this took, since the exact provenance of SHA inside the NSA is still classified), but enjoyed at least a two year honeymoon in the public cryptographic community before the attack was replicated [5]. The honeymoon is clearly now over for this class of hash function, with papers describing new and improved attacks being published in virtually every recent cryptology conference [2,7,8]. Examples of these are shown in figure 2.

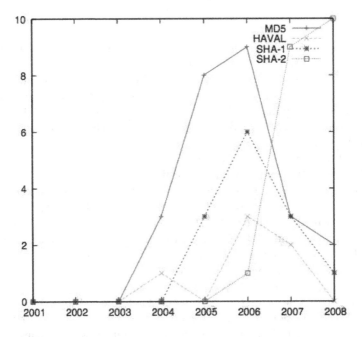

Fig. 2. Numbers of attacks on various hash functions by year

Honeymoons also appear to apply to security architectures as well as security protocols and algorithms. Virtual machines as an isolation mechanism appear to be a particularly salient example.

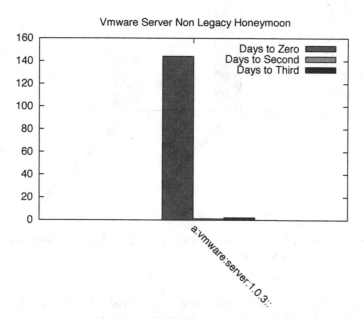

Fig. 3. Honeymoon (Days to first vulnerability/Days to Second Vulnerability for VMware Server

The concept of virtual machines has been in commercial use since the IBM 360 model 67. Since then it has been proposed as a panacea for a wide range of computer architecture issues including security. The idea of isolating systems in their own virtual worlds protected from outside interference or kept from interfering outside themselves is an important one, but even VMs must interact with their host systems in some way. For instance, virtual machines are software systems and therefore have the same security life-cycle properties as any other software systems. This includes the honeymoon effect. Figures 3 and 4 show the days to first vulnerability against the days to next vulnerabilities for one popular virtualisation product's server and workstation editions. Both graphs show a significantly longer period from initial release until the discovery of the first vulnerability than from the first vulnerability until the discovery of the second. As you can see from figure 4, the workstation edition also follows the exploit, patch (issue new version), re-exploit cycle common in most software products.

An additional security consideration for virtual machines is that the host/guest interaction itself is vulnerable. At Black-Hat Las Vegas 2009 Kostya Kortchinsky demonstrated that he could leap from the virtual machine to the host machine

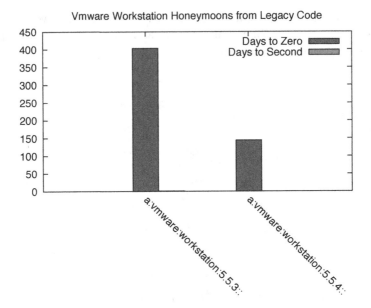

Fig. 4. Honeymoon for VMware Workstation: note that these represent honeymoons broken as a result of legacy code

and vice versa exploiting a memory leak in a shared frame-buffer [3]. In other words, for virtual machines, the honeymoon is clearly over.

4   Panic or Resignation?

Should we take comfort in this, or be frightened? Perhaps the answer is yes to both.

References

1. August, G.L.: An attack on the Needham-Schroeder public-key authentication protocol. Information Processing Letters 56, 131–133 (1995)
2. Chabaud, F., Joux, A.: Differential collisions in SHA-0. In: Krawczyk, H. (ed.) CRYPTO 1998. LNCS, vol. 1462, pp. 56–71. Springer, Heidelberg (1998)
3. Kortchinsky, K.: Cloudburst: A VMware guest to host escape story. In: BlackHat (2009), `http://www.blackhat.com/presentations/bh-usa-09/KORTCHINSKY/BHUSA09-Kortchin%sky-Cloudburst-PAPER.pdf`
4. Lowe, G.: Some new attacks upon security protocols. In: Proceedings of the 9th IEEE Computer Security Foundations Workshop, pp. 162–169. IEEE Computer Society Press (1996)
5. Biham, E., Chen, R.: Near-collisions of SHA-0. In: Franklin, M. (ed.) CRYPTO 2004. LNCS, vol. 3152, pp. 290–305. Springer, Heidelberg (2004)

6. Syverson, P.: A taxonomy of replay attacks. In: Proceedings of the 7th IEEE Computer Security Foundations Workshop, pp. 187–191. IEEE Computer Society Press (1994)
7. Wang, X., Yin, Y.L., Yu, H.: Finding collisions in the full SHA-1. In: Shoup, V. (ed.) CRYPTO 2005. LNCS, vol. 3621, pp. 17–36. Springer, Heidelberg (2005)
8. Wang, X., Yu, H.: How to break md5 and other hash functions. In: Cramer, R. (ed.) EUROCRYPT 2005. LNCS, vol. 3494, pp. 19–35. Springer, Heidelberg (2005)

Blood in the Water
(Transcript of Discussion)

Sandy Clark

University of Pennsylvania

A couple of years ago when we were analysing voting machines we came across a question for which we didn't have an answer, namely if these machines are so bad why aren't they being attacked left and right? These machines were full of vulnerabilities, they were trivial to exploit, and yet it strikes me now there's been no documented case of an attack on any voting system by exploiting a software or a hardware vulnerability.

Peter Ryan: Perhaps you're coming onto this anyway, but there have been documented attacks on eVoting systems.

Reply: Yes, we'll explore that in just a second. So there's some sort of honeymoon, there's some sort of protection that these machines are enjoying right now, and we wanted to find out what it was. We went into possible explanations including things like lack of incentive (do you go to any bother on a US election), or maybe the bad guys are just a lot better at this than we are (that's possible, but I have no way to test it).

It did occur to us that one major difference between eVoting computer systems and other kinds of computer systems is that eVoting systems are really only accessible to the general public about two days a year, so maybe the secret to protecting voting systems, that right now is giving them this honeymoon, is the fact that attackers simply aren't familiar enough with them to have developed a set of attacks, or to make those attacks undetectable.

So we thought about familiarity, and one of the problems with that is that it goes against the whole standard of software engineering philosophy. This picture is from Brooks "The Mythical Man-Month", and the standard software engineering model believes that when we release a software product it has all of these bugs, and you find the easy bugs really fast, and you patch those bugs, and then you find the slightly harder ones and you patch them, eventually you get to a point where it's too hard to find any more bugs and you consider the software secure.

So what we did to try and find out whether familiarity mattered, whether or not the Brooks model worked, is we scraped the bug lists, we got over 30,000 vulnerabilities, we correlated them with bug traffic, we even manually checked about 3,000 of them, to make sure it was correct. Then we picked the popular server apps, the user apps, with both the Open Source and Closed Source code, and we correlated the vulnerability with the release state of the product, and the release state of each specific individual version of the product, and then we looked to see whether or not it matched Brooks model, or whether or not there was some sort of honeymoon effect going on. And what we found was a model that looked much more like this. There does indeed seem to be this

B. Christianson and J. Malcolm (Eds.): Security Protocols 2010, LNCS 7061, pp. 18–24, 2014.
© Springer-Verlag Berlin Heidelberg 2014

honeymoon period where a client seems to be protected, and then this first primal vulnerability, that genesis vulnerability is found, and then like blood in the water attracting sharks, a whole bunch more vulnerabilities appear until you reach this sort of levelling off effect, and that could be as a result of end of life of software, or a new version is released, or something like that.

So if there's a honeymoon effect for software, where else might we see it? Because the interesting thing about the idea of familiarity is that it is extrinsic to the quality of the product itself. After a bunch vulnerabilities are found, and people get used to it, or the learning curve is over, then whether or not you've written a program seems to matter, but if voting machines are an example, and this honeymoon effect really exists, then properties that don't have anything to do with the quality of the software are what matters. So we thought maybe there'd be certain protocols, maybe some in firmware or hardware, or security architectures, and we just chose the first three that came to mind. So we chose, one security protocol, one algorithm, and we looked at the VMware, and surprisingly all three of them had something similar to a random effect going on.

So the first thing that we looked at was the Needham-Schroeder protocol, and at some basic differences between protocols and software. First of all, nobody releases a protocol that they know to be buggy and then says, stick it behind a firewall. Secondly, there's really no new version, no-one says, buy my new security protocol 2.0, it's got video, so the life-cycle of a security protocol is going to be much, much smaller. And in the case of Needham and Schroeder, when it was released, in the late 70s, early 80s, it had this long, long honeymoon. And then all of a sudden in 1994 there was an attack. In 1995 there was another attack, and then there were four all in one year. It was as if the security community had to learn how to attack the security protocol. Now especially important is that the attacks didn't attack until after the paper about the BAN logic came out, so once there was information on how to analyse a security protocol and a tool available to use to analyse it.

Virgil Gligor: There was a 1981 attack that was the first one which pointed out the vulnerability of the third message effect.

Reply: Thank you. So the sharks attacking came after we developed a tool to do it. And now of course there are things like protocol fuzzers, and attacking protocols is pretty well understood.

George Danezis: The 90s, when all these attacks are appearing is a special time, right, because these protocols are deployed and used on public networks.

Reply: For the first time in any wide scale.

George Danezis: Yes. We had lots of protocols in the 80s, but if you are an academic you were not quite sure if you are going to really have a career out of analysing them, breaking them, building better ones, or if they're just there, and they're using some military network, or some intranet, and you will never basically see them.

Reply: And that brings up an interesting point, are the sharks attracted because it's suddenly become a good research interest, is now the time that everybody should be looking at something? You see that a lot in the hacker community, because someone will find a really interesting hack against something, and now everybody wants to jump on that bandwagon and then get props for finding another hack, so everyone starts to look at it.

So after we looked at the protocols we decided to look at hash algorithms, and we looked at MD5, HAVAL and the SHA family. And the SHA family is particularly interesting because of course it was the NSA who popped up with the message that SHA-0 was flawed, and you should put this here fix in and use SHA-1, and that was the blood in the water, that caused everybody to start looking at the SHA family and just to see if they could figure out what the NSA knew and they didn't. And then there is kind of a feature creep because you start to do larger and larger keys, we've got SHA-256, SHA-512, so there is kind of a new version of a hash algorithm released. But we really do understand now how you attack with hash algorithms. And the other interesting thing about the SHA family was Crypto 2005. I was there, I watched it on streaming video, and there was a paper in the main session that discussed attacks against SHA-1 on a reduced set. And then at the end of the conference in the rump session there were three more papers about SHA attacks, it's as if everyone had focused on it all at the same time, including that one by Wang et al which, when she'd finished talking, she got a standing ovation. So as far as we're concerned, with these algorithms anyway, the honeymoon is over, we're going to have to develop something new. All we're doing right now is getting by until we can find something new.

And the last thing that we looked at were virtual machines, and virtual machines have been given as the answer to everything. The answer to users who want to try something kind of risky, or they need special privileges, stick them on a virtual machine. You want to test malware, do it on a virtual machine, anything you want to do, virtual machines will save us. Except last summer, BlackHat, when Kostya Kortchinsky gave a wonderful talk on how you use the SVGA buffer as a memory leak to break out of the virtual machine onto a host, and to go back the other way around. And then a week ago last Tuesday, Core Security Technologies came out with the press release that they had broken Microsofts Virtual PC, in particular that they had been able to exploit the safe execution handlers, the memory randomisation, inside the virtual machine. If the operating system was running as the actual host, these would not be exploitable, but inside the virtual machine they are. And what's interesting about all these attacks even though they take place on two completely different software, you know, virtual PC and VMware, is that they both exploit the same idea, the fact that in order for a virtual machine to run it has to have special privileges that it might not otherwise have, and if you mess around with special privileges you can break out of the system.

So I expect if the pattern follows as it has been that we're going to see a number of attacks against virtual machines very soon. I think this is a flaw.

Alex Shafarenko: If I may interrupt. It is true if the virtualisation software is flawed, then there will be vulnerabilities that any guest operating the system could exploit. But the advantage is that once you've fixed the virtual hardware, you fix it for all virtual machines, whereas whatever you do with individual operating systems, it will only work with that operating system, you'll have to do similar checks and certification processes with every other operating system. So virtual machines do not eliminate concerns, they concentrate them in one place.

Reply: That's an interesting observation, however, they're also running on another system, and you've got unexpected interactions that you can't plan for.

Alex Shafarenko: Only due to errors in design, not anything else.

Reply: Couldn't you say that about everything?

Alex Shafarenko: No, because every other design is variable, this one is fixed, once it's done, it's done. If you manage to find the last bug, it's still possible, it's a very localised design, because a virtual machine has a very focused job, it tends to its hardware, it doesn't do anything else. And it only emulates one type of hardware, because all these virtual machines ride on Macs for instance, like yours, right, they presume a certain hardware structure, and they don't give you a lot of choice or freedom. A physical PC would have a hundred choices, a choice of one of a hundred graphical cards, one of a hundred disk drives, etc, but in a virtual machine it would be just one set.

Virgil Gligor: Have you looked at the size of the virtual machine drivers and hyper drivers, in practice, and the size of the PCP for the virtual machines, like for example Xen, which is a pretty good design, over 120,000 lines of code VMM, and probably a million in the route from A0. Now if you don't have the variability there I don't know where you'd find variability.

Alex Shafarenko: What kind of variability are you talking about?

Virgil Gligor: Well variability in terms of software, and in terms of bugs that could be exploited, as Sandy points out. Even before, what she said, NSA ran an analysis study of VMware and Xen, and they found numerous bugs.

Alex Shafarenko: Due to the size of the product you will find bugs in it. My point is slightly different. You can freeze a virtual machine without detrimental effect on performance, because it's not a real machine.

Anil Madhavapeddy: Sorry I have to disagree. The issue for all emulation is the notion of power virtualisation, which is to run as much on the bare metal as you can, so you're actually running on the hardware without any protection. I think this is the reason for a honeymoon period: our assumption is changing, we're going from wrapping everything in a nice container to actually running stuff in the bare metal as much as possible.

But this leads to a very wide interface with the hardware, so it's actually not possible these days to take a virtual machine and run VM on an Intel chip, and run the same VM on an AMD chip, because you're running so much in the micro code concerned, and the actual interface is very different. So I think we're going to get a lot of attacks because our security researcher looked at this a decade ago and found a nice contained system, and now you come back to it even five years on and all of a sudden there's a new hardware support for VT and AVSVM.

Bruce Christianson: And the membrane was gone.

Anil Madhavapeddy: Exactly. The membrane's gone, it's just different now, so it's almost a case of security researchers don't have the bandwidth to look at all these evolving systems.

Reply: Well it's also that we set our perceptions based on one thing, and then it takes attackers to change our perceptions.

Alex Shafarenko: It also may be due to the fact that virtualisation is not added with the support of a firewall, because the hardware was not intended for any virtual machines, so with a suitable change in that design you may find your that your problems have a limited scope.

Reply: And that comes to a version of feature creep, well it can do this, why don't we see if it can also do this, it's the standard evolutionary model that everything follows.

Jeff Yan: Actually I can probably offer a possible explanation to the effect of the honeymoon effect extracted from a social psychology perspective. Basically human beings follow trends, our researchers are also humans.

Reply: Yes, I think that is a huge point, that's kind of the follower effect which we'll get to in a second.

So it looks like when you're looking at a security problem, during the very beginning of any vulnerability's life-cycle, or any product's life-cycle, extrinsic properties matter a lot more than we've ever given credit for. I think we as security community have long known intuitively, that vulnerabilities have different properties than bugs do. And I'm looking right now at some ways to test this. There are some people at ATT that have built a bug detector that's about 80% accurate on the software that they tested it on, as long as they have access to the source code and access to all of the bug tracking they can predict with 83%, 85% probability, which function is going to have the next bug. We're going to see if we can test that looking only at security vulnerabilities, and see if the same pattern applies. I'm hoping that there is some difference, I would like to believe that security vulnerabilities are different. The second point is that extrinsic properties are much more important. And something that we don't really think about, the first vulnerabilities found in a system are not necessarily the whole proof, and this again goes against the software engineering model.

When you're looking at something like a vulnerability, the first vulnerability in a product, and it's a result of legacy code, that's not "low hanging fruit", that legacy code existed in the previous version and wasn't found. And by the way, our forthcoming paper has a lot of information on this, about 50% of the vulnerabilities found in software are the result of legacy code, and a good percentage of the primal vulnerabilities are also the result of legacy code. And then the other possibility is, as you just said, people do what other people do, we follow trends. So this honeymoon effect we found, it seems to apply all over. Security protocols, crypto algorithms, seem to follow exactly the same pattern. Virtual machines follow the same pattern as software. But what's surprising is that superficially this isn't software, a security protocol is not software, there's some fundamental differences, which basically means that security patterns are alike no matter what, but the actual implementation is different.

And lastly, we asked the question, why should we care about the honeymoon at all? Well in the paper we just submitted we found the result that over the last years of looking at vulnerabilities and the products affected by them, nobody is winning the arms race. The last ten years the rate of vulnerability discovery has been just linear, which surprised all of us, we thought we would see spikes like an ECG. And in the past ten years there have been massive changes in the attacker and defender cyber-space. On the defender side there have been 300 plus new security initiatives. There's type-safe programming languages, there's automated patching, there's new types of firewalls and honeypots, and a lot of money spent to try and invent systems. And on the attackers side there are all of these great attacking frameworks that are available, many just point and click. And the minute a vulnerability is exposed it's announced the next day, you know, every patch Tuesday is followed by exploit Wednesday. There's also a change in the motivation, no longer is it just kids in their basements, but now you've got highly trained professionals profit motivated, or patriotism motivated, or whatever. So the balance of power shouldn't be the same, but any static system, any stalemate, always favours the attacker, because defenders have to defend against everything, but the attacker only has to find one new thing.

So we've got to figure out a way to change the arms race, and we only have two models. In the Centre for Disease Control model, you inoculate yourself against every known possible attacker that's out there and you stick yourself out in the wild and you wait to get attacked, and you clean yourself off and you do it again. The other model that we have (that tends to be used by military and our government) is the castle and moat model, where you build this huge fortress and you put a firewall outside and around you, and you stick yourself out there and you wait for the attack, and then you clean yourself off and you do it again. If we're going to change this, the only way to change the system is to change the rules of how we play, and that means we have to focus somewhere else. So let's focus at the beginning. Let's do offensive security codes. That's it. Any questions.

Dieter Gollmann: The first attack against the hash function was about 1993 by Hans Dobbertin on MD4, and at that time he told everyone who wanted to know that the same methods would work for MD5, but it would be difficult, and therefore for a very long time cryptographers preferred to do the easy things and not the difficult things, until they finally ran out of other problems to look at. So there might be an issue that it takes a long time until certain analysis methods become so well understood and so easy that lots of PhD students can do something and get enough research they can write papers about. It was the same story in the mid 1990s with protocols. Once there were tools, you could specify the protocol, throw it into a tool and see what comes out.

Reply: Yes, that's familiarity again, that's when you learn the system and then you attack it, and you're protected until then.

Bruce Christianson: I think it's an interesting observation that breaks on the BAN logic started after the first proof that it was correct. A cynic would say, well OK the countermeasure is obvious, just don't prove that the product is secure. But the thing about a proof is it tells the attacker where to look because the proof holds under certain assumptions, so to find the attack I've got to break one of the assumptions.

Reply: And the same with hackers, because hackers always succeed by violating assumptions. So it's almost exactly the same model you would see with someone attacking software, saying do it again, go around the system, or the same with the exploit Wednesday, you're looking at the patch to see where you should focus your attack. Same model.

Bruce Christianson: Yes, picking what to change.

Reply: Well one thing we found is that old attacks come around again, old attacks are always new again. I have a friend, his name is Mike, and Mike was laughing a few months ago, and the reason he was laughing was he said it was an attack he hadn't seen since the 90s, but it was working again because of something somebody had changed. They never go away, they just evolve or recycle.

Saša Radomirović: Don't you have that also with infectious diseases, you have a while before they actually smoke.

Reply: Smallpox is back again, Polio is back again in the US, yes.

Bruce Christianson: Yes, even a very small population smouldering away below the inoculation threshold is enough to break out again soon.

Reply: They worried about those parents that won't inoculate.

Bruce Christianson: That's exactly it, yes.

Digital Immolation
New Directions for Online Protest

Joseph Bonneau

University of Cambridge Computer Laboratory

Abstract. The current literature and experience of online activism assumes two basic uses of the Internet for social movements: straightforward extensions of offline organising and fund-raising using online media to improve efficiency and reach, or "hacktivism" using technical knowledge to illegally deface or disrupt access to online resources. We propose a third model which is non-violent yet proves commitment to a cause by enabling a group of activists to temporarily or permanently sacrifice valuable online identities such as email accounts, social networking profiles, or gaming avatars. We describe a basic cryptographic framework for enabling such a protest, which provides an additional property of binding solidarity which is not normally possible offline.

1 Introduction

Throughout history, new forms of technology have been adapted to facilitate and advance social movements and protests [9]. The potential of the Internet to revolutionise social movements by providing low-cost global communication has been analysed by scholars in a wide range of disciplines [7]. In their influential 1996 essay "Electronic Civil Disobedience" the Critical Art Ensemble argued that the Internet enabled powerful organisations to avoid having a conspicuous physical location such as a castle, capitol building, or corporate headquarters, and thus effective protest would eventually have to be carried out by electronic means to be effective [6].

Dorothy Denning's 2001 essay introduced three broad categories of online social movements: activism, hacktivism, and cyberterrorism [3]. Online activism describes using computer-mediated communication to aid in peaceful, legal social movements. Activism techniques include fund-raising, gathering and disseminating information, and signing online petitions. These tactics utilise the de-centralised nature of the web to facilitate grass-roots movements whose dispersed supporters may be difficult to organise in the offline world. The low cost of Internet communication can also harm online activism, as individual protests struggle to compete for attention online [9].

The recent growth of online social networks and virtual worlds has opened up new means of activism and non-violent protest. For example, millions of users declare their devotion to various causes on social networks by joining groups or adding icons to their profiles [14], while virtual world participants conduct online

B. Christianson and J. Malcolm (Eds.): Security Protocols 2010, LNCS 7061, pp. 25–33, 2014.
© Springer-Verlag Berlin Heidelberg 2014

pickets outside unpopular organisations' virtual property [1]. Such protests are different from those typically analysed in past academic literature in that they use the existence of online identities to show support for their causes. Social networks have also been widely hailed for their role in organising offline protest. In this function they serve as a highly efficient communication medium, enabling qualitatively different types of movements such as flash mobs which are organised on very short notice.

In contrast, hacktivism entails directly harming an opposition's online resources. A variety of tactics exist [2,15] including defacing or disabling web sites, blocking access through denial of service attacks, manipulating search engine results, or harassing individuals through email floods. The ethics and legality of such tactics are complicated. Adherents claim that such means are ethical because, as they are not intended to cause any physical violence or harm, they are a modern instantiation of the long and widely-accepted tradition of non-violent civil disobedience [12,17]. Opponents argue that such tactics violate property rights and are the online manifestations of violent protests [8].

In either case, the results of these protests have been mixed. The earliest large-scale movement, a series of denial of service attacks in 1998 by a group called Electronic Disturbance Theatre supporting the Zapatista movement in Mexico, brought large-scale media attention to its cause [10], but subsequent movements have not always received favorable news coverage. A central problem remains that such tactics demonstrate technological expertise but do little to demonstrate the extent of a cause's support.

Cyberterrorism is distinguished from hacktivism in that it attempts to initiate real-world harm by using the Internet to destroy physical infrastructure. An act of cyberterrorism might be using a remote exploit in a control server to destroy a power station, or cause an airplane crash by disrupting air traffic control systems. Despite the large potential loss and the stated desire of known terrorist groups to conduct such attacks, there have been no successful incidents and the threat remains largely speculative [4].

1.1   Common Problems

Both online activism and hacktivism have drawbacks which are increasingly limiting their effectiveness. Online activism struggles to gain attention given the enormous quantity of information available online and the ability of Internet users to filter out information from groups they disagree with [16]. Hacktivism suffers both from increasingly effective technical defences and the possible loss of public support due to its adversarial nature.

In the abstract, a protest aims to demonstrate both *commitment* and *morality*.

Commitment. Commitment requires demonstrating both the existence of a large number of supporters and a serious level of support from each user. For example, a street rally shows that a large number of adherents are willing to expend free time marching in support of a cause. Viewed as a commitment signal, the importance of numerical turnout makes sense. Indeed, protest organisers routinely claim higher turnout than official estimates.

Numbers alone don't prove commitment, there must be a real opportunity cost for participating members. Benefit concerts may attract large numbers of attendees, but still not demonstrate commitment if attending the concert is desirable independent of the specific cause. In contrast, street rallies in inclement weather or with a high risk of arrest demonstrate higher commitment.

Online protests struggle with commitment due to the extremely low cost of signing an online petition or joining a social networking group.[1] Detecting the commitment of protesters is related to the computer security challenge of preventing spam. The low cost of email allows individuals to overuse attention resources for personal gain, requiring automated filtering techniques. Similarly, the low cost of organising an online protest means that many movements can gain a token level of support online. People have limited attention resources for social movements as well, often relying on the mainstream media as a filter to ignore online protests unless they can demonstrate sufficient support.

Ideally, we desire a mechanism for online protesters to send an unforgeable signal of dedication to a cause. For email spam, proof-of-work schemes allow senders to show that a message is genuine by performing costly work before sending. The idea has not caught on in practice and economic analysis has suggested that spammers can expend more effort to send spam messages than ordinary users can for real messages [11]. We avoid computational work as a signal for dedication to a protest because some individuals have much greater computational resources than others. Protests traditionally embrace an ethic of equality, enabling all participants to contribute equally to the signal of commitment.

The innate desire to show commitment can be seen in the creative attempts of some social networking movements to strengthen their signal. An informal protest movement over perceived discrimination against Barack Obama's 2008 presidential campaign saw thousands of users changing their middle name to "Hussein" in solidarity. Anger over NBC's 2010 firing of talk show host Conan O'Brien similarly saw thousands of users changing their profile picture to an image of O'Brien. Such methods show slightly higher commitment, as they diminish the core purpose of the user's profile to showcase information about themselves. Furthermore, they can only be used for one cause at a time, in contrast to group memberships of which users can hold dozens. Still, the level of commitment shown is relatively low and more effective protests would allow a signalling from a much larger spectrum of commitment.

Morality. Many protest movements aim to maintain a moral high ground by maintaining an ethical code which they consider superior to their opposition's. Certainly, protests which aim to succeed through media coverage rather than by inflicting direct harm frequently attempt to claim a principle of "non-violence" to demonstrate that they are being oppressed by some opposition group. There

---

[1] Hacktivism can be even worse at demonstrating commitment, as a single competent hacker may be behind an entire denial of service attack if he controls a large botnet.

is a vigorous scholarly debate over the ethics of some forms of hacktivism, and adherents frequently attempt to follow a "hacktivist ethic" to avoid such criticism [17]. The FloodNet software introduced in the Zapatista protests and since used in many others, for example, requires many users to download and install software to generate web requests, which they claim makes their protest akin to a virtual "sit-in" with each user consuming only a reasonable amount of resources. Regardless of technical specifics or definition of violence, however, hacktivism remains combative in nature which can prevent its adherents from gaining public sympathy as an oppressed party.

1.2 A New Direction

We draw our inspiration from the history of non-violent social protests which were effective because participants faced risks of serious personal harm. This harm could either be from an opposing power structure, in the case of street marches being violently suppressed, or from the participants themselves. Hunger strikes remain a powerful symbol of dedication in that participants provide a real threat to starve themselves to death in support of their cause. An even more extreme example is self-immolation, such as the public suicide of the Buddhist monk Thích Quảng Đức in protest of the Vietnam war.

We propose that online protests can prove strong commitment in a morally-acceptable way by enabling users to temporarily or permanently sacrifice their online identities. We propose a basic cryptographic framework for such a protest and described the key divergences from its offline inspiration.

2 Protocol

2.1 Assumptions

We assume that all participants in the protocol hold an online identity which they are willing to suspend as a part of the protest. This identity may be a social networking profile, and email account, an avatar in a virtual world, or a reputable account in an online market. Each user u_i holds some secret password x_i which controls access to their online identity. Each user also has a separate public/private key-pair $(k_i^{\mathrm{pub}}, k_i^{\mathrm{priv}})$, with all public keys known by all users.

We further assume that a password oracle $\mathcal{O}$ exists which maintains a password table $T : \mathbb{Z} \to \{0,1\}^*$ mapping each integer user ID i to an arbitrary password. $\mathcal{O}$ allows any user u_i to change their password after completing a zero-knowledge proof of knowledge of x_i (for example, a challenge-response protocol) and sending a new password x_i' to $\mathcal{O}$. It is critical that $\mathcal{O}$ is indifferent to the protest and will not actively oppose it, as we will discuss in Section 3.1.

2.2 Initiation

We require a trusted protest initiator P. The initiator does not need to be the actual leader of the group, but needs to be trusted by all protesters to faithfully complete two critical initialisation tasks. We envision that it is best if P is in fact indifferent to the cause, serving the role of an elder statesmen or neutral arbiter.

In signing up for the protest, all participants send their secret knowledge x_i to P along with k_i^{pub}. After all n participants have signed up, P then completes the password update process with $\mathcal{O}$, changing each participant's password to a random value x_i' and then deleting the original value x_i. At this point, all participants have lost the ability to access their accounts, as only P knows the current passwords.

P generates a master key pair $(k_*^{\mathrm{pub}}, k_*^{\mathrm{priv}})$ and n shares $s_1 \ldots s_n$ of k_*^{priv} using a threshold decryption scheme [5]. P then creates a symmetric escrow key k_e, and publishes:

$$\left\{ \mathrm{E}_{k_e}\left(\mathrm{E}_{k_i^{\mathrm{pub}}}(x_i')\right) \Big| 1 \le i \le n \right\}, \quad \mathrm{E}_{k_*^{\mathrm{pub}}}(k_e)$$

This information includes a doubly-encrypted version of each user's new password, under both the escrow key and each users' individual public key, and an encryption of the escrow key to the distributed master key. Upon publishing this information, P has completed its organisation of the protest and can destroy all of its secret knowledge, in particular the new passwords x_i' and the master private key k_*^{priv}.

2.3   Completion

Participants can agree to end the protest by decrypting the escrow key (k_e), enabling all users to securely recover their new passwords, after their demands have been satisfactorily met or they have received sufficient media attention. The threshold scheme parameters can be chosen to require some desired threshold m of n users to agree to end the protest.

It is important to recognise technical differences between threshold decryption and voting. If participants may hold multiple votes and change their votes between rounds, it is necessary to use a homomorphic threshold scheme [5], which enables users to update their shares after each vote so that information cannot be combined from multiple votes.

This protest protocol differs from most of its offline inspirations in that the solidarity of participants is binding. Participants cannot back out of the protest without a quorum willing to end it, unlike traditional protests which rely on maintaining a strong esprit de corps to prevent defection. One binding example from the real world is protesters chaining themselves around a tree, though this can usually be broken by any two participants.

2.4   Variants

Suicide Option. The basic scheme only allows voters to end the protest by restoring access to all. It may go on forever if m voters never agree to end it. In a real-world hunger strike, there is a biological deadline limiting the maximum length of the protest. This is difficult to translate into an online protest, but we might assume that the password oracle $\mathcal{O}$ will enable the setting of an account destruction key y_i for each account. In this case, P will generate two escrow keys, k_{e+} and k_{e-}, publishing both $E_{k_*^{\mathrm{pub}}}(k_{e+})$ and $E_{k_*^{\mathrm{pub}}}(k_{e-})$, and then for each user publish $E_{k_{e+}}\left(E_{k_i^{\mathrm{pub}}}(x_i')\right)$ and $E_{k_{e-}}(y_i')$.

Thus, users can vote to end the protocol either by restoring access to all or by exposing each users' account destruction key. In practice, we might assume y_i' is in fact just x_i', the user's password. In this case, upon a successful decryption of k_{e-}, there would be a race to take over the newly exposed accounts. The protest may rely on the action of griefers to quickly destroy or hijack the participants' accounts.

Individual Escrow. It may be desirable for the crowd to be able to vote individually to unlock or destroy individual user accounts. This can be accomplished at some expense by using individual escrow keys k_{e+}^i and k_{e-}^i for each user and then publishing $E_{k_{e+}^i}\left(E_{k_i^{\mathrm{pub}}}(x_i')\right)$ and $E_{k_{e-}^i}(y_i')$ for each user in addition to the previous information.

This would enable a protest in which random accounts are destroyed regularly, giving the protest urgency and a limited time frame. The random account to destroy can be chosen by a distributed shared-randomness protocol, or P can specifically enable random deletion by randomising the destruction-key escrow, publishing $E_{k_{e-}^j}(i, y_i')$ such that the protesters don't know which account i they are exposing if they reveal k_{e-}^j. This can be considered a digital version of a crowd of street protesters exposed to random gunfire.

3   Limitations

3.1   Platform Neutrality

This protest will not work if $\mathcal{O}$ chooses to interfere. In particular, $\mathcal{O}$ can prevent password changes, choose to remember old passwords and give users the option to back out of the protest using their old passwords, or can restore accounts that users have attempted to delete. The significance of this is that such a protest cannot be mounted against the service provider itself, or any party which the service provider has a vested interest in defending. In the real world, users have often used Facebook itself to protest changes to the site, which would not be possible in this setting.

3.2   Platform Minority

Such a protest requires that the n participating members represent only a minority of the total population of the online service for two reasons. First, the service provider would probably interfere with the protest as described above if threatened with losing a majority of its members. Second, the effect of a large number of users losing their accounts might actually be less damaging, as they could collectively migrate to a different service. If only a small number participate in the protest, then the suicide option would be more damaging as participants would risk losing access to a still-popular service.

3.3 Value of Identities

Most offline protests hold the central principle that all human lives are irreplaceable and of equal value. In an online protest, some identities may be much more valuable than others. In particular, some protesters may have new or little-used accounts which they are much more willing to lose than users with well-established accounts. The only realistic defense against this is to establish participation rules enforced by P during initialisation, such as a minimum age of accounts, and bar others from participating in the protest.

3.4 Infiltration

A protest could be hijacked by individuals not interested in the social aims of the movement, or indeed opponents of it. The hijacking could also take the form of a Sybil attack, where one user with many accounts gains a large amount of voting power. Again, there appears to be little defence against this except to rely on P to vet candidates carefully. Cryptographically, it is desirable to use a robust threshold scheme, wherein a malicious user cannot poison the results of decryption by intentionally submitting an incorrect share. This ensures that malicious users cannot block legitimate votes to end a protest.

3.5 Central Trust

The protest organiser P can interfere with the protest in various ways, and also hijack or destroy participants' accounts itself. It is difficult to de-couple P's dual roles of re-setting users passwords and generating key shares, because we wish to ensure that only participants who have provided a valid account gain voting rights. Schemes do exist for threshold cryptography without a trusted dealer, but they would require giving all participants shares before a public key was available to escrow keys with. Such a scheme would yield great exposure to Sybil attacks and infiltration because shares could be acquired prior to submitting valid credentials.

We appear to have little choice but to assume a benevolent initiator exists whom protestors are willing to trust in the role of P. Note that we have attempted to design the protocol so that P can go offline once the protocol has begun. This would allow P to in fact be a trusted elder or non-profit organisation who may not be particularly attached to a specific protest, but is trusted in general for organising social movements.

3.6   Splinter Coalition

If serious disputes arise within the protest community, it might result in m users intentionally destroying the accounts of their opponents within the movement. This is particularly problematic in the "individual escrow" scheme whereby individuals can be targeted for destruction by design. Even in the basic scheme, a malicious coalition could secretly decrypt the escrow key, restore their own accounts, and refuse to share it with a targeted minority. Such a conspiracy would be inherently unstable, as it would require electing a new trusted leader and any defector could blow the whistle on its existence. If this is a significant concern, it may be necessary for P to maintain the master private key k_*^{priv} to respond to any allegations of conspiracy.

4   Conclusions

We have presented a novel protocol to enable digital protesters to engage with larger and graver issues. Ultimately, our proposal still relies on public perception and it is difficult to tell if an online protest can ever generate the same level of human compassion as physical suffering. Certainly, it would be disrespectful to compare the mortal sacrifices of history's great social advocates with the loss of a social networking profile.

However, there is evidence that online identities are becoming increasingly valuable, and indeed many users would be reluctant to give up access over a cause. Thus, we speculate that there may be some value to this approach in enabling a protest to demonstrate strong commitment by its members while remaining completely non-violent.

References

1. Blodgett, B.M.: And the Ringleaders Were Banned: An Examination of Protest in Virtual Worlds. In: C & T 2009: Proceedings of the Fourth International Conference on Communities and Technologies, pp. 135–144. ACM, New York (2009)
2. Costanza-Chock, S.: Mapping the Repertoire of Electronic Contention. In: Opel, A., Pompper, D. (eds.) Representing Resistance: Media, Civil Disobedience and the Global Justice Movement (2003)
3. Denning, D.: Activism, Hacktivism, and Cyberterrorism: The Internet as a Tool for Influencing Foreign Policy. In: Networks and Netwars: The Future of Terror, Crime, and Militancy (2001)
4. Denning, D.: A View of Cyberterrorism Five Years Later. In: Himma, K. (ed.) Internet Security: Hacking, Counterhacking, and Society (2007)
5. Desmedt, Y.: Some Recent Research Aspects of Threshold Cryptography. In: Okamoto, E. (ed.) ISW 1997. LNCS, vol. 1396, pp. 158–173. Springer, Heidelberg (1998)
6. Critical Art Ensemble. Electronic Civil Disobedience and Other Unpopular Ideas. Autonomedia (1996)

7. Kelly Garrett, R.: Protest in an Information Society: A Review of Literature on Social Movements and New ICTs. Information, Communication and Society 9, 202–224 (2006)

8. Kracher, B., Martin, K.: A Moral Evaluation of Online Business Protest Tactics and Implications for Stakeholder Management. Business and Society Review (2009)

9. Kreimer, S.: Technologies of Protest: Insurgent Social Movements and the First Amendment in the Era of the Internet. University of Pennsylvania Law Review (2001)

10. Lane, J.: Digital Zapatistas. The Drama Review 47 (2003)

11. Laurie, B., Clayton, R.: "Proof of Work" Proves Not to Work. In: The Third Annual Workshop on the Economics of Inforomation Security (2004)

12. Manion, M., Goodrum, A.: Terrorism or Civil Disobedience: Toward a Hacktivist Ethic. SIGCAS Comput. Soc. 30(2), 14–19 (2000)

13. McPhillips, F.: Internet Activism: Towards a Framework for Emergent Democracy. International Association for Development of the Information Society Journal on WWW/Internet (2006)

14. Neumayer, C., Raffl, C.: Facebook for Global Protest: The Potential and Limits of Social Software for Grassroots Activism. In: Community Informatics Conference: ICTs for Social Inclusion: What is the Reality (2008)

15. Rolfe, B.: Building an Electronic Repertoire of Contention. Social Movement Studies 4, 65–74 (2005)

16. Sunstein, C.: Echo Chambers. Princeton University Press (2001)

17. Thomas, J.: Ethics of Hacktivism. Information Security Reading Room (2001)

Digital Immolation
(Transcript of Discussion)

Joseph Bonneau

University of Cambridge

How did I get to this topic? I thought about the biggest problems in the world: inequality around the globe, climate change, baby seals being hit over the head by Canadians, and Conan O'Brian, my favourite talk-show host, fired by NBC. I only see two people nodding so I guess he didn't catch on internationally, but in America people were really upset about this. So seriously (and sadly) young people in America, especially college-aged students, were probably equally upset about Conan being fired and the Haiti earthquake, which happened around the same time and generated a similar online buzz.

The question is, what do people do about it? After the Haiti earthquake, this long thread popped up on Facebook: for some reason people said that for everybody who posted this message, Facebook would donate $5 to the Haiti relief, and so thousands of people got onto this one thread and kept replicating it, and it got to the point that Facebook had to actually have a press conference to issue a statement that they were not donating money to Haiti. So this was a very ineffective protest. There's also a group that's trying to save the seals, which is great, we all want to save the seals, nine people joined and they raised $25. So this also failed.

So people want to protest things online, but there really isn't a good way to do it. Why do you want to do protests online? One reason is, if people want to get married online, then essentially everything is online and it makes sense that protests should go online. But here's actually the serious part of the talk. There are reasons that people have been writing about for a long time now for why protests need to be online in the future. There are two compelling reasons to me. First, a lot of organisations now don't have a physical presence that you can really picket or boycott. An investment bank is a company that people don't really understand: they don't have storefronts, people don't buy anything from them, but they're a very powerful group that people might get angry about. And on the other side you have social movements, for example the Pirate Party, which managed to win a seat in the EU Parliament; they're equally dispersed, so this is an organisation that doesn't really have a physical presence. It basically doesn't exist outside of the Internet, it's a bunch of people who have met online. They've got to the point where they have offline meetings now, but there's a lot of social movements that really only exist online, so naturally they want to do their protests online.

So people have been writing about how online process will work for about ten years now. Dorothy Denning wrote the fundamental paper and she came up with basically three ideas. Online activism is basically just an extension of normal organisations, fundraising, getting petitions, spreading information to

B. Christianson and J. Malcolm (Eds.): Security Protocols 2010, LNCS 7061, pp. 34–44, 2014.
© Springer-Verlag Berlin Heidelberg 2014

the online space. For example the "Stop the Digital Economy Bill" campaign in Britain had people signing online petitions, emailing members of Parliament, trying to raise funds online. So this is kind of innocuous and harmless. There's the hacktivism movement which is doing things like denial of service, sending a lot of emails as a form of protest, trying to get groups you don't like to rank highly on Google for negative search terms, things like that. They actually did it with George Bush: a group of people managed to get the search term, "miserable failure", to go directly to his biography page, so that's one thing people have done kind of for fun. It kind of varies on the levels of seriousness, so this group that came during the last Israel/Gaza conflict, a lot of people downloaded software to do denial of service on pro-Gaza websites from their home computers. This was pitched to people outside the conflict, not in Israel, who felt like they could donate their computer to this cause. And similarly people like to hack websites and replace the website with something else, so Twitter has a really bad track record of getting hacked about every two months, and last month it was some group called the Iranian Cyber Army. I have no idea if they're really Iranian, but that's what they did.

And then the final level of digital protest, cyberterrorism, this would be actually exploiting computers to cause physical violence in the real world. You notice this is a movie poster for a movie that came out before I was born, that shows how relevant cyberterrorism has been in the real world, basically it's never really happened so it's kind of still a movie type threat.

I'm going to reduce all this to just two dimensions now, which is a huge over-simplification. In a protest movement (in contrast to warfare, or rebellion, or an insurgency movement, where you're trying to actually harm people and cause damage), you're trying to prove two things. You're trying to prove some sense of morality, that you have the moral high ground compared to the other side (which is why principles like non-violence, solidarity, democracy, equal representation of all people, in the protest are usually important). And you want to show a commitment, so you're trying to show that you have a number of supporters, and that they're dedicated to this cause. So morality is probably the less controversial one, if you look at the history of protest movements they almost always have a moral code that they espouse, that shows that they really believe that what they are doing is good. Non-violence in particular has come up over and over again in a lot of different cultures, and I won't get into a long debate about whether or not non-violence is effective or right, but for most protest movements this is what they want to achieve.

And there's a question about whether the hacktivism stuff that you heard about earlier qualifies as non-violence. In some sense it's non-violent in that you're not physically causing harm to people or machines, but you are causing harm to websites, so in some sense it is online violence, I would argue that's how it's been viewed. When people that push hacktivism try and make the opposite case and say it's actually peaceful, they try to make the analogy that doing a distributed denial of service attack is like a sit-in, where you have a bunch of people all sending requests to a website at once. And they actually design and talk about their systems specifically around this analogy. But I'll leave that to the side today and say that I want to be even more non-violent than that.

So commitment is the interesting property, as I've looked at a ton of protest movements it's really popped out at me. So these are marches on Washington just this past autumn, in September, and it's really interesting to see how over and over again when you look at protest movements, they make a really big deal about the number of people that turned out. On the left this is a website that's in favour of these people marching on Washington essentially to lower taxes and a few other things, and they claim that two million people turned up. The New York Times said fifty thousand, so a factor of twenty difference on the number of people that turned out, which seems pretty amazing. This really matters, because the protest is trying to show commitment, trying to show that people really care about this cause of lowering taxes, two million send a much stronger signal to the general public, and says that they should pay attention to these people.

Numbers aren't always perfect. Here are two pictures; one is a protest and one of them isn't. One of them is the Live Aid Concert in London, and the demonstration said look, we have hundreds of thousands of people turning out for the cause of debt cancellation for Africa. The other one is just a free concert that the New York Philharmonic put on in Central Park. So I'd argue that getting numbers to turn up doesn't really mean anything if the people aren't sacrificing anything, it doesn't show any commitment if people are willing to spend the afternoon listening to music in a park, because clearly they're willing to do that voluntarily. So it actually shows a much higher commitment if people are putting up with some pain or inconvenience. In the famous civil rights marches in the US, people got sprayed by hoses. The World Trade Organisation protesters in Seattle were famously violent, and there was tear gas, and people were having chemicals sprayed on their faces. This again demonstrates much higher commitment to the cause. And then the highest level of course when people get shot at protests, that really tends to draw attention to their cause.

So those are good ways of showing commitment, but they rely on somebody actively opposing your protest and trying to harm you. I've actually found a surprisingly large number of creative ways that protests try and demonstrate commitment by making it essentially more inconvenient to participate in a protest than to just go march around on a nice afternoon. Animal Rights activists like to protest nude, and the way they do that is by getting a ton of people to lie naked covered in fake blood on the street to show what it would look like if people were in a slaughterhouse. And it's interesting because even if you think their protest movement is crazy, you can agree that they're more committed to their cause than the people watching a concert. There's a recently started movement in the US, this is by Pro-Life people who want to make abortion illegal, where people commit to cover their mouth with a piece of tape and not speak for an entire day; it can be fairly powerful if you notice several people in your day that are willing to make that sacrifice.

Then last week, perfect timing for this talk, in Thailand the protest organisers got people to donate blood in massive quantities. They have set up tents to collect blood from the people participating in the protest, they collected on the order of a thousand litres of blood, human blood, and then they marched through the streets with their containers of blood, and poured it all over the steps of the president's palace. This is basically brand new, I don't think that anyone's ever tried the "pouring blood" protest before, but without knowing anything about Thai politics, you can tell that people are really upset and willing to draw blood out of their body and pour it on the ground.

Malte Schwarzkopf: What was the government response to this protest?

Reply: To be honest I don't know, I don't feel qualified to break down Thai politics, I don't even know what these people want, or who they're protesting against, but they definitely proved to me that they don't like them because they're pouring blood out.

So if you take this to the extreme you get a hunger strike where you say that you're willing to starve yourself to death to demonstrate your opposition to something. Even more extreme than a hunger strike, people who are willing to burn themselves to death. Actually, if you do a quick web search, the number of people who have burned themselves to death is surprisingly high, maybe a dozen people do it every year for various causes. I was shocked at how many do it.

Right, so my goal for the talk is to try and figure out how we can do this online, doing something that's non-violent essentially, you're not making any attempt to harm your opposition, but you're proving commitment by sacrificing something that's of value to you. And actually looking around I think that there are signs that people are trying to do this. The basic protest that I showed earlier where you join this Facebook group that says, I want to save the seals, the reason it's ineffective is that you've proved zero commitment, because it essentially takes no time, and people have joined several hundred of these groups, so it's not impressive if you say that a hundred thousand people have joined your seal group.

This movement that started on Facebook in response to racism against Barack Obama, people, en masse, in the order of tens of thousand of people, changed their middle name on Facebook to be "Hussein" as a show of solidarity. And even though the number of people that did this was a lot smaller than the people who joined the big protest groups, it actually got a lot of coverage, because at least it is a very real sign of commitment, that you're willing to put something on your profile, and you can only change your middle name once. And similarly for Conan O'Brian, who I mentioned earlier, this image of Conan O'Brian spread around Facebook, and several hundred thousand people actually changed their profile picture away from themselves to the image of Conan, which again is a very slightly higher level of commitment to just joining a group because you're willing to in a sense make the service a little less useful because you no longer have a picture of yourself, you're replaced it with a symbol of your dedication to Conan O'Brian.

Right, so the actual security protocol that I want to describe to you basically takes this to the next level and asks, are you willing to sacrifice your entire profile over a cause that you believe in? The basic idea is that a group of protesters get together, they all say that they're willing to sacrifice some account that they have, this could be social networking, webmail, virtual role gaming, essentially I think the protest should work equally in those different environments. While the protest is going on all of these identities are locked so people can no longer actively use their account. There's a vote, so people have to vote to end the protest and unlock, which gives it kind of the unique property in that the commitment to the protest then becomes binding: there's the possibility of permanently losing your profile as part of this protest.

So say that there's a platform provided that controls access to these accounts, it's basically just an oracle that maintains a table of passwords, and it allows you to update. This is pretty simple, I think the only interesting security property is that I assume the platform owner is indifferent to the protest, so this is not a protest against Facebook or Gmail, in which case they would be an unwilling participant.

So you have your N protesters, each one of them has an account registered, and it can be from any of these different platforms. And then the funny kind of thing I have in the design right now, there's a protest initiator who is essentially a trusted third party, which I've tried to limit to trust in them a little bit, but this kind of dependency that means that you need to have a strongly trusted protest initiator, I'll come back to the trust assumption in a second.

So here's how it works: the initiator generates a master key for the entire protest, and then they generate shares in the private key and one symmetric escrow key. The people who want to join the protest have to send their password to the protest organiser who then verifies it's a valid password, and if it's a valid password they then go to the password oracle and reset that person's password, so the protest organiser now knows the new password for that person's account, so it's effectively locked and the original account owner can't log into it. And then the protest initiator sends back to that person a share of the private key, and then they're enrolled in the protest. So once everybody who's going to participate has joined, the protest organiser signs and publishes this big mass of stuff. For every protest participant, the new password that they need to recover their account is encrypted twice, once with the escrow key for the whole protest, and once with that participant's individual public key. The escrow key, which will let everybody get back into their accounts, is encrypted with this master key that everybody has shares of. So to end this protest, the participants all have to agree to end it so that they can collaboratively decrypt the escrow key. Once they've decrypted the escrow key then they can peel off this layer of encryption, and then each individual person will have the encryption and the password to get back into their account.

Audience: Is there some threshold of how many people it will take to decrypt the escrow key?

Reply: Right, the threshold is just a parameter, you can say it depends on what the social cause of the protest would be, what majority of people need to agree to end it, and you can do secret sharing with arbitrary thresholds if that's what you want.

Malte Schwarzkopf: So I see how this is nice and useful because the protest initiator can then destroy the private key, and then give access to all the passwords that are going to be with you all again when they all bind their shares. But my question is, is that necessary because people trust the protest initiator anyway because they give their clear text password to them. So if I'm going to give my clear text password to them, I trust them enough not to just ignore me later, so I don't need cryptographic assurance that they're not going to screw me over.

Reply: Well you can't really get cryptographic assurance that they've destroyed the key anyway. The only situation where destroying the key, it's possible you can think of the protest organisers being some machine or some hardware secure module, that everybody then takes sledgehammers to afterwards. But essentially, yes, I agree that it's fairly weak, there's a lot of trust in the protest organiser at the beginning. The important thing though is that they can go offline, I mean, they can organise this protest then wash their hands of it.

Malte Schwarzkopf: No, it's not at all a question, I'm just wondering if this whole framework is actually necessary because you can just have trusted machines that gather all the passwords. But I assume that you're going to be developing this.

Reply: Yes.

Alex Shafarenko: I think there's a better answer to those questions. Any protest that critically depends on a single individual is vulnerable, this is a protocol that uses that vulnerability. So if the secret police make an arrest, the protocol is broken.

Reply: That's a good point, yes. So let me introduce a few variants on this, and I'll try and give it inspiration, so the basic protocol I just described was a boycott, everybody has their accounts locked for some time, and then eventually, hopefully after the demands are met and you end the protest, so the boycott has succeeded. And then, like I've been saying, since you have this cryptographic binding before the protest can break, it's at best a little bit unusual for offline protests, the best analogy I could think of is when the protesters chain themselves around some object, like these people did on the streets of San Francisco, essentially those people can't withdraw from the protest because they are physically bound to all the people around them.

The first extension, if you want to, the last protest, the only way for it to end, I guess it could go on forever, in which case nobody will ever gain access to their account because it's impossible for it to end negatively, which is different than a hunger strike. So one of the reasons hunger strikes can be effective is that they impose a time by which point people will start dying for health reasons, and with a lot of hunger strikes there will be a countdown on how long that people have been fasting, which is aimed to put pressure on decision makers to cave in to demands. So if we add one thing to this protest, to this protocol that I propose, there need to be two escrow keys, so essentially there's a positive escrow key and a negative escrow key. And the positive one is, if you decrypt that means end of protest and everybody gets their accounts back, and if you collaboratively decrypt the negative escrow key then everybody's account is destroyed. And the account destruction is a little bit strange, so you notice the differences that, if the positive key encrypts, encryption of the person's password, so once you decrypt that only that person can get it back. And with the negative account, with the negative escrow key encrypted this y_i directly, which I said is an account destruction key, so maybe the platform allows you to register a specific password just to destroy the account, more likely that is actually just the password, and you assume that if this process is happening then it's probably known, and people vote to end it with the suicide option, then everybody's password will be publicly known, and griefers will come and essentially destroy those accounts for you.

And then there's another modification that you might want in case you don't want just one vote to unlock everybody or destroy everybody. You can do them individually, so you can wrap a different escrow key around each person's destruction key. I'm not really sure how useful this is, it will allow you to do a protest where individuals are sort of dying at some continued frequency, so maybe everyday you erase an escrow account to try and put pressure on the people you're negotiating with. There's kind of an analogy between doing that and doing a protest where gunfire is coming randomly hitting people, but I think it's a little bit weaker.

Right, so that's the basic variation that I was going to propose. I guess I'll try and start some discussion by just saying that the limitations that I recognise in this protocol now, and I'd be interested to hear more. I believe that you can't use this protest to protest against the platform operators themselves, because obviously they have the power to block, they can block the account destruction, they can undo account destruction, they can not let the protest organiser change passwords, and all sorts of other things. And then in the real world people do want to use Facebook to protest Facebook itself, so that's not something that I think would work here. There's also a pretty important limitation that George actually brought up a couple of months ago, which is that you have to have a minority of all the people on whatever the platform is, like if you had two thirds of Facebook participating in your protest, then even if Facebook was indifferent to what you were trying to achieve with the protest, they would block it because they can't afford to lose that many users. And the sacrifice is actually much lower, if everybody leaves Facebook at once then you haven't really lost anything valuable because Facebook no longer exists, and Facebook will start again somewhere else, which is basically what happened. Does anybody recognise the logo? This is Friendster, which was Facebook before Facebook, with all the media buzz and people thinking it was the next big thing, friends who disappeared, and all their friends were people who were on Facebook, and that wasn't a protest, that was just a technological evolution.

There's another problem which is that in the offline world everybody's life can be taken to have roughly equal value, and if a person dies in the process it's a person who's died, and everybody knows essentially what that means. In different places where this online protest might happen, online identities are worth less or more depending on how long they've been around, how much people are dedicated to them. In the market for World of Warcraft accounts, values vary a lot: an account that's been around for longer and has more experience is worth a lot more than a new one. And I think there's no real defence against this at the protocol level, you have to trust the protest organisers not to let anyone join the protest if they have an account that is really new and not worth anything.

Malte Schwarzkopf: There is a real life analogy about that surely, and that's that if people protest in different parts of the world, it's not a question of the value of their life, but their protest is going to be noticed in different place. So if someone starves to death in Africa, it's probably not going to make a big difference to someone who does a hunger strike and starves to death in the US or in Europe, where it will get lots of attention, so the identity of different value in different parts of the world, I think that's the analogy that you can draw there.

Reply: Yes. I mean, that's definitely true, I feel like it's for slightly different reasons that media covers both those things.

Malte Schwarzkopf: Or if a celebrity took part

Reply: But isn't that still because they're famous or because they're lives are valued more?

Malte Schwarzkopf: But how did they become famous, they became famous by building up their identity over time.

Reply: OK, I mean, I guess, I mean if a person's who's life is really terrible starves themselves to death in a protest, the reaction wouldn't be, well that doesn't seem very nice, we're going to ignore this, because his life was bad anyway.

Jonathan Anderson: Well the Cambridge Academics sort did that when they said, we're going to have draconian IP, and then it took Ross and some other people to say, well we'll leave if you do this, and maybe if it was all junior faculty members nobody would care.

Reply: OK, yes, so maybe there is more of an analogy then.

Reply: So trust in the organizer is essential, and I guess I'm sort of weakly saying that this might, the protest organiser hopefully isn't a strong activist in causing some mutual third party it's trusted this sort of overseeing process, which is why I was thinking that it might be like EFF, or maybe Amnesty International, some organisation like that, who oversees this protest, and does the crypto in the beginning of it. There's kind of an analogy for this in the offline world: Jimmy Carter, Nelson Mandela, Kofi Anan, several other very famous diplomats who are all near the end of their lives, formed a formal organisation called The Elders. It's about ten or fifteen people who joined the club who are all very well respected statesmen around the world, so that they can collaboratively weigh in if there's a disputed election in some country. The elders will issue a statement basically saying, we as respected statesmen, who don't have much directly to gain in this, are all on this side. So that's kind of more what I was hoping would be the people who would take essential trust, people who essentially I guess have nothing riding either side.

I think that voting, I mean, there's some technical issues which, the difference between voting and doing this threshold decryption, I think the more interesting problems are how you deal with Sybil attacks, people trying to register multiple accounts in a protest so they can have more votes, whether the protest is being infiltrated by the opposition with a bunch of fake accounts. And again, essentially you have to rely on some vetting process to determine this a real account that's being committed in the protest so we're comfortable giving them voting rights, or else it's not, and that has to also follow the protest organiser.

Michael Roe: The Facebook policy is people are supposed to use their real names for an account. We know that the account should be a real person's account rather than a pretend account.

Reply: Absolutely, but if you're having a protest against a powerful company, they can find ten thousand people who don't care about Facebook, slip them a little bit of money to start a Facebook account and join the protest, and then they will have infiltrated it. It helps if the accounts aren't freely created, and require proving identity somehow, but it's something that you have to check for I guess.

So to return to the criteria I set out for how I wanted to design an online protest system, does this scheme demonstrate morality, I think so, it's definitely non-violent. I think the main way that this would be attacked socially is that whether or not people really understood how the scheme worked, and if they understood the cryptographic implication of things, if there was too much trust in the organiser herding people into the protest. In terms of commitment, does this really demonstrate, if people have sacrificed their Facebook over some cause, does that really demonstrate a commitment. That depends on your point of view, I think for a lot of people it seems silly and maybe even insulting to be comparing giving up online accounts to real hunger strikers, but on the other hand, if you go around and look at the way a lot of people use social networks and other things online, these are really important to people, and the prospect of giving that up is actually, is a fairly big sacrifice for a lot of people.

Anil Madhavapeddy: I guess there's an assumption here that having a sacrifice makes for an effective protest, but what effect would this have on media coverage.

Reply: So I kind of, yes, my opinion, I mean, protests really, they need media attention and shame to work, right, I mean, the reason people are burning themselves to death is effective because it gets in the paper, and then people will go and read about the cause and care about it, right. So this is, in a sense this is no different, the goal of this whole thing in the end is to get a lot of coverage in the press, and for people to say, well young people really care about this issue, and they're willing to sacrifice this. If people actually did this protest, how the press would view it, would they cover it, I have no idea, it would be a really, really interesting social experiment.

Alex Shafarenko: I think there's a flaw in this because what you have to assume is that by giving out your password you're sort of blocking the identity, all you're blocking is access to certain files and certain webpages. Now if I were to be a malicious protester who wants to participate for the purposes of promoting myself, but not sacrifice anything what I would do, I would tell all my connections a month in advance that my reserve identity is Alex Bryant, and if you don't see Alex on this system because, you know, there was a suicide mission, then please check that, and if you see somebody with that name, that's me, only, you know, reincarnated. What would have been useful is a monitoring facility, what I've been thinking about for the last ten years is whether this could be de-centralised. The major flaw is this proposal is the trusted third party, and this has already been said, if there's a trusted third party there's no need to do any of this, and that trusted third party could be an intermediary for all of it, including the end of the protest or suicide and just send messages at some point that say, OK, so-and-so is under house arrest. Well yes, so-and-so under house arrest, and basically your identity is already screwed because they have found the database, and they've already delivered all your identities no matter what you do, and you can't get them back.

Reply: I mean, it is possible for the protest organiser to destroy everything and then go offline and disappear.

Alex Shafarenko: Well you need a threat model basically, and a more precise threat model, and a more accurate description of the third party. What would be interesting is to find a technological basis on which a third party becomes unnecessary, because the way things are at the moment on, social networks are like computer accounts where you will be without a password. These will not provide an adequate technological basis for transferable accounts. Maybe there's a way accounts become transferable, and those sort of events become easier without transferring?

Anil Madhavapeddy: If I just follow up your answer, it seems this is a weird case. So if you take the Digital Economy Bill, there's a kind of really big commitment to immorality as well, where all of the companies that closetedly wanted it to happen, the corporate interests and lobbying to do, they spent a lot of time and effort constructing their agenda in order to do a bad thing. Should we be setting up corporations that would also try to find the same turf?

Reply: Well so you're saying that the way the Digital Economy Bill got proposed was through whatever lobbying and influence and that people should be essentially responding in kind?

Anil Madhavapeddy: Well just why have the asymmetry?

Reply: Well, that's an old question, right. I mean, why did Ghandi say, be non-violent, when the other side is violent? I mean, philosophers have addressed this problem for a long time, and the standard argument is that everybody in power resorts to violence and we have to rise above them. If you don't believe that, that's completely fine, if you want to advocate violence in certain cases, and in some sense violence is maybe the wrong word, because then it gets into these issues of morality and things, the question maybe is tactically, would it be better to do the same sort of dirty tactics as the other side.

Anil Madhavapeddy: Yes, it's not necessarily destructive as violence, especially online.

Reply: If the long term goal is to gain the support of the general public, there is advantage in claiming that you're the moral side.

Malte Schwarzkopf: I think in this model you're trying to prove that you are moral and for everyone to realise that you have a point. But the dimension I think this lacks, but I think is hard, potentially impossible to do in online protests, is to inconvenience whoever your protest is against. If I go and poor blood on the steps of the president's palace, that is inconveniencing government, not just because of the media attention (well mainly because of the media attention), but it's not just that some people have a moral point, it's also that they are doing something nasty, though not actually violent, to the government. There's a more direct link between the entity that they are protesting against and the protest than if I try and protest against seal clubbing by locking myself out of Facebook; that's like if I protest against seal clubbers by not eating bananas.

Reply: If the Thai protesters poured soda on the steps of the palace instead of blood, the inconvenience of cleaning the soda would not have mattered, and it's not that it's harder to clean than blood, the only reason it matters is because it's blood, and it's hard to get blood. So in some cases it would be a better to be more directly confronting people and going after the seal clubbers physically, but I guess I'm looking for forms of protest that are effective without doing that, and in the blood case, the actual harm caused is very minimal.

Malte Schwarzkopf: I'm not arguing about the harm done, but the link to the cause of the protest.

Relay-Proof Channels Using UWB Lasers

Bruce Christianson[1], Alex Shafarenko[1], Frank Stajano[2], and Ford Long Wong[2]

[1] University of Hertfordshire
[2] University of Cambridge

Consider the following situation: Alice is a hand-held device, such as a PDA. Bob is a device providing a service, such as an ATM, an automatic door, or an anti-aircraft gun pointing at the gyro-copter in which Alice is travelling.

Bob and Alice have never directly met before, but share a key as a result of secure hand-offs. Alice has used this key to request a service from Bob (dispense cash, open door, don't shoot). Before complying, Bob needs to be sure that it really is Alice that he can see in front of him, and not Mort.

Mort and her accomplice Cove are planning a wormhole attack along classic man-in-the-middle lines. They wait until Alice is in a situation where she expects to be challenged by Bob, and then Mort pretends to Bob that she is Alice, while Cove pretends to Alice that he is Bob.

Mort and Cove relay the appropriate challenges and responses to one another over a channel hidden from Alice and Bob, in order to allow the dual masquerade to succeed, following which Alice waits impatiently in front of a different ATM, or the wrong door, or another gun.

How can such an attack be prevented? Obviously it suffices if Alice and Bob both have a secure way of identifying their (relative) location to sufficient accuracy. But how can they do this?

Suppose that we could enclose Bob inside a Platonic Faraday cage, which blocks all information-bearing signals, not just the RF ones. At the end of the protocol run, Bob could be confident that Alice was also inside the Faraday cage. Provided the Platonic Faraday cage was of sufficiently small size and shape to satisfy the appropriate proximity requirement, Bob could proceed.

One way of providing such a Platonic Faraday cage is to use the laws of physics: for example distance-bounding protocols use the fact that the speed of light is finite[1].

In this position paper, we argue that the laws of information theory can be used instead. The key insight is that it doesn't matter if the Platonic Faraday cage leaks some information[2], provided the amount of information that Mort and Cove need to exchange is greater.

Previous work in this direction has relied upon restricting the rate at which Mort and Cove can communicate, essentially using a variant of covert channel analysis to reduce the rate of leakage. We propose the converse approach, using Ultra Wide Band (UWB) lasers to transfer so much information from Bob to

---

[1] Although there is some doubt in the case of entanglement: imagine a Josephson junction 30m wide changing state.

[2] Even Plato allowed for some information leakage.

B. Christianson and J. Malcolm (Eds.): Security Protocols 2010, LNCS 7061, pp. 45–46, 2014.

the location where he believes Alice to be that only a fraction of it could be relayed by Mort.

The real Alice knows where to look for the crucial signal bits, which are hidden at different time and wavelength positions according to a pseudo-random series seeded by the shared key, but Mort is stymied.

The use of UWB is widespread at microwave frequency bands, but we believe the use of it in visible light spectrum (where the information packing density is higher) to be novel. The continuous pulse rate is high (Pbps) and the power is very low. Normally in UWB receiver and transmitter are matched. Here the objective is that they should be deliberately mis-matched, with the transmitter sending more pulses than it is possible for the receiver to distinguish.

Consequently, by the Nyquist-Shannon Theorem (Signal to Noise Ratio version), a receiver who does not know precisely which pulses to capture will be unable to capture more than a small proportion of them. Effectively the attacker cannot relay the whole side-channel signal without amplifying the noise to the point where the signal is undecipherable. The beam contains too much information for a feasible transponder array to re-broadcast, and cannot be reflected using known mechanical or optical means.

This makes the proposed UWB laser approach ideal for use outdoors: simultaneous use of two[3] narrow beam directional lasers from different positions on a baseline of suitable direction and length allows the position of a remote object to be accurately determined in three dimensional space.

In contrast, although the use of multiple simultaneous distance bounding protocols allows triangulation within the convex hull of the base points[4], objects cannot be located outside the convex hull with the distance bounding technique.

At the other extreme, on the small (tabletop) scale, the use of a single UWB laser allows a Platonic Faraday cage to be provided by a cardboard box.

References

1. Christianson, B., Shafarenko, A.: Vintage Bit Cryptography. In: Christianson, B., Crispo, B., Malcolm, J.A., Roe, M. (eds.) Security Protocols. LNCS, vol. 5087, pp. 261–265. Springer, Heidelberg (2009)
2. Clulow, J., Hancke, G.P., Kuhn, M.G., Moore, T.: So Near and Yet So Far: Distance-Bounding Attacks in Wireless Networks. In: Buttyán, L., Gligor, V.D., Westhoff, D. (eds.) ESAS 2006. LNCS, vol. 4357, pp. 83–97. Springer, Heidelberg (2006)
3. Damgård, I.B., Nielsen, J.B., Wichs, D.: Isolated Proofs of Knowledge and Isolated Zero Knowledge. In: Smart, N.P. (ed.) EUROCRYPT 2008. LNCS, vol. 4965, pp. 509–526. Springer, Heidelberg (2008)
4. Stajano, F., Wong, F.-L., Christianson, B.: Multichannel Protocols to Prevent Relay Attacks. In: Sion, R. (ed.) FC 2010. LNCS, vol. 6052, pp. 4–19. Springer, Heidelberg (2010)

---

[3] In the variable position case it may be necessary to have three fixed-position lasers and choose which two to use depending on the desired position of Alice.

[4] For example, an accurate upper bound on distance from four non-coplanar points allows the responder to be located accurately within the tetrahedron which is their convex hull.

Relay-Proof Channels Using UWB Lasers
(Transcript of Discussion)

Alex Shafarenko

University of Hertfordshire

This talk is about the mechanics of security as well as protocols for security; what I am trying to do is to work out some general principles of a certain technology that is necessary for a certain type of security protocol.

This is an authentication problem with a twist. There's a prover and a verifier, they talk to each other, they use standard protocols for the prover to prove its identity to the verifier. The twist is that both the prover and the verifier have spatial coordinates, and the goal is not just to verify that the prover is who he says he is, but also that he is there in person.

The verifier verifies the identity of the prover, but also the prover has some assurance that the verifier is talking directly to the prover. So there are two physical entities involved in the protocol, whether it's explicitly by actually finding where they are, or implicitly by providing assurance that they are where they are assumed to be. This turns out to be an incredibly subtle problem. It's not a new problem, there's been research in this area, but the way that this tends to be looked at is distinctly logical and not technological, and the trouble with logic is that it is, by necessity, a model, and the model throws something away, and people have to support the model with technology finally. And that's when you discover that you threw away something that needs to be there in the model. If I manage at the end of this talk to convince you that there's something fishy about all these systems then I have achieved my main goal, but I might be able to do a little more.

So why this is important is due to the so-called relay attack, which probably you know. What happens here is that the genuine principals, Bob the verifier and Alice the prover, have two impostors, two men-in-the-middle, spliced in, that are two agents of Moriarty, Mort and Cove, and although Alice believes she is talking to Bob, in fact she is talking Cove, who is relaying every message from Alice to Mort, who is talking to Bob, and vice-versa.

There's nothing wrong with the messages sent, the integrity is not compromised, authenticity is not violated. What is violated is the binding between the message and the principal, because Alice is in the next room, and Bob faces somebody who appears to be Alice, does as Alice would, except Alice is not there, it's Mort, who is an agent of Moriarty.

But why is it so important? It is important because sometimes material goods are involved in this transaction, like I am going through the door, this is the door, this is me going, except it's not me, it's Mort who goes through this as a result of this authentication transaction. And I am actually going through a door somewhere else, into an entirely unimportant place, not knowing that I am actually letting somebody in elsewhere.

B. Christianson and J. Malcolm (Eds.): Security Protocols 2010, LNCS 7061, pp. 47–53, 2014.

Now if I could include spatial coordinates in the protocol, then that attack would not work, because I would be saying, I'm Alice located here, and Bob would check the coordinates to see that whoever appears to be talking to him is at that location. But what reliable method do we have for coordinate verification? Obviously if you give me three numbers, that's not much use for me, they have to have landmarks, as part of the scene, and I have to reference the principals with the set of these landmarks, and these landmarks should be sufficiently prominent, and sufficiently dense in the environment, not to allow Mort to mingle with Alice somewhere, and confuse Bob so that he can't distinguish one from the other.

George Danezis: Isn't the case that if you just include coordinates in the messages, you can't actually authenticate to something that is further away? So if my car knows where it is, because it has some GPS in it, and then I'm opening the door with a hand-held remote, and that door relays the message to a door that is further away, if within the encrypted shell of the messages both sides introduce coordinates . . .

Reply: Absolutely, then the attempted relay would not work.

Bruce Christianson: Provided you have a foolproof unspoofable unbreakable un-denial-of-service-able trustworthy GPS within your security envelope.

Reply: But what is a reliable method to do coordinate verification? What if I think that you have this set of coordinates, in fact you have a different set of coordinates, just because my coordinates system is off, and it is off enough to allow as the impostor to share the square that's recognised as one coordinate on the coordinate system.

George Danezis: Ah, I was a bit confused about what the problem was.

Reply: Now if you use electronic means of positioning, they have to be authenticated, effectively you introduce a third party, you don't want to do that, the whole point of this type of protocol is not to rely on third parties, you want to be able to verify locally that the principals are actually bound to the cryptographic entities that represent them. You could instead focus on the communication technology and use it in order to achieve the properties that you want. So you have your options, you can make relay strictly impossible, or you can make relay prohibitively expensive, or alternatively you may just make it detectable, in which case it's ineffective. You don't have any other options if you want to look into verification.

So start from the top here, what is it to make a relay impossible? Well you can use a physical principle, for instance, the speed of light is limited, so any delay would lengthen the communication path, therefore it will increase the communication delay, and there are so-called distance bounding protocols, Kuhn etc, which are based on this principle. The trouble with this whole approach of distance bounding is that what we measure is not just the propagation delay, we measure the sum of the propagation delay and the processing delay, whatever time it takes to run the tiny little protocol. So they simplify that protocol tremendously, in fact all that most distance bounding protocols do is an XOR with an incoming message, which doesn't take much time.

But if you are operating in a very small confined volume, you will need to differentiate between communication over say ten foot distances and twenty foot distances, right, and we are talking about units of nanoseconds. And what these people don't allow for is that delays in the receiver and transmitter of that order are not to do with the distance, they're to do with electronic processing, you have to charge up a line to trigger a latch at the end of it, and that's not the propagation time, it's the time associated with the capacitance of that line, which could be significant. So when you are in a nanosecond range, the variation of delay could be significant. Now Moriarty has a lot more resources than Alice, so Moriarty could have a huge parallel receive and processing system, and could try to reduce that capacitance delay so much that it will mask the difference in propagation time.

There are protocols that try to accommodate those possibilities, there are some partial solutions, but they're never completely satisfactory. OK, another option is make relay detectable, how do you make relays detectable, this is an old problem, how do you make a copy distinguishable from the original. Now if we're talking about copies of bits, that's pretty hard isn't it, because all zeros are the same. There is technology called quantum fibre where you have individual photons propagated in a coherent quantum mechanical state, and if you try to measure that photon then you change it. So if you try to relay it, you have to first measure it, and then reproduce it, and that changes the original, which is detectable. That is in a price bracket that I don't want to consider for supermarkets, for instance. It is a possible way of going about this, but I don't think this is necessarily the cheapest way. What I would like to focus on is something that is practical, cheap, and reliable. If Moriarty has all the resources of the world, and I want to be be a hundred years future-proof, then I fail, but if I am developing this technology for today, and maybe five years from today I redevelop it quickly and cheaply, then maybe that will work. Most security assurances are cost-based anyway.

What we need for a practical approach are some universal principles, so that whenever the culture changes, and we want new technology to support this approach, then we can check it against certain principles on a checklist, and if we satisfy those principles, then we are more or less assured that this would work as advertised. So are there such principles? OK, this is the core strategy, I call it OWM, overwhelm Moriarty. There's Moriarty somewhere, he's trying to listen on all communications to relay them, we're trying to make it very hard for him to do that. How do we overwhelm Moriarty? We, the verifier, offer a massive challenge, not a few bits but a few tens of terabits, of which the real challenge that the honest receiver should receive is a tiny proportion, a tiny fraction, that only the true Alice knows where to find, because that information is part of the shared secret between the prover and the verifier.

Now how does Alice get to that portion of data? Alice would use passive selection of this significant part sent by the prover, passive selection that does not involve detection, amplification or retransmission. Passive selection does not distort anything, it is totally safe to use. For instance, when you listen to the radio, you tune your receiver, you're choosing the wavelength that you receive, you're not distorting any other wavelengths, and you're not using any machinery for signal amplification in order to select. Moriarty does not have this luxury, Moriarty does not know where the signal is, where the actual challenge lies, because the actual challenge is small. So Moriarty would have to relay the whole huge amount of information without changing any tiny bit of it. And that would require a huge communication capacity. Communication capacity is not the same as channel capacity, channel capacity refers to the ability of channels to sustain a certain number of data bits per second. Communication capacity includes the capacity to receive, detect, communicate, and then return a message, so includes all processing both ends. And whereas you can have a significant channel capacity, communication capacity would be more limited.

So it looks like we have two requirements here. Requirement one is to prevent passive relay. Otherwise Moriarty does not even have to be there in the scene, because whatever signals are sent from the verifier to the prover may simply be received further away, and I call this a passive relay, something that acts as a relay due to the core properties of the original channel, so you have to prevent the passive relay. So examples of passive relays include mirrors or waveguides, between the verifier with a laser beaming light at the prover, so these things should be prevented.

They could be prevented passively or actively. Passively by putting things in the proverbial Faraday cage, I say proverbial because what people use this phrase for is not exactly what Faraday meant it to be, Faraday cage is an isolation unit in security models. So how do we isolate this completely so that the source of the signal and the receiver are in some closed volume, or we actually physically block the signal outside a certain volume. But there are also active ways of preventing passive relays. One active way which I find very useful is when you create a noise. Just create a lot of noise outside the area of communication, if it's optics we're talking about, bright light everywhere, except in the little tiny volume of space where you have the prover and the verifier talking to each other. So if Moriarty wants to passively eavesdrop on that he will have to contend with this huge interference. You can also focus a signal on one point in space. If you focus light on one point and put a mirror there you will disperse that light all over the space.

Requirement two, the transmitter must be able to achieve a greater dynamic range than any feasible receiver, and that sounds paradoxical because people think that a transmitter and receiver share the same kind of technology, in fact they don't, receiver technology is much more subtle and much more difficult than transmit technology. A radio 4 transmitter on the Isle of Wight here radiates one Megawatt of radio frequency power in long-wave, and you can build a circuit that emits only 1 nanowatt, and you can use them together on slightly differing frequencies, that gives you 12 orders of magnitude, 150 dB dynamic range. Now if you can build a radio receiver that can receive 150 dB dynamic range, i.e. a waveform accuracy of more than 24 bit, you will be a rich person very soon, because all I know is possible at the moment is 60 to 80 dB maybe.

So how do we do that, what sort of graded dynamic range? You can build different physical parameters, you can have verifiable limits on the receiver size, that's the easiest of all, whatever the receiver technology, if you demand that the prover produces a miniature receiver, say you've given them a slot in which to plug it, then you will limit the ability of that receiver to receive very much, because receivers have to be large if they have some reasonable dynamic range. Physical limits to linearity I've already mentioned, if you have to contend with huge signals and small signals, you will distort either the huge signals by saturation, or the small signals by limited challenge capacity. That's the more subtle one, limited challenge capacity because the sensor has a transmitter, OK, so you have a sensor, it receives signals from the verifier, but then if you are Moriarty, there's a huge demand for information that you have to relay, and the stream that you have in this relay system to the transmitter can't be narrowed by the channel if we're going to sustain that level of communication.

So these are the principles. Now I'll show one example that illustrates all these principles in one go. Suppose we decide to use an optical channel between the verifier and prover to make the communication unrelayable. So we are sending the challenge from the verifier to the prover over a beam of light. Now to make the transmitter overwhelm the receiver I use all sorts of wavelengths first of all, it is quite feasible for visible light (400 to 800 nanometres) to have a laser that is capable of radiating 400 nanometres broadband light, so from red to blue. Here I will have about 400 colour channels, each colour channel will carry easily 100 megabits per second. The information will be noise, except for certain very narrow spectral windows, the position of these windows will be governed by the shared secret that the prover and the verifier have, OK. So this is the window for the green channel and I see a signal here, this is the window for the red channel, I see no signal here, and this is the window for the blue channel, I have a signal here, so I have received one green, zero red and one blue, that's the code that I have received. If I can collect about 100 bits over a second, I'm OK. Over the same second Moriarty will receive 100 billion times 400, about 5 TeraBytes. If he has to relay that, I don't think that's easy.

Example: sensor nib

Fig. 1. The prover

Now this is the prover's device, it's a pen with a nib, the nib is one cubic millimetre in size. The verifier has a lot of space available, so the verifier has lots of lasers shining at different angles, and the prover has installed a sensor in one point here, but where that point is Mort doesn't know. So we have wavelength, time and angle. That, in my view, can give me two orders of magnitude more, so that would probably push me up to half a PetaByte per second, communicated over that short distance. If you're Mort you'll have to retransmit that. Now Mort can't do that for the following reasons. Mort can't do it over the radio, it really doesn't carry that kind of bandwidth. Mort can't do it over another beam of light that she shines from her device to Cove's fake verifier. The reason for that is that it wouldn't travel in empty space because of the huge bandwidths, it will actually disperse, you can't focus it here. Here it doesn't need to because Alice's sensor is thrust against Bob's light source, there's no propagation.

Jonathan Anderson: What if Mort's sensor in fact is a whole big bundle of fibres, and at the end they all go in different directions and so Cove can re-create ...

Reply: One cubic millimetre, and a whole bunch of fibres, which you have to coordinate, you have to make a parallel beam of light, this is focused now on this point. So you have a tiny little microwave, and behind it one fibre, yes, you can have one fibre, but I can make this volume as small as I want because this is light, so we're talking here, 10, 20 microns. Even if Mort has a perfect fibre channel, because Moriarty is a genius, right, then where does this fibre go to? Mort is standing in front of a till and she has this huge cable full of optical fibres coming out from under her petticoats, and trailing along the floor to Cove's trouser leg. It's not really practical. I work with Aston University Photonics Group, they are actually my experts in the physical side of things, and they assure me that there's no such thing as mobile fibre optic communication, they said that if that was possible a lot of people would be a lot richer. At the moment it's practically impossible.

This is my device, this is the area that we've flooded with light to avoid free space propagation. This is my little cavity with a nib. And I use every physical parameter I can. My main ones are time and bandwidth, that I can always do, I can have a lot of different wavelengths. Now the problem is, whenever I show a diagram like this I need to prove to you that I have passive filtration facilities, remember the principals have to be passive because otherwise they wouldn't reduce the effect of noise and extract the signal. Do I or do I not have them? In fact I would not have been able to do this thing only two or three years ago, the reason for it is that in astronomy there's a similar problem. You have a telescope looking at a far galaxy in the sky. The light from that galaxy is in fact almost completely masked by the scattered light of the sky, right, and this scattering only happens in very narrow spectral windows that correspond to spectral lines of the primitive elements there, oxygen, hydrogen, maybe molecules like water, etc, so there are about 150 lines in total that all the blue sky light energy sits in. So astronomers had to set their telescope in the mountains or in outer space because they couldn't deal with that, because the amount of light that they get from the sky exceeds by 20 orders of magnitude the weak light from the stars. So then they did not have good optical filters, but now they do.

I have a publication from 2009 on my desk where they report a filter with 102 dB efficiency, and the spectral windows that they deal with are exactly 100 1nm channels, that's what I want to do. So they can now slice portions of 1nm of visible spectrum and suppress everything else by a factor of 102 dB, which is about four billion. So we can have a passive filter for this system sitting here, the filter by itself is very portable, essentially a piece of portable fibre, and there's a diffraction grating inside, and that grating is very high tech. To calculate where the elements of the grating need to go requires a supercomputer, and they're very, very impenetrable computational schemes, they have only just found a way of implementing it, many months of computing because this is a very poorly defined problem.

Now all I need is to wind this fibre into a small volume, put it behind the sensor here, the sensor is just a lens essentially, and then here I have only 1 millimetre width, one channel, 40 Petabits per second, I use a timer to slice up little pieces of it, and then put these pieces together. That's my message challenge. And I reply by radio or by, I don't know, by voice, it doesn't matter, because the channel is already unrelayed. If it's unrelayed all one way, that's enough to bind the principals to the endpoint. That's it, OK, thank you.

George Danezis: There are related approaches using spectrum, that effectively have similar properties, where you share a key ...

Reply: Indeed, this is spread spectrum essentially.

George Danezis: So you could have used it maybe over RF as well?

Reply: Well you can use it over RF, but that's not enough, because RF can be relayed over optics. I wouldn't have been saying that five years ago, but now we have software defined radio, which can sample a large chunk of radio spectrum with a digital converter. We didn't dream about that five years ago, that wasn't even remotely possible, now it's just a commodity problem. So we can't use radio any more as it's now relayable, even the microwave portion is generally relayable over optics, but optics cannot be piggybacked on anything else yet, I mean, I'm not aware of anything. Maybe X-rays.

Bruce Christianson: Preventing relaying is a matter of having an appropriate Faraday cage to enclose the protocol. Low energy frequencies are easy to stop: wire mesh will stop RF (including microwaves), and black paper will stop visible light (including IR and UV). Higher energy frequencies (such as X-rays) have a low background level, so it's easy to detect if they are being used with sufficient bandwidth to relay the entire challenge[1]: as Alex pointed out earlier, for a Platonic Faraday cage relay-detection suffices[2].

---

[1] Remember, Moriarty is evil and doesn't care about fatalities.

[2] We might also need some Tupperware to slow down the nano-bots.

Using Dust Clouds
to Enhance Anonymous Communication

Richard Mortier[1], Anil Madhavapeddy[2], Theodore Hong[2], Derek Murray[2], and Malte Schwarzkopf[2]

[1] Horizon Digital Economy Research
Sir Colin Campbell Building, Triumph Road
Nottingham NG7 2TU, UK
richard.mortier@nottingham.ac.uk
[2] University of Cambridge
15 JJ Thomson Avenue
Cambridge CB3 0FD, UK
{firstname.lastname}@cl.cam.ac.uk

1 Introduction

Cloud computing platforms, such as Amazon EC2 [1], enable customers to lease several *virtual machines* (VMs) on a per-hour basis. The customer can now obtain a dynamic and diverse collection of machines spread across the world. In this paper we consider how this aspect of cloud computing can facilitate anonymous communications over untrusted networks such as the Internet, and discuss some of the challenges that arise as a result.

Most anonymous networks act as a *mix network*, creating hard-to-trace communications by using chains of proxy servers. For example, Mixmaster[1] is an anonymous re-mailer based on the mix-net protocol [2], MorphMix [10] is a peer-to-peer circuit-based mix network, and the popular Tor [4] network is onion routed.

Tor faces a major challenge: the pool of nodes available to route other people's traffic is limited. Individuals often desire anonymity for their communications, but they may be unwilling to route other (potentially illegal) traffic through their personal machines, and expose themselves to legal action in doing so. In addition, user-provided nodes are often short-lived and unreliable because they run on home machines or laptops, which can only route traffic when they are powered on and connected to the Internet.

In this position paper, we introduce the concept of a *dust cloud*: a dynamic set of short-lived VMs that run on cloud computing platforms and act as Tor nodes. Users can join a dust cloud when they require anonymous communication, and incur charges only while participating. We outline the core architecture and benefits of dust clouds (§2), before considering some of the challenges for successful adoption of dust clouds and suggesting avenues for development and research (§3).

---

[1] http://mixmaster.sourceforge.net/

B. Christianson and J. Malcolm (Eds.): Security Protocols 2010, LNCS 7061, pp. 54–59, 2014.
© Springer-Verlag Berlin Heidelberg 2014

2 Dust Clouds

To use a dust cloud, we assume that users have access to public cloud computing facilities, e.g., Amazon EC2 or Rackspace. When a user wants to communicate anonymously, they spawn one or more *dust motes*, cloud VMs that run Tor and are configured to survive for fixed periods of time (possibly all different). These Tor nodes receive the user's traffic as possible ingress points, as well as routing for other nodes as normal. When the user finishes communicating via a particular dust mote, they disconnect from it, leaving it to continue routing other traffic until its allotted time expires and it is destroyed.[2]

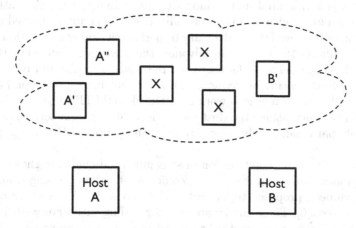

Fig. 1. Dynamic VM-based Tor nodes in the cloud. Host A spawns two VMs (A' and A'') and Host B spawns a single VM (B'). All VMs are full Tor routers.

How is this better than the existing model of the user's host directly acting as a router?

Privilege Separation. It is no longer the user's host computer that routes other traffic in the Tor network, but their dust motes instead. In case of, for example, complaints about abuse originating from the user's Tor node [8], the user can terminate the dust mote and demonstrate from the code image (also hosted on the cloud) that the offending traffic came from a participant in the mix network. This is considerably more difficult to do when Tor is installed directly on a personal computer, which typically have multiple applications that can generate traffic. Privilege separation also makes it more convenient for users to run exit routers, an important benefit as the Tor network currently suffers from a lack of exit bandwidth.

---

[2] A real-world analogue uses ionization trails of meteors during atmospheric entry to establish short-lived communications paths [7].

Storage Separation. A dust mote can run independent processing and has some storage, enabling it to buffer traffic to improve mixing. Doing this efficiently requires protocol proxies inside the dust mote that understand the application traffic to some extent. For example, an SMTP proxy could receive e-mail, and hold it for a random amount of time before passing it along to the next Tor node. Crucially, this delay does not require the user to be online and connected—the dust mote continues running for its allotted time without the original user being connected.

Processor Separation. Running proxies alongside nodes enables other interesting use models. Streaming large video files is currently impractical since the regular traffic patterns and limited node bandwidth make anonymising the paths difficult. Viewing a long video or, more generally, performing any long-lived transfer over Tor makes it easier for an adversary to perform a timing correlation attack. If the user requests the content in advance, the dust mote can cache the content from the origin server. The user then re-connects to Tor and retrieves the content for offline viewing anonymously, but without having to be online while it is assembled. Similar methods work for PDF files (HTTP range requests) and peer-to-peer networks, since the dust mote's local storage can serve as a buffer. For the truly paranoid, the dust mote could even connect to Freenet [3] to store its data.

One extremely useful combination of streaming and clouds might be to provide anonymous audio, and even video, conferences. Self-organising transcoding systems have been proposed to let real-time audio scale with network capacity in multicast trees [6]. These can be adapted for scaling with *anonymity* in mind, by introducing jitter when routing audio to the participants so that everyone receives a slightly different signal. The CPU capacity for this would be provided by dust motes owned by those participating in the call.

Usage Accounting. Each dust mote that the user creates is paid for, and helps to grow the network as well as anonymise that user's traffic. Thus, a heavy user will naturally pay more by spawning more dust motes, and since these dust motes *must* route other user's traffic in order to preserve anonymity, it also helps to grow the network as a whole.

Ease of Use. The provision of pre-configured VM templates makes it easy to create and destroy Tor nodes in the cloud. Ease of use is important for mix networks in order to grow the set of users, and hence the size of the anonymity set and the relay bandwidth available. Using pre-defined templates which can clearly be shown to act *only* as Tor nodes and *not* to manipulate the data also helps to achieve plausible deniability.[3]

---

[3] There are cases of arrests due to running Tor exit nodes, e.g.,
http://bit.ly/5WAflQ

3   Challenge/Response

Cloud computing is a promising platform for a mix network such as Tor, but it also presents several interesting challenges. In this section, we discuss some of these challenges, and suggest potential mitigations wherever possible.

3.1   Longevity

Challenge. Dust motes are relatively short-lived and exhibit a high churn rate. This can disrupt Tor usage: a dust mote might be terminated while still in use as a relay.

Response. As a cloud VM's lifetime is paid for and fixed ahead of time, dust motes can advertise their scheduled termination time, allowing users to manage the effects of termination. Tor circuits are pre-emptively constructed and rotated frequently, so clients can stop using a dust mote that is about to shut down without disruption. Indeed, in many ways the predictable life expectancy of dust motes makes the cloud a more suitable platform for Tor than personal computers, which may be turned off at any time without warning.

3.2   Diversity

Challenge. There are two associated diversity challenges for the dust cloud, provider and geographic. At present there are relatively few significant cloud computing providers such as Amazon or Rackspace, and these major providers have restricted geographical diversity—and hence applied jurisdiction—of their data-centers. For example, Amazon EC2 has data-centers in only three regions: California, Virginia, and Ireland. Both effects make it relatively easy to monitor or block access to the cloud for a set of users.

Response. In response we note that there is a similarly limited number of major ISPs, and as cloud computing takes off we can expect the number of cloud computing providers to increase from its current level. Indeed, previous studies of location diversity [5] have indicated that the best places for nodes may be at points that are connected to a large number of other ASes. Cloud providers are likely to be positioned at such locations in order to provide good network connectivity to their customers.

3.3   Billing

Challenge. As cloud instances are paid for by users, billing records may provide a way to link individuals with their dust motes.

Response. We note that the same is also true for residential ISP connections and standard use of Tor. This effect could be mitigated in at least two ways. First, by building an exchange where users can swap access to dust motes. For example, user A pays for one dust mote but allows user B to use it as a cloud node, while user B pays for a different dust mote but allows user A to use it. Second, by providing coarse-grained pre-payment options so that users' detailed usage need not be tracked by the cloud provider. If the user then multiplexes "legitimate" use of cloud nodes with their use as dust motes, it may help them to attain plausible deniability.

3.4   Traffic Mixing

Challenge. As the number of dust motes might easily scale in proportion to the number of users, it could be difficult to ensure a sufficiently rich mix of traffic to provide effective hiding.

Response. Again, we propose two ways in which this can be addressed. First, by establishing the market proposed above for dust motes, in order to restrict the dust cloud's rate of scaling and ensure that, while providing acceptable service, it does not scale up so fast that the level of mixing is too low. Second, by using the fact that dust motes have compute and storage available to generate spurious mix-in traffic. Doing this effectively is an open problem, but the extra resources available to dust motes might make it more tractable in this environment.

3.5   Attack by the Cloud Provider

Challenge. Having both physical access to the cloud VMs and control of the virtualization stack, the cloud provider can potentially inspect a dust mote's memory and storage, compromising private keys and modifying code [9].

Response. There are two layers of trust here: (*i*) the provider controls the host machine and can inspect memory, network and disk; and (*ii*) other users on the same cloud infrastructure may snoop on traffic via timing attacks [11]. At some level protecting against the provider is impossible to prevent: with physical access to both computing and network infrastructure, the provider can do anything it so chooses without the user even being aware.

In order to mitigate the second risk, we require some cooperation from the provider. By using trusted computing techniques [12] or disaggregating the virtualization stack [9], the provider can limit the opportunity for compromise. In practice, the user can make it more difficult for a particular provider to compromise the system (*i*) by ensuring diversity in placement among their set of dust motes; (*ii*) by frequently and randomly hopping dust motes between cloud nodes; and (*iii*) by taking care with items such as private keys, e.g., avoiding storing them on the disk to which they are applied. We believe one of the biggest dangers to anonymity in Tor remains the shortage of exit nodes and the possibility of malicious snooping on them [13]: a dust cloud would greatly increase their number and help mitigate this problem.

We would like to thank Christian Kreibich, Alastair Beresford and Jon Crowcroft for useful discussions on this paper. This work was partially funded by the RCUK Horizon Digital Economy Research Hub grant, EP/G065802/1.

References

1. Amazon EC2, http://aws.amazon.com/ec2/
2. Chaum, D.L.: Untraceable electronic mail, return addresses, and digital pseudonyms. Communications of the ACM 24(2), 84–88 (1981)
3. Clarke, I., Sandberg, O., Wiley, B., Hong, T.W.: Freenet: A distributed anonymous information storage and retrieval system. In: Federrath, H. (ed.) Designing Privacy Enhancing Technologies. LNCS, vol. 2009, pp. 46–66. Springer, Heidelberg (2001)
4. Dingledine, R., Mathewson, N., Syverson, P.: Tor: The second-generation onion router. In: Proceedings of the 13th USENIX Security Symposium. USENIX Association (2004)
5. Feamster, N., Dingledine, R.: Location diversity in anonymity networks. In: Proceedings of the 2004 ACM Workshop on Privacy in the Electronic Society, pp. 66–76. ACM (2004)
6. Kouvelas, I., Hardman, V., Crowcroft, J.: Network adaptive continuous-media applications through self organized transcoding. In: Proceedings of the 8th International Workshop on Network and Operating Systems Support for Digital Audio and Video, pp. 117–128 (1998)
7. Mahmud, K., Mukumoto, K., Fukuda, A.: Development of MBC System Using Software Modem. IEICE Transactions on Communications (Special Issue on Software Defined Radio and its Technologies), 1269–1281 (2000)
8. McCoy, D., Bauer, K., Grunwald, D., Kohno, T., Sicker, D.: Shining Light in Dark Places: Understanding the Tor Network. In: Borisov, N., Goldberg, I. (eds.) PETS 2008. LNCS, vol. 5134, pp. 63–76. Springer, Heidelberg (2008)
9. Murray, D.G., Milos, G., Hand, S.: Improving Xen security through disaggregation. In: Proceedings of the 4th ACM SIGPLAN/SIGOPS International Conference on Virtual Execution Environments, pp. 151–160. ACM (2008)
10. Rennhard, M., Plattner, B.: Practical anonymity for the masses with MorphMix. In: Juels, A. (ed.) FC 2004. LNCS, vol. 3110, pp. 233–250. Springer, Heidelberg (2004)
11. Ristenpart, T., Tromer, E., Shacham, H., Savage, S.: Hey, you, get off of my cloud: Exploring information leakage in third-party compute clouds. In: Proceedings of the 16th ACM Conference on Computer and Communications Security, pp. 199–212. ACM (2009)
12. Santos, N., Gummadi, K.P., Rodrigues, R.: Towards Trusted Cloud Computing. In: Proceedings of the 1st USENIX Workshop on Hot Topics in Cloud Computing. USENIX Association, Berkeley (2009)
13. Sassaman, L.: The Faithless Endpoint: How Tor puts certain users at greater risk. Technical Report 2007-003, ESAT-COSIC (2007)

Using Dust Clouds to Enhance Anonymous Communication (Transcript of Discussion)

Malte Schwarzkopf

University of Cambridge

This presentation is about dust clouds in third party anonymity, and the fundamental technology that we're building on is mix networks, which I assume most of you are familiar with. The idea is Alice wants to anonymously communicate with Bob. She does not want to be anonymous to Bob, but wants to be anonymous to some evil Eve that's observing the network, and to do that she sends her data to a mix network, it goes into hiding from the ingress point to the egress point, and then comes up to Bob, and Eve observing parts of the mix network can't tell what's being said or who's talking to whom, because it all lies encrypted in the network. However, that does not solve the problem if Eve is able to look at both the ingress and egress point of the network, then she can still see what's going on, so if some evil overlord has a view of the entire Internet (a global passive adversary), we can't be using a mix network. That's the basic setting we're looking at, and the specific mix network that we are concerned with is Tor; we think that our strategy would pretty much work with any mix network, but Tor is the example that we used in the paper.

So you are familiar with the structure of Tor, you go through onion router relays, you do a bit of cryptography, and Eve looking at these two connections can't figure out what's going on. The only place where they start sending cleartext is from the exit node of the Tor network to whatever the destination point is, where the web server may be, or whoever we want to talk to. And then obviously there's a symmetric channel going the other way with an exit node at the other end where we send stuff in the clear again. So that's the basic technology. Now Tor is active, lots of people use it. I checked; last night there were 1,677 Tor routers online, and whilst there are no clear user statistics, it is being used, a lot of people route a lot of traffic, so clearly there's demand for this sort of technology. However, Tor is facing a bunch of challenges, I know some people might be thinking this is old news. But one of the challenges that Tor is facing is around capacity of exit nodes, there are a lot of people who are willing to route traffic for them, providing data anonymity, but no-one wants to be this guy who's exposing their IP address to the web server sitting here, and who's not anonymous. Because the exit node, appears to be the node communicating end-to-end with the web server, and the IP address will turn up in the logs, and also anyone monitoring this can consider they're talking to the web server. And the reason why people don't want to do this is that there are potential legal implications because if someone does something illegal through Tor then the exit node will get the blame.

B. Christianson and J. Malcolm (Eds.): Security Protocols 2010, LNCS 7061, pp. 60–70, 2014.
© Springer-Verlag Berlin Heidelberg 2014

Before I explain how our concept of dust clouds is improving on this, I'll just briefly touch on what dust clouds are. We start off with the traditional view of Tor communication, which is, Alice wants to talk with Bob, she calls for a number of onion routers and gets talking to Bob via the exit node here. Now traditionally when using Tor these intermediate hosts are personal computers, people just install a Tor client on their computer, and voluntarily share some of their bandwidth and computation time for the benefit of anonymity of other people, they allow other people to route traffic on their computer. That's nice, but obviously any of these can go away at any point in time, because if I just close my laptop no-one can route traffic through me anymore. And in fact, in the early days of Tor, that meant that all circuits were broken and had to be re-established, and TCP streams were broken, which is not great.

The big buzz word in computing nowadays appears to be cloud computing, so let's bring the cloud into this in order to improve on the traditional model that I've just outlined: Alice and Bob spawn so-called dust clouds, they spawn virtual machines in the cloud, they just go to Amazon EC2 or Rackspace and just spawn a few machines with a pre-defined image of one's Tor, and they get these guys sitting in a cloud, and we call the actual virtual machines dust motes, and an aggregate, then, i.e. the ones that Bob spawns, are a dust cloud. The idea is that you are hiding in the dust cloud, you're using the dust cloud for Tor communication, and so the Tor communication, instead of going through a bunch of personal computers owned by a bunch of people, now goes through a series of virtual machines. And these are in no way different from ordinary Tor nodes, they can run as their client, no-one changes the protocol unnecessarily, they just sit there and do their thing in the cloud.

Now why is this a good idea? I'll go through a couple of benefits in a minute, but basically one big advantage we get from this is that machines in the cloud have got good connectivity, high bandwidth connections, and are much more reliable than someone's personal computer sitting somewhere on a thin piece of string in some random country. There's some challenges which I'm going to get onto later. But as a starting point, these are better Tor routers than personal computers might be. So, the big problem, the capacity of exit nodes, how can we address that using this architecture? One benefit that we believe you get from running these virtual machines in the cloud is that you are basically separating your personal computation and the stuff that you're doing on your computer from your Tor usage of the computer when running a Tor node. The virtual machine in the cloud could just run the Tor node, it's not doing anything else, you just have a very lightweight virtual machine just with Tor, and no other applications, no SSH, no other Internet traffic coming out of it. So if then you run an exit node and you have trouble, you get sued, you can very easily — where very easily is relative to the difficulty that you have if you were talking about your personal computer — you can very easily prove that you've only been running a Tor node, whereas if you're trying to explain what generated traffic on your personal computer, there's lots of options, and it's quite difficult to put out a convincing proof that it was Tor and not some other application like your web browser. However, if your Tor node in the clouds is clearly not running anything but Tor, which you can prove just using a binary image, then you're in the clear. Now making this case in court is probably going to be difficult, because the court is not going to understand cloud computing, but that's a separate issue that can easily be addressed by legislation, or rather education of the people doing legislation, rather than technology.

Another opportunity that this gives us when running exit routers, which is of a bit more practical nature, is that we can just terminate the exit and re-spawn it on a on a different IP. So let's say someone has been doing something illegally here, or someone sends you an abuse complaint, then you just say, OK, well I disconnected the IP, I shut down the VM and we spawned it somewhere else, and you're in the clear again, that's a bit more practical than the first idea.

The second benefit is to do with long-lived transfers. Currently one issue that Tor is facing is if you are running a longer transfer on the Tor network, as in say downloading a long video stream, you give an attacker who's analysing traffic on the network an opportunity to do timing correlation attacks because you are running a long TCP string and they can attack into the network at certain points and from the timing that they see packets going past at they can work out what might be going on. There are some papers showing that this is possible[1], and that you can actually do quite a lot using timing correlation attacks. So Tor is not currently suitable for anonymous viewing of long running streams. In order to solve this you could (although this would require modification to the Tor protocol) tell your dust cloud, go and fetch this thing on my behalf for later viewing, and then it breaks it down to a series of small requests, and because your virtual machines are running in the cloud, they just do their thing, and a bit later using an encrypted connection, you can view the file that they've downloaded. And because the virtual machines have got storage, they can buffer it for you, and potentially (again this would require a protocol extension) talk to one another, and distribute the download job between them.

Another application for streaming that we thought of, is audio video conferencing. Currently doing video or audio conferencing over Tor is not particularly practical because what ends up happening is, if you've got more than three people involved, you're sending the same data to a variety of different places, and again that gives an attacker many more opportunities to do traffic analyses. So what the virtual machines in the cloud could do on your behalf, is that they could introduce some jitter, not exactly jitter, but they could reorder packets a little bit and just make sure that the streams don't look the same, and hence make life more difficult for an attacker. This is not something that normal Tor couldn't do, but by the virtue of being a cloud and having dedicated computer power and bandwidth, they can do it more easily.

Anil Madhavapeddy: If you wanted to do an anonymous audio conference today, how would you do that? Let's say you have a bunch of folk all over the

---

[1] See Steven J. Murdoch and George Danezis: "Low-Cost Traffic Analysis of Tor", in 2005 IEEE Symposium on Security and Privacy Oakland, California, USA.

world who wanted to have a conversation? It's really hard to do things like audio conversations anonymously, am I right?

Alex Shafarenko: I wouldn't want to do that on the router. It requires a lot of bandwidth first of all, if you really want the bandwidth to communicate over audio, then you need a server somewhere that aggregates all the streams into one, otherwise each and every one of you have an upstream obligation, which the current systems would not be up to.

Reply: You can imagine kind of a store and forward, right, I talk and my voice gets recorded, and then forwarded to some service that re-forwards it.

Alex Shafarenko: That's an entirely different kettle of fish. And the audio server would create a tremendous vulnerability because if it compromises just that server, nothing else, then everybody's in trouble, and without it you can't aggregate all those streams.

Reply: One other thing that virtual machines can do more easily than personal computers is padding. Traffic padding, sending some bogus traffic that you hide your actual traffic in, is an ongoing challenge in anonymity research. One reason why normal nodes don't do it, is that normally their bandwidth is limited, and they are already piggybacking on someone's Internet connection, so sending out a constant stream of traffic to hide traffic in is not going to be practical. However in a data-centre environment, like in the Amazon data-centre, that's a lot more easy to do because internal bandwidth within the data-centre is free anyway, and external bandwidth is charged at a very low rate, and the machines have got high bandwidth connections, so they could feasibly do this, whereas it's not possible on personal machines.

Then also, elaborating on the advantage of placing machines in the data-centre, you can actually get a fairly interesting benefit from placing some of your virtual machines with one cloud provider, and some with another. So let's say we've got Amazon here, Google there, they're both offering virtual machines. So the idea here is that you enlarge an anonymity set, i.e. the number of people that could be you. Currently, with personal computers, the anonymity set is probably the people using the same ISP, because your IP can be tracked back to your ISP using reverse lookups. Jumping to cloud computing, your Amazon VM is going to have an ID that's registered to Amazon Web Services, so you could at that point be any user of Amazon Web Services, so that's a pretty large number for me to search already. And you can also pop IPs in there in order to obscure your traffic a bit more. Now if you heterogeneously replace some of your dust motes on the Amazon cloud, and some of them on the Google cloud, and then jump between the two in the process of going through your Tor network, you're basically creating a union of the two anonymity sets, because you could now be any user of any of the Google cloud users and any of the Amazon cloud users. Obviously there's going to be some interception, but there are also going to be some separate bits of set, so you get a very large anonymity set. That's obviously assuming that Amazon and Google do not collaborate and exchange their customer details, if they did then this wouldn't work, but I think it's reasonable to assume that they're mutually distrusting each other.

There are also some other minor benefits like the ease of users is greater than installing a talk line from your own machine, because basically you have a one click button that you just click and it spawns, and which enters into the cloud and routes the traffic through them, in fact you could even build a browser extension that gives you enhanced private browsing, by clicking a button you just configure your browser to use a proxy, and you could also have an exchange at the end for different people, where people put in Amazon EC2 instances and exchange them between one another, so that you can also cross jurisdiction boundaries and make things more difficult, and keep your anonymity.

Now I'll mention a couple of challenges that this model is facing and our responses to them. The responses are not necessarily conclusive in the sense that there's always remaining doubt, but these are the obvious challenges that we came up with. So one of them is longevity of nodes, and one of the benefits that I mentioned was the fact that virtual machines persist for longer and more reliably than person computers. Now obviously at some point they are going to go away because that's the whole concept, you launch an instance, it remains there for some amount of time, and then it goes away again. But, and again, this is a slight modification of the protocol, they know for definite how long they're going to persist, so if you're launching a virtual machine and you're setting its binary time to be an hour from now, then you do twenty minutes of the longest communication, and then it then hangs around for another forty minutes to do traffic for other people. It definitely knows when it's going to go away, so it could communicate its own death time to other machines, and Tor, in the current protocol version rotates its circuits every ten minutes, so in the process of doing that it could check whether all machines at the next swap are still going to last for another ten minutes; if it's not then it will use a different path, so you avoid the scenario where a machine goes down and its circuits and streams break, because you have a defined end-point.

Second challenge that we came up with is the geographic diversity. Now cloud computing providers have big data-centres, their locations are in places, I believe Amazon has got two in the US and one in Ireland, but they're not as spread across the whole world and across jurisdiction boundaries as personal nodes are. So that's both a benefit and a curse at the same time. It's a curse because you become a lot more traceable, and if all the virtual machines that you're using are in the US, then you're not crossing a jurisdiction boundary, and even if some of them are in Ireland, it's still not a huge gain. On the other hand, they live in a data-centre environment, they live in a well connected environment.

Virgil Gligor: I think Australia would be the best choice and it's completely anonymous.

Reply: In terms of legislation or in terms of bulk?

Joseph Bonneau: Well China is also kind of missing this.

Reply: And some bits of Russia. But yes, the advantage that we can get from it is that they're in a data-centre environment, which is a highly connected environment, connected to many ASes. And there is previous work indicating that you want to put your nodes in places where there's high connectivity, because then there's many paths that the data could have come from previously.

Joseph Bonneau: So I'm not sure, if all of your nodes are within Amazon's network, it doesn't really matter if some of them happen to be Ireland, if the US government, which is where the company is based, really wants at them they can then make strong threats to the company.

Reply: Which was my point on the curse side of this. Now if you did POP providers, if you did have Google and Amazon, they're both US companies, but you did have a European provider as well, and then you heterogeneously placed some of your VMs with Amazon and some of them with a European provider then you'd have a jurisdiction boundary cross, and actually one that you can control because you can just go spawn a few dust motes here, spawn a few dust motes there, whereas currently with Tor you just get some random people in a random country saying we'll be in the same country as you, but here you actually get control.

So third challenge is probably the most obvious one, your account provider knows who you are, and if they become under pressure from the government then they're probably going to surrender the data and not protect their customer, simply because they have to in order not to be shut down. However, there are a few ways of dealing with this; one I touched on earlier, is to have a public exchange, with a principle that goes, OK, I'm putting five dust motes into the exchange, and then that gives me the right to take five out of it. And other people also put theirs in and basically just trade them. So if you get five dust motes from five different people then you get fairly good anonymity because they could all be anywhere, and there's no way of really tracing you, or to provide a billing record, or at least any way of tracing you is going to take a huge amount of effort. And the other way of dealing with this, which might be economically viable and interesting, and hence, we think it could happen, is to have a prepay cloud model, a coarse-grained pre-payment model where you just pay Amazon, say, at some point I'd like to be using some virtual machine but don't track which ones I'm using, i.e. keep no records. There might be sufficient demand for such anonymous cloud computing, and if they came under legal pressure it might go away, but it is an option.

Jonathan Anderson: But you can buy prepaid credit cards and things, pay in cash and then you have this card that just works until it runs out.

Reply: I think Amazon currently verifies your phone number in the registration process; I guess you can get a prepaid mobile number and register that. And actually one point I've got on a later slide is, you could potentially have a sort of recursive construction of dust clouds, and you could go through Tor, through the dust cloud to make another dust cloud, so that if you had an anonymous way of paying, you could just be perfectly anonymous and Amazon couldn't even trace where that was created from because it was created from within the anonymity structure. They can place you within the infrastructure, but if you go through a different cloud provider then it suddenly becomes quite difficult for them to find out who you are.

So the fourth challenge is traffic mixing and scaling this whole thing up. We anticipate with this model that, because it's got some advantages over just running on your laptop as a Tor node, many people are going to do this, and at some point the number of dust motes is just going to overwhelm the number of ordinary hosts on the Tor network, and also because you can scale this much more easily, you can just fire up a hundred dust motes if you suddenly have a pressing need to do a lot of anonymous communication. But an effect of that is obviously going to be that as it scales up you might not be able to get sufficient traffic mixing anymore because maybe there's just a few actors that are the majority of the nodes on the network, in which case they lose some of the anonymity, or they are all located in certain data-centres, and then you again lose some of the anonymity and some of the nice path properties of Tor. That challenge can potentially be overcome by the idea that I outlined earlier, the sort of public exchange of virtual machines, because then at least you've got different identities associated with them, and that gives you back some of the anonymity. And if I've got a hundred VMs in there and someone else has also got a hundred, and a few other people have, then you can just exchange them, so that we still get sufficient mixing. And the other idea, again, I've also mentioned before, is that you can generate spurious mix and padding traffic, because in a high bandwidth environment that's OK, and then you again get dense traffic mix because some of your traffic because some of your traffic is just bogus.

The fifth and final challenge is if your cloud provider is evil and attacks you. On the first level, if they're inspecting the main memory of their machines, there's nothing you can do — they can always do that, but if you use any cloud resources, even you use hardware trusted computing, then they can probably still do something, you have to trust them to an extent. But if you're running Tor on your laptop, that's true of your ISP, because your ISP can monitor your traffic. And if you're using Tor in the current way then anyone along the way can also look at their main memory. They're only going to have encrypted data in their main memory but really it's no different from the access that the cloud provider gets, except that the cloud provider in this case would get access to more nodes than anyone owning a few personal computers and connecting them to Tor. So that's part of the trade-off, and to an extent there is very little you can do about it. You could potentially introduce some sort of common trusted cloud computing and do de-aggregation of the virtualisation stack, there is some existing work on that too, but it's not going to overcome it entirely in the end.

So prospects, what else can this be used for? So far I've concentrated on saying how can we make it better for using dust clouds and dust motes. There is some other work that we're currently doing, looking at what we call personal containers. It's a separate concept, but somewhat linked, and the idea is that you have a virtual machine somewhere in the cloud that's entirely yours, and that holds all of your personal data on the Internet, and has actually got plugins that connect it to different data providers, such as social networks, and to your mobile phone, and it just sucks in all the data, aggregates it in one place in the cloud. The other argument here is that it's better to have a virtual machine that you own that aggregates all your data than having Google aggregate all your data, because then you're selling your soul to Google, whereas if you've got your own virtual machine the only entity that you're kind of selling your soul to is your cloud provider, but if you use encryption there are some limits to what they can do, subject to what I said on the previous slide. And one of the plug-ins in a personal container is a Tor plug-in, so a personal container can be connected to Tor. Now the interesting benefit that we get from that is that personal containers can then communicate anonymously using Tors in the services feature where you announce service using a notification at introduction points, and then someone talking to the server says something, and they talk to one another in an anonymous way. You could get personal containers talking to each other perfectly anonymously and passing information on from one another, assuming that everyone has a personal container in the cloud. So you can get personal containers talking in the mixed network. And then this slightly weird figure was supposed to introduce the idea of recursive construction of dust clouds, and I don't think it's really actually obvious from it, but if you have an anonymous way of doing payment then you can use Tor to set up more Tor nodes and get perfect anonymity from that, or almost, well not perfect, but very good anonymity. And that's all I've got to say.

George Danezis: I think that you're trying to stretch a bit too far. In effect Tor is used for low security applications that require effectively a user to be anonymous with website servers, so I visit the hospital; my insurance company is operating and it does not have any legal right to go and request records from my ISP, but I still don't want to expose my own address because that might give out information. Or traders in an investment bank, for example, where I'm in the same situation. And then there is also the sort of medium security where you have a bit disorganised adversaries that don't have any kind of technology, and all that stuff that it might protect you against. Against really highly motivated adversaries it doesn't really offer any protection because they can basically look at the network patterns and then find out which communication is which. So I think the way I see your argument here is that there is really no reason to do anything as complex as Tor for the low security requirement. If you're a trader in Goldman Sachs, you can just fire up an Amazon virtual machine and then start accessing the Internet with that, and as long as all the other bankers do basically the same, it should be fine, no-one's going to know which bank you're from, what you're looking at, and so forth. So why do Tor, just use the one hop relay, that's fine.

Reply: Yes and no. I see your point. I think you can approach this from two sides. You can approach it from the side of saying, OK, I basically want low to medium security, anonymity, I use a one hop relay, fine, wonderful, it's not going to protect me against the NSA or the US government, but it's going to protect me against the website knowing who I am, OK, fair enough, you can just use an anonymous proxy in your browser then. And you probably want to do that in fact because Tor is not particularly fast. Now the other direction that you can approach this from is to say, we have Tor, it's a nice architecture because we have this free hop relay, and also you can cross jurisdiction boundaries, and you get anonymity, but it's kind of slow. So we can either say we build something less complex than Tor, or we can say we'll make Tor faster, and to an extent this is saying that we're going to make Tor faster because we introduce lots of bandwidth nodes. And I think in the end you're going to meet in the middle with a similar result, you are anonymous versus the website, Tor probably gives you a little bit more anonymity than just the one hop relay, and you can get some other benefits from it. But I agree with you, that if you just want to hide your identity versus the website you don't need Tor, but then again, you can just use an anonymous proxy.

Anil Madhavapeddy: I think the question is, why don't you always want to have security, and we know the answer is that it either costs you a lot or you lose a lot of utility, so with Tor, when you actually use it, I had eight seconds response times, and Google can re-route me to Kazakhstan, so you lose a lot there. But why can't Tor scale up to both sets of users, which in theory should be the super fast response if you're just going through one or two hops that are quite diverse. But the question is why does anyone care about anonymity at all, so does anyone actually use Tor on a daily basis. Do you actually do all your shopping on Tor?

George Danezis: No, no not on a daily basis, but it depends what I'm doing.

Anil Madhavapeddy: Right. So you choose.

Reply: I mean, who in this room uses security for nuclear command control, we're not in the business for doing it for nuclear command control, right. I mean, the Human Rights activists and agents have a use for it, but, you know, these are human rights not security rights.

Anil Madhavapeddy: That's true, yes. It feels like one of the biggest reasons for using this sort of thing is just to make it easy to use for other people who do not worry about all the details.

Jonathan Anderson: Well you do kind of guarantee the existence of a global adversary who is a little bit stronger than passive, because they can do things like look at the memory of all of your VMs. You're talking about different providers, but let's assume that all the data-centres are hosted in countries where the Western Governments could get at them if they wanted to.

Reply: But, yes, in a similar way they could get at normal Tor nodes if they happen to all be in Western countries, they just bust the house and get the computers. I agree you're putting a bit more trust in commercial entities here.

Sandy Clark: That would actually require I think a warrant, whereas getting the data just requires a letter saying who you want to ask for the data.

Reply: But if the provider complies, they can.

Sandy Clark: Which they almost always do.

Reply: Yes.

George Danezis: There is another aspect. So Tor and other modern communications are designed with forward secrecy in mind, so if you do bust the door down and you get keys, you will not be able to replay the traffic in the cache. I mean, one can of course argue about, can some people put software on other people's computers and effectively have the same capability as monitoring the memory, the machines, so that would come down to the same. But the threat there is, if I give you your computer, might be in the hands of your adversary all the time, which means that you might as well not be anonymising if that is your adversary.

Reply: Yes.

George Danezis: This is what I'm saying, if this is your adversary you lose in this architecture, and that's OK, because most applications might not need that.

But also there is another threat model that hasn't been mentioned which is that if you're extending this to the cloud your adversary can just buy more dust motes than you have, and then your probability of routing through them is quite high, and then you get the sense of the situation. There is also a technical challenge in that currently Tor's directory service broadcasts the available routers, and control, you can join the network, and I think the protection level there is IP ranges, they would probably be somewhat unhappy about allowing the entirety of Amazon involved in both cloud infrastructure to join because precisely of that, because anyone can just buy loads of nodes on there.

Saša Radomirović: Is there an interest of having exit nodes, when we have the three strikes law? Unless I'm completely anonymous, if I have an exit node, and there is a three strikes law in the country, which means if I'm caught three times misbehaving I'm being cut off the Internet, so since I have no control of the exit nodes I will be blamed three times.

Reply: Well currently if you're running your laptop and people are doing really nasty things from your laptop, then your ISP is eventually going to crack down on you and say, we will kick you off, or we'll report you, or whatever, stop doing this. And the same thing obviously applies in the cloud. I'm not sure what the answer is really, but my gut feeling is that you're better off with a cloud provider because you can always hop from one VM to the other, change your IP address many times, and what's going to happen is if someone complains about abuse, they're going to write to Amazon, who, if your VM is still running, will terminate it and they would just disconnect the customer and it's locked, the US government is not going to cut off the entirety of Amazon just because some people on Amazon are misbehaving. There are currently spam bot VMs on Amazon that sends bandwidth from PCG, and nothing particularly is being done against that because you can't just drop the IP range because there's lots of genuine email being sent from Amazon. So you're optimising a bit and that is harder to be cut off entirely, to be blocked entirely, but yes, it's not perfect.

Joseph Bonneau: I guess my question is, it seems like you're assuming that Amazon will know that this is going on and be sort of indifferent to it?

Reply: Yes, they get money.

Joseph Bonneau: It seems like if they're going to get money for it, and they reckon that they somehow can get around it, but they have the problem too that they don't want to be the final exit node, and that if Amazon is the source of all this bad stuff, eventually they will get blocked and bad things will happen, and it will detract from the usability of their cloud as a service to everybody else, which will probably still be most of their profit. But I just want to question this.

If Amazon is OK with this then there's a more efficient way they can architect, they can build a huge server that just does anonymous communication, doesn't require people to go through setting up the virtual machine and their files, and it serves no other purpose. And perhaps Amazon and Google, and a few others, could set up this huge dedicated Tor node. They're not interested in doing that for a couple of reasons: the liability, and the fact that there may not be a market for it. So it's strange to think that they would allow this to happen in a cloud.

Jonathan Anderson: I just wanted to comment on the conflation of the cloud with the aggregation of all the ISPs. The huge difference is that instead of dealing with thousands of ISPs people might have to deal with four cloud providers, and if that's the case, the cloud providers would have a very good incentive to optimise the route for people outside to get at your data. Whereas the ISPs, well you have to talk to them, they've never done this before, and it's a whole deal that they don't know how to do, and it's not worth pulling teeth. But Amazon or Rackspace, or whoever, will say, oh there's the letter, here's the data, have a nice day.

Reply: I'll address the questions in reverse, I think that's easier. So yes, that's true, there are apparently only a few major cloud providers. One of the assumptions that we're making in this work is that there are going to be more in the future, probably not as many as there are local ISPs, but in terms of major ISPs, there aren't that many that probably want to nationalise these in every country. And then you could imagine cloud providers evolving in a similar way, either could happen, it's possible. The point before that was about Amazon stopping this and kicking off this customer. I send to the ISP with the difference that you can actually, as Jonathan pointed out earlier, set up new VMs anonymously using anonymous credit card payment, whereas it's going to be difficult to get an Internet connection sorted out anonymously, because no ISP is going to connect your house without you telling them who you are. So in that sense it's similar, but you are probably slightly better off here. And then the first question was about ...

Joseph Bonneau: I was just saying if they were interested in doing this, and wouldn't cut you off, they would probably commercialise it rather than leave it to people to make a value added service themselves.

Reply: I contest that, because there's a difference between them actively commercialising and actively offering it as a service, and potentially ignoring the government, and them tolerating it because they're indifferent, they get money out of it, and it's not affecting them hugely, they sometimes get a few complaint letters and shutdown a few VMs. It's similar to a peer-to-peer on the Internet, ISPs obviously aren't offering peer-to-peer access as a service, because that would be taking the Mickey, but they're kind of tolerating it because it makes them money. We think similar economics could apply here, but we don't know for sure because it's not been tried yet.

Generating Channel Ids in Virtual World Operating Systems
(Extended Abstract)

Michael Roe

Microsoft Research

Introduction

Two of the most popular software platforms for creating virtual worlds–Second Life and Metaplace–both use a message-passing architecture. *Objects* communicate by sending *messages* on *channels*. The channel's name or identifier acts as a capability: a program that knows the channel's identifier can send and receive from the channel.

1 Second Life

In Second Life, all users are placed in one very large virtual world where everyone has the ability to create new objects and attach programs to them. (In reality, Second Life's security model is more complex than this. For example, users who are below 18 years old are isolated from users who are 18+ by being put into an entirely separate virtual world. There are also discretionary access control on who may enter particular parts of the virtual space. But for the purpose of this explanation, we can ignore these details). This means that the main protection mechanism that stops an attacker sending control messages to your objects is that the channel ids are secret.

Metaplace, which was in open beta test from May until December 2009, has a rather different security model, which we describe later. The cryptographic protocol described in this paper was designed for platforms that are similar to Second Life, although they can also be applied to Metaplace.

The security of the system clearly relies on keeping channel ids secret. This usually works because the scripts run on a central server cluster owned by a single organization, not on the client, and the client never learns the channel ids. (In both Metaplace and Second Life, the client is assumed to be untrusted).

Channel ids are often embedded in the source code. This is not immediately a security problem, because the access permissions on scripts can be set so that a user of the script cannot read it.

However, there are two problems with embedding capabilities in scripts. Firstly, it makes the access permissions on scripts more security-critical than they would be otherwise. A compromise of the secrecy of a script (the attacker learns what algorithms it uses etc.) is perhaps not very serious. It is rather more

B. Christianson and J. Malcolm (Eds.): Security Protocols 2010, LNCS 7061, pp. 71–73, 2014.

serious if the attacker uses the capabilities embedded in the script to attack the authentication and integrity properties of the running system (e.g. by sending spoofed control messages to objects).

Secondly, it makes it difficult to organizations to run their own servers (or, more precisely, run other people's scripts on their own servers).

If servers are run by multiple organizations that do not trust each other, secret channel ids embedded in the source code are no longer a viable option. The operators of one server cluster can use their physical access to find out the channel ids used in their own cluster, and then use this knowledge to launch an attack on a rival organization's server. (This assumes that the same scripts are in use on both servers, and each organization has user-level access to the other's system).

Proposed Solution

- Each software publisher has a private key, K_A^{-1}, and corresponding public key K_A.
- Scripts are signed: Program, Sign(program, K_A^{-1})
- Clusters of servers each have a secret key, K_{S_i}.
- Within server cluster S_i, each program computes its channel ids as follows: channel=H(K_A, name; K_{S_i}), where H is a keyed hash function and name is a name for the channel used within the program.
- Each server cluster checks the signature on a script before running it. This check need only be done once, the first time the script is uploaded to the server.

With this approach, we can use the underlying message-passing layer without modification, just changing how we generate the channel ids. It has the advantage that one server cluster (and the organization controlling it) cannot compute the channel ids that are used in a different server cluster. Authors of scripts retain the ability to write scripts that communicate with each other, by using the same K_A to sign each program.

2   Metaplace

Metaplace, an alternative software platform for virtual worlds, was in open beta test from May until December in 2009. For Metaplace has an additional layer of protection. Each user gets their own miniature virtual world, that is isolated from the others (in particular, an object in one world cannot send a message to an object in another, at least not without using a different message-passing mechanism that is specifically for talking to untrusted things in other security contexts). Users can enter someone else's virtual world, but unless they have "superuser" privilege in that world, they cannot introduce new programs and attach them to objects.

Metaplace has an additional complication, that a single object in the visualization of the virtual world can have multiple programs (known as *scripts* in Metaplace) attached to it. Scripts attached to the same object can communicate via shared memory; locks are not needed to guard against concurrent access because the scheduler guarantees that at most one thread of control is active in the object at any one time; the object acts as a *monitor*. In Metaplace, the channel id is actually the name of the function that is called when a message is received on the channel). In Metaplace, read-only scripts are referred to as *closed source*. This should not be confused with the more common use of the term, which refers to a particular kind of software license.

Acknowledgements. I would like to thank George Danezis for discussions while I was writing this paper, and for presenting the paper at SPW XVIII.

Generating Channel Ids in Virtual World Operating Systems
(Transcript of Discussion)

George Danezis

Microsoft Research Cambridge

This is Michael Roe's work, but Mike has kindly asked me to present it so that I can be here today, and so that he can also present some different work tomorrow. You can ask questions, and check how well I understand the discussions we've mostly had by the coffee machine over the last years.

The world of gaming has changed since the 80s; a lot of us are familiar with pac-man, but things have progressed quite a bit. Games became more elaborate, then they went online, and as the games went online people started generating modifications of games, and there was a lot of creativity until today we've effectively stopped having games per se, and what we really have is online platforms, online communities.

The platform offers some basic services, but the content (the actual games being played online in the spaces) is generated by users or by third parties, and not the actual games platform itself.

So two key examples of this, Second Life and Metaplace, offer a virtual world, where you are represented by some 2 or 3-D character, and you go around and you interact with things that are created by other users. So in this setting we will see that there are some new security problems, but let's first offer some background with one of these examples, the oldest one, which is Second Life. So in Second Life you enter effectively a 3-D world that is hosted somewhere by Linden Labs, which runs the whole service, and each user is represented by a little 3-D character going around. Now there are details, there are two different places you can be, one for grown-ups and one for children, but since we're all grown-ups here let's assume you go straight for the adult part of the Second Life. And the world as it offered by Linden Labs is actually pretty boring, you know, there are some islands around, there is a sea, and there is this pretty basic boring person you are represented by; pretty much all the content (to a first approximation) is generated by users, which is amazing.

This is actually what made the web go crazy, because all content was not generated by the Tim Berners-Lee himself, but by everybody else, and the idea was that by allowing users to generate the content, including active content, which also contributed to the web becoming really cool rather than just static pages, it would become big. So effectively in this virtual world what is really important is that there are, in your impressions with the world, all the time three parties: yourself (represented by a client and a connection to the server), the actual server (which is the platform that runs all the logic), but then there are also the creators of the objects that you use. So if for example you have a car,

B. Christianson and J. Malcolm (Eds.): Security Protocols 2010, LNCS 7061, pp. 74–81, 2014.
© Springer-Verlag Berlin Heidelberg 2014

you are the owner of that car but you are not the creator of that car, someone else has created the car, which involves the 3-D design, and the code that describes how this car goes around, and how you can race it with other people if it is a racing game, and so forth. And in this particular case, you are the owner, but you're not maybe allowed to do everything that goes in the car. Now you of course are attached to these objects, and sometimes these objects effectively encapsulate state that the owner should not really be allowed to interact with. So if we, for example, take a game, a shooting game, and we have two objects that facilitate the shooting game, one that represents effectively your level of energy left, and the other one that is a gun that you're allowed to shoot other people with, all the logic effectively in the state of the game object, despite the fact that you're their owner, is encapsulated in this object, and you shouldn't really be allowed to mess with it, otherwise you could cheat, for example, by aiming better, or by decreasing more energy from the other players as you're allowed to, or by increasing your own levels of energy, and so forth.

So how is this done in practice? What are the mechanics of having this kind of three parties effectively interact in this world? Everything happens through messages, all the objects in the world effectively communicate with each other on channels. So in the particular example of the shooting game that I described, the object that is the gun tells the object that is the energy of the other player, I have shot at you, reduce your energy level by ten, and if by the way it reaches zero, the player dies and goes back into the beginning of the game. And the players just buy these systems, buy these objects, and put them on effectively, and start running around shooting at each other without being able to modify their state. Now of course, as we understand, this messaging has to somehow be secure, because if anyone can write and read messages from these channels they would be able to pretend that they are shooting other players whereas actually they haven't, or they would be able to make other plays reset effectively and go to the beginning, and so forth. And in practice how is this done today on Second Life, it is done by using 32-bit channel identifiers, which are effectively just an integer. So if you can guess an integer, you can start communicating with these objects and modifying presumably through these channels that are secret state, and then doing all sorts of weird things to other players of these games.

Now so far this isn't a problem, because if you just have a relatively small number which has to be done online, so you cannot take it home and try all 2^{32} combinations, so it's kind of moderately hard but not impossible, but what mitigates really this problem is that for the moment the whole world is really run on the trusted clouds and servers of Linden Labs. But this is about to change. First of all it's going to change for scalability reasons: if the web were to only run on Tim Berners-Lee's servers probably it wouldn't be as big as it is today, so decentralisation would actually help scaling up. But there are also other reasons to run code on servers other than the servers provided by the infrastructure. One of them is policy: Linden Labs has very particular culturally-specific policies about how they interpret what pixels can do to other pixels, including games relating to adult themes, or gore, or violence, or whatever else, and they are under increasing pressures in all the jurisdictions, they are to change this according to the local customs, and so forth. So it would be a good idea not to have one big global infrastructure that manages all this, but actually allowed people to run their own local servers with their local games, and their local customs, as they wish. Actually the Linden Labs rules are a bit vague right now, and I'm not sure, maybe Mike you know, if they have actually planned particular games, but an interesting meta game would be to try to effectively build games that would get you back there.

Another reason why you might want to run your own servers is that Linden Labs servers give you very little control. So if you are McDonald's and you want to effectively create a virtual burger restaurant online, it is a bit embarrassing if you have to rely on this third party infrastructure that is slow and unreliable, and gives users a really poor experience, and you cannot fix it. And you cannot maybe have a VIP area where you can allow some people and not some other people depending on whether they pay you, or depending on whether they bought a Big Mac yesterday, and so forth. Similarly for authorisation, or if you are trying to have an intranet kind of virtual world as well, for example where only Microsoft employees can participate in meetings. You might want to run your own infrastructure for all these reasons.

Now what are the problems when you start decentralising the infrastructure where these things run? So far the security paradigm is that objects run code that contains secrets, and the particular secrets are the channel ids that these objects are communicating on. If now this code starts migrating onto untrusted platforms, and the source code reveals which channel ids are used to communicate between the different objects, it means that as soon as the code touches a rogue server, the channel ids will become known to the adversary, and then they can go to another world and start abusing them by sending messages that they shouldn't be sending. So we are not particularly concerned about what a rogue virtual world would do, because it can do anything that it wants. What we're really concerned about is that they learn information about third parties, objects and scripts, and then go off to the otherwise honest infrastructure, and abuse that information there.

So what is really our idea here is that, or our key security requirement is that, if you run your own infrastructure you should be able to get a lot of third party code, lots of third party content, and logic, and so forth, and then allowing your users to use it, but that shouldn't really give the adversary, if it is indeed the adversary that runs such an infrastructure, an advantage to go and violate security properties of code value on the honest infrastructure. And in particular, since we want to think of a way of keeping the same kind of security paradigm as Second Life has, namely objects communicating on channels as the main way of actually achieving secure communication, we better make sure that we won't have these kind of fixed channels ids that the adversary can learn and reuse to abuse effectively the objects somewhere else.

Now, this is opening a second problem here, which is that currently, because all the games are effectively hosted in one single place, players are allowed to roam around, and to effectively reuse their objects, and so forth. So if I have a gun and it has six bullets, which is the example here, and I shoot three of these bullets, then I have three bullets left. And this might be actually quite an important property in that a particular game designer might decide to actually charge me for bullets, so their particular business model might not be to sell me the gun, or to sell me the access to the game, but their business model might be that you have to pay for the bullets. So I would find basically I go and buy a bullet, it would give a unique id to the bullet that will be transmitted to the victim, and the victim will give it back to the server, and then make sure that the energy then goes down, otherwise it doesn't, I mean, there could be a scheme like this. And of course it would be really ideal if we decentralised the infrastructure effectively, and allowed users to run on different servers, to still maintain this property, but a simple thought experiment really allows us to see that this is very difficult. If I have an adversary server that is allowed to modify arbitrarily the state of objects (not following the logic that is embedded in the algorithm), how can I make sure that the state that comes from the adversary's servers is correct. This is a very difficult problem, and unless we go down the multi-party secure computation route, which is extremely expensive given the fact that we just want to have little avatar playing around, it is very difficult to accept state that comes from a different (untrusted) security domain into our servers.

So here for this solution that is being proposed. What we're saying is that effectively we're going to classify servers according to the security domain they're in. So we're going to say that some servers are effectively trusted within a particular domain, but effectively we're not going to allow any mutable state to go between the different clusters effectively of servers, effectively partitioning the world in terms of side effects, so any effects that exist in one world will not go anywhere else when it comes to access content. I mean, for images and such things, it's not such a big deal, except when it comes to intellectual property protection.

Bruce Christianson: Is there not a way out using proxies? As long as the mutable state itself doesn't actually move, why can't I just redirect the messages back so that they're always processed on the same server?

Reply: If you do different interfaces that might be the case. For reasons of speed the idea here is, and actually we have discussed exactly this architecture before, we could have an architecture where you effectively have the client, the virtual world server, and then a server that is a third party that manages and runs the scripts of the objects, and this is within the security domain of effectively the creator of the objects, so the guy who created the guns and the energy level indicators, and all that stuff. The problem there is that you automatically introduce a level of indirection that is a network operation, so if you fire a gun, you have to send a message to this third party saying, I fired my gun towards that direction, the other person will then have to check every so often, did anything hit me by the way, and then, you know, please decrease my energy; it could become very difficult to have that three-way indirection and still be able to play interactive games.

Bruce Christianson: I wouldn't advocate doing that generally, it's just that you just need to do it until the next time you reload.

Reply: So effectively have an audit, like have a trace that you then can give to this third thing, it is certified as being an honest trace, because it is indeed given the inputs and the outputs, the thing that the programme would run, and then go ahead, yes, that is maybe a way. And let's not forget, there are interesting sub-problems that may have efficient solutions, such as payment, right, I mean, so for some things it might actually be impossible.

Anil Madhavapeddy: The original Quake World when it first came out did a bunch of really good stuff on the basis that cheating was far rarer than actually just predicting stuff and redesigning it. So if the assumption here is that if there are too many attackers it would prevent the game being played, so if you did an audit on it that would actually provide quite a good incentive, right? Because let's say five seconds after I cheat the audit system catches up and exacts a penalty, or maybe it terminates the game if someone cheats, so there's no point cheating in the first place.

Reply: Yes, but let's not forget that these virtual worlds are not only about people shooting each other and getting hit. Sometimes you have objects that contain messages and such things, so you may have confidentiality issues also, because I might use it for having an online meeting within my company, because flying tends to be more expensive. Sometimes you actually have an integrity violation that might be difficult to reconcile later on as well. So it's not just availability and playability issue like in traditional gaming, these things are meant to be virtual world platforms for all sorts of interactions, so it's more difficult.

So the idea behind this protocol is really, how do we extract ids that allow very efficient user partitioning, and the actual technical scheme is rather straightforward. Each creator of objects effectively has a signing key and a verification key, and this is pretty much the same as for signing software patches. And of course, they use the signature key to sign any software components they give out as part of their objects, so the logic behind shooting, driving, and so forth. Then each cluster of servers within the same security domain actually share a symmetric key, KSi, and then what we say is that within that cluster any programme that communicates gets assigned effectively a security channel, so it asks for a security channel with a particular name, and then the actual id that this channel has is a hash of the signature key used to sign the programme, this is the multiplex across different provider effectively of code. The secret key of the cluster, this is to do multiplex between different security domains, and then the name, and this is to do multiplex between different channels within the object. And of course H is a key hash function, and actually it is the key that is KSi. And this way effectively we do multiplex across all these three dimensions, allowing each script to run and be tied in, and each id to be tied in per creator of script, per security domain, and per name of channel, so that we can actually use them for different things.

Now in practice this gives a really nice and simple interface for the game designers, because they don't have to care about any of the crypto, the only primitive they need to say is, could I please pull from the channel, fire bullet, and this is effectively the name, and everything else just happens behind the scenes, and at the time of the execution of the script, they don't have to care about anything else. Fire bullet is just the name of the channel, it's not the secret, so anyone that actually inspects the source code does not learn any information that could allow them to go then to another virtual world and be able to infer the channel ids that will be used there. Which means that additionally, since all of this binding happens at execution time, . . .

Paulo Verissimo: But the time at which you fire the bullet should be a secret? Because, you know, if it's a game where you're trying to kill someone, if that is not a secret then . . .

Reply: Yes, so what is still secret at this point (if the adversary has the KSi), is which is the correct key, the symmetric key that Macs can give as the channel id when this script is executed. So assuming that the adversary doesn't know that key, they will not be able to rewrite what is in some different channel, they will not be able to send a message on that channel on that server. Since the binding actually happens quite late, at the time of the execution of the script, this means that the KSi keys of the clusters are effectively private, and whether there is a key compromise, or a key rotation, and so forth, it can just happen transparently, it's just that people would have to just re-route all their channels and bring them up again, and everything else will just work fine. And this is the basic idea, and probably a lot of the questions will have to be redirected towards Mike, since it is his work, I'm just presenting it.

Bruce Christianson: This seems like a very nice generalisation of Li Gong's iCap system[1], where what he wanted was for capabilities to have different bit pattern representations in different domains, and that is precisely why caching the capability of the secret depends on the domain you were in. If you want to move from one server to another, do you have to reboot your channels, or is there a way that you can kind of push them through a firewall and have them mapped?

Michael Roe: The servers have their own virtual space, so you're never sending a message where the sender is on one server and the secret is on another, and so effectively across domains you have a separate instance, a new channel.

Reply: Migrating within the same security domain has a problem because the ids are the same, migrating across has a whole different set of problems as well, because then you run on state that is potentially corrupt.

Bruce Christianson: 32 bits doesn't seem like very much.

Michael Roe: So, easy to increase the number of bits. In Metaplace there's an arbitrary string.

---

[1] A Secure Identity-Based Capability System by Li Gong in Proceedings of the 1989 IEEE Symposium on Security and Privacy.

Bruce Christianson: Then it's not going to be sparse.

Reply: But just increasing the width is not sufficient, you also need some platforms to do with the multiplex, because if you rely on having a fixed, large, unguessable id, it's only going to be unguessable once the script runs on the trusted server.

Jonathan Anderson: This is also a usability improvement from the programmer's perspective, because then your time channel identifies to some sensible name like, the channel that I shoot bullets over, instead of a fixed concept.

Michael Roe: Yes, this is right. In Metaplace you can get yourself put in a slightly different security architecture perception to a certain amount. So the threat model is that the games don't trust each other, so one game wants protection, other games are nervous, the operators of server clusters don't trust each other, and operators of server clusters are usually only multi-party on a weaker service, so what you're really connecting to is someone who owns their own servers, then the secret is out of the range of using that user level access on somebody else's server to damage the integrity of the system.

Malte Schwarzkopf: I think the idea is that I, as the Second Life operator, get the source code and work out the channel ids, then I use that to write a book that goes around in another server, and it duly does something that benefits me in some way, kills people and takes their treasure.

Michael Roe: Yes, so that's supposed to be the protocol?

Bruce Christianson: But the crucial thing is that the person I'm shooting at is never on another server, right?

Reply: Yes.

Michael Roe: So you get to the second of these things called private islands where there's not so much sea as vacuum between you and the mainland, in other words, a part of the three-dimensional virtual space that nothing can get to.

Bruce Christianson: A cordon sanitaire.

Michael Roe: And so you have to have something similar to this, that when you're in a separate security domain you can't continuously move into some place where you would meet to compete in.

Bruce Christianson: My suspicion is this solution could actually be generalised to the multi-domain requirement.

Anil Madhavapeddy: So the whole virtual world context here is a red herring, you could apply this to a website, for example.

Bruce Christianson: This is the point, yes.

Anil Madhavapeddy: Yes, I mean, it sounds like it's essentially containing the threat.

Reply: I think that Facebook with its applications, sharing the same kind of security domain at the browser level, you know, similar things could be used there. You could be contained within the domain effectively, have a different key proved in and say, if you actually share a security domain you will end up with the same channel communicating with it.

Bruce Christianson: Or even if you just talk to a gateway that knows the translation protocol, then it will map you but enforce the security policies as it does so.

Censorship-Resilient Communications through Information Scattering

Stefano Ortolani[1], Mauro Conti[1], and Bruno Crispo[2]

[1] Vrije Unversiteit Amsterdam, The Netherlands
{ortolani,mconti}@few.vu.nl
[2] University of Trento, Italy
crispo@dit.unitn.it

Abstract. The aim of this paper is to present a new idea on censorship-resilient communication Internet services, like blogs or web publishing. The motivation of this idea comes from the fact that in many situations guaranteeing this property is even matter of personal freedom. Our idea leverages: i) to split the actual content of a message and to scatter it through different points of retrieval; ii) to hide the content of a splitted message in a way that is clearly unidentifiable—hence involving encryption and steganography; iii) to allow the intended message recipient to correctly retrieve the original message. A further extension on this idea allows the recipient of the message to retrieve the message even if: i) some of the retrieval point are not available; ii) some retrieved data have been tampered with—their integrity has been violated.

1 Introduction

Allowing people to communicate privately is important in many context. Guaranteeing the anonymity of the source of a message is a way to obtain communication privacy. The concept of anonymity refers to the fact that a given subject is concealed among a set of subjects—the anonymity set—as taking part of an action. However, anonymity is not enough if the communication channel is censored. The act of publishing information establishes a direct communication between the publisher (e.g. http://www.blogspot.com) and the user (e.g. the corresponding IP address).

Different works addressed this problem by loosing the correlation between the IP address used by the user and the user itself. For instance, in Tor [1], the user accesses the World Wide Web by means of multiple identities provided by a network of nodes. Tor is able, to some extent, to anonymise the user and even the publisher (by means of Tor hidden services) within the Tor network. Hence, it seems that the problem of guaranteeing the anonymity of an individual has been already addressed and solved. We observe that the solution provided by Tor works only if the information are retrieved from within the Tor network. However, not all the users are now using the Tor network—and we cannot force them to do it. Moreover, if someone wants to publish something using Tor he has to deploy a server to employ these hidden services.

B. Christianson and J. Malcolm (Eds.): Security Protocols 2010, LNCS 7061, pp. 82–89, 2014.

As an example, let us consider a non democratic authority censorship. It might i) identify the publisher and subsequently ban it—forcing the publisher to stop its activity, or ii) check the user traffic and filter the one directed to the publisher. In the remaining part of the paper, we describe our solution with respect to a blog post service. It is however straightforward to extend the described solution to other Internet services, such as other type of web sites.

Our solution counters censorship by dividing the content of the message into chunks, then publishing them in multiple locations as comments to blogs. In such a way, censoring a publisher does not prevent the content published through other publisher to be retrieved. The scattered content is shared by means of a link including all the necessary information to retrieve all the post fragments. An application running inside the browser of the client (e.g. a Firefox extension) provides then the logic to i) re-assemble the content and ii) display it as a web page inside the user browser.

Moreover, the content can be concealed by means of steganography. Hence, it will not be easy to identify a publisher as the one publishing a specific content. However, any steganography technique requires the definition of what is known as the cover signal. In other words, we have to provide the message acting as the envelope for our secret message. Since such envelopes shall resemble already published content, we retrieve the cover signal from website such as wikipedia: the meta keywords included in the publisher's site can be easily used as query terms.

Finally, we consider only blogs that are not moderated and do not require any registration. This would pose another defense to the users privacy in the case the publisher collude with the censorer.

Organization. The rest of the paper is organized as follows. Section 2 reports on the related work in the area. Section 3 presents a brief overview of our approach. We introduce some preliminaries in Section 4, while our solution is described in Section 5. Section 6 gives a brief discussion on the key points of the proposal. Finally, Section 7 concludes the work.

2   Related Work

A wide range of solutions have been published on the anonymity of communications. Among these, Tor [1] is probably the most practical one. While Tor could partially solve the problem we address, it would require the following. One one side, it would require all interested users to use Tor. On the other side the Tor node that wants to act as publisher must manage a server in order to offer a Tor *hidden service* [2]. Furthermore, we observe that the *directory servers* used to announce the hidden service represent points of failure and a weakness by itself—identifying the *introduction points*.

In our solution, we leverage on the information scattering concept [3]. Furthermore, we make use of the text steganography [4] to hide the message M intended to be sent within other text. As a property of the steganography, it is not possible to detect that the resulting text contain an hidden message. A further extension of the proposed solution could also make use threshold cryptography [5]. This would make the solution more efficient and resilient: the message M could be splitted and scattered into n different points and retrieved contacting just $t < n$ of these points.

3   Our Approach

We are interested in publishing a message in a way such that it is not easy to censor the message itself, or even censor the publisher that keeps the message on line and available to visiting clients. The main idea is to split the message M intended to be sent into n message chunks m_i ($1 \leq i \leq n$), and publish these separately. Furthermore, each single message chunk m_i can be published hidden with steganographic techniques. We recall that we assume the publication is done through posting on blogs. A censorer would not be able to get the real meaning of an actually posted blog's comment as well as it will not be able to reconstruct the intended message M. In fact, only the intended message recipient will be provided with the actual information required to retrieve all the required published comments, and get out from them (hidden with steganography) the actual chunks for M. Hence, only the intended recipient will be able to reconstruct the message M, while the censorship will not be able to selectively ban a message or the publisher of a specific message.

The message chunks m_i are scattered to different n publishers p_i ($1 \leq i \leq n$). In our example-driven discussion a publisher is a blog server and the publication is made throughout comments to pre-existing blogs. We consider blogs that do not require any registration, nor a moderator approving the comment itself. In the following, we refer to a publisher also as a repository. Furthermore, we assume that the number of comments are not bounded and that a specific blog's post is identifiable by the combination of URL (Uniform Resource Locator) and comment id. Without loss of generality, we also assume that no CAPTCHA mechanisms are in place on the publisher. However, we can relax this assumption considering that for our scenario a user already qualifies as motivated. Hence, solving a set of CAPTCHAs does not pose any hindrance to our system. The effort of solving a set of a CAPTCHAs is therefore considered acceptable.

The basic approach of publishing just a "piece" of the given text can be enhanced by means of steganographic techniques. In this case we aim to choose as an "envelope"—the object that hides and carries the actual "piece" of message—a text that matches the blog's topic. This process can be automatic, since a web site provides the meta keywords. Upon hiding through steganography we can look in a texts source website (e.g. wikipedia) the topic of the web page and retrieve a consistent text snippet. Upon decryption we just need the key.

In order for a user that wants to get the actual message scattered and hidden through steganography among different unknown sources, the user need the appropriate "link", that is a set of information (URL, comment id, key) for each of the used repository. All these information can actually be assembled in a link in a way similar to how it happens for P2P protocols (e.g. eMule).

4   Preliminaries and Notation

In this section, we present some preliminaries required for the rest of the paper. In particular, we give the definition of a publisher and some other related concepts. Table 1 summarizes the notation used in this paper.

Table 1. Notation Table

M	Message that is intended to be sent.
n	Number of chunks a message is divided into.
m_i	A chunk of message M, $(1 \le i \le n)$.
p_i	The publisher (repository) of chunk m_i.
url_i	URL that identifies publisher p_i.
m'_i	Message that hide (through steganography) the message m_i.
ID_i	Identifier of blog's comment m'_i.
$meta_i$	The first meta keyword in the HTML page of the blog of publisher p_i.
E_k	Steganographic function with key k.

Definition 1. *A publisher p_i is a blog server where we can publish information. The blog is not moderated and it does not have bound on the number of posts. Any publisher p_i is univocally identified by its URL url_i. Given a publisher p_i, we identify with $meta_i$ the first meta keyword included in the HTML page of the blog.*

A blog is composed by a set of posts (or comments), i.e. pieces of text.

Definition 2. *A blog's post (or comment) for a publisher p_i is a text message bounded by the max length accepted by p_i.*

Definition 3. *We define as $Cover(meta_i) = t_i$ the function that, given a keyword $meta_i$, it returns a text t_i from a texts source website, where the topic of t_i is in accordance with the keyword $meta_i$.*

An example of a texts source website is Wikipedia. One other component that our system requires is the steganographic primitive.

Definition 4. *Given a message m_i, and a meta keyword $meta_k$, we conceal m_i as follows: $E_k(m_i, Cover(meta_i)) = E_k(m_i, t_i) = m'_i$, where E_k is a steganographic function with key k.*

Intuitively, the message $m'_i \approx t_i$ conceals the message m_i. Since E_k can be implemented through encryption followed by the application of steganography, in the following we also refer to E_k as just encryption. Publishing the obtained message m'_j is defined as follows.

Definition 5. *Given a message m_i' and a blog url_i, we define the function $Publish(m_i', url_i) = ID_i$, as the function that publish m_i' in url_i. The value ID_i is the identifier of the resulting added blog's comment.*

To ease the retrieval of the scattered information we define a URI (Uniform Resource Identifier) resembling the one adopted in P2P systems, such as eMule.

Definition 6. *The URI of our protocol, namely `info-URI`, is defined accordingly to the following ABNF notation:*

```
info-URI     = info-scheme "::" info-publish [ "||" info-publish ]
info-scheme  = "info"
info-publish = http-URI "|" info-cid "|" info-key
http-URI     = The publisher URL
info-cid     = The comment ID
info-key     = The key of the encrypted content
```

A message scattered among two different publishers, p_1 and p_2, respectively in two comment ID_1 and ID_2, has the following URI:

$$info : url_1|ID_1|k_1||url_2|ID_2|k_2.$$

The last corner-stone of our approach is the definition of the function in charge of retrieving the so-scattered content. A browser extension is enough to carry out this task. The assembling phase is defined as follows.

Definition 7. *Given a URI $info : url_i|ID_i|k_i$ the decryption part works as follows: $D_{k_i}(Retrieve(url_i, ID_i)) = D_{k_i}(m_i') = m_i$ where the function $Retrieve(url_i, ID_i)$ retrieves the comment ID_i from the blog at url_i.*

5   Our Solution

In Section 3 we gave an overview of our approach. In this section, we describe its architecture.

The overall architectural design is depicted in Figure 1. We immediately identify the two main actors interested in the communication: the publisher (repository) and the visiting client. The three repositories are in turn identified by url_1, url_2, and url_3. Even if the figure depicts just one visiting client, the same mechanism applies for any number of them. Last but not least, the source of cover signal is represented by the Wikipedia web site.

Let us now assume that a client wants to publish a message M in a way such that the message will not be censored. First, the client selects the repositories— i.e. blog sites—satisfying Definition 1. These are identified by url_1, url_2, and url_3 in Figure 1. The client hence splits M into message chunks, one for each selected repository. In the example, we have three chunks: m_1, m_2, and m_3. For each of the selected repository, the client gets the meta keywords from the blog HTML page and, depending on these, it selects a text of the same topic from the texts source (e.g. Wikipedia). Let us call this texts "envelops" (t_1, t_2, and

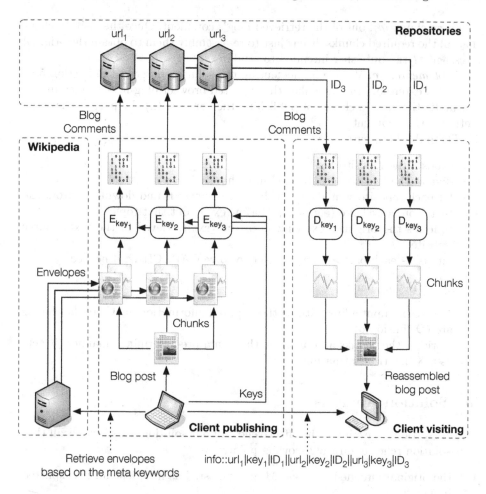

Fig. 1. Architecture of our Information Scattering solution

t_3). Now the client selects a different key k_i for each message chunk m_i. A key k_i is used to hide by mean of steganography the message m_i into envelope t_i (text steganography tools [6] are used in this step). The resulting text m_i' is then posted as a comment on the repository url_i. Finally, the publishing client uses a side channel (e.g. email) to send the information required to a visiting client to correctly retrieve the original intended message M. In particular, for each message chunk m_i, the publishing client will state the URL of the repository url_i, the blog's comment id ID_i within the given blog, and the key k_i required to hide m_i within the comment ID_i. The overall resulting string will be a string accordingly to Definition 6, $info :: url_1|key_1|ID_1||...||...$.

Once the URI string is received (by means of the side channel), the visiting client acts as follows. For each element (url_i, key_i, ID_i), it retrieves from the repository url_i the blog's comment ID_i. Then it uses the key key_i to get the message chunk m_i, out of the retrieved blog's comment. Once the visiting client has all the required chunks, it has just to re-assembly them to obtain the original message M the publisher intended to send.

Implementation. We are implementing the solution described in Section 5 as a Firefox extension. In particular, the expected browser plug-in is divided in two parts: (i) the part in charge of publishing the content; (ii) the part in charge of retrieving the content.

The publishing part:

- chooses the repositories;
- divides the text to be published into chunks;
- for each repository, it retrieves the meta keywords and downloads from the texts source website (e.g. wikipedia) a text about that topic;
- conceals the original text chunks in the text retrieved in the texts source website;
- publishes each part asking the user to solve CAPTCHAs, if needed.

The retrieving part:

- receives in input a link with all the required information on where the chunks are (Definition 6);
- retrieves the chunks and organize them in a pre-determined manner (it acts as a XSLT transformation).

6   Solution Analysis

In this section we evaluate the effectiveness of our solution. First, we recall that our solution relies upon the following points:

1 the original intended message M is not posted as it is, instead it is splitted in chunks m_i;
2 each chunk m_i is not posted as it is, but it is hidden by means of steganography within another text;
3 the text used to hide the original chunk m_i is chosen in a way such that the resulting post looks like a plausible blog's comment, related to the topic that is actually discussed in the blog—thanks to the meta keywords;
4 the information required to retrieve the chunks and compute the original message M are transferred to the visiting client throughout a side channel that is outside the distribution mechanism.

The point 1 is used for practical reasons. In fact, the message M intended to be sent could have an arbitrary length that is over the bound of a single post accepted by a blog server. Furthermore, the steganography function works better when the text to be hidden is small.

The steganography function (point 2) is used to avoid the censorer to identify a message chunk m_i as not desired and to ask the publisher p_i to ban it. Also hiding the chunk m_i within a text t_i with a similar topic (point 3) is done in order to avoid the censorer to understand that a blog post might contain some hidden message.

The last point is used to transfer to the visiting client all the required information to get M. We assume that the side channel used for this purpose is secure, e.g. mail could be encrypted with public key crypto allowing confidentiality and authentication. While guaranteeing the security of this channel is out of the scope of this paper, one might argue that if such a channel exist the message M could be convoyed just using this channel. However, we observe that the information could be passed before the actual message is generated. Also, once some initial secret data are shared among the sender and the receiver, the information required for the messages sent after M, could be auto generated without requiring any further communication—e.g. using chain of hash function.

Furthermore, using techniques like threshold cryptography the original messages could be splitted in a number of chunks n such that a smaller number w out of n are sufficient to retrieve the original M. In this way, even if $n - w$ repositories are identified and blocked, the clients will still be able to retrieve M.

7   Conclusion

In this paper, we presented a new method to achieve censorship-resilient communications. We presented a solution for sending generic text messages, using existing server, thus not requiring any special software (e.g. Tor) at the server side. Furthermore, we depicted a way to hide these messages through blog posting. The presented idea can be easily extended and even optimized for specific type of messages (e.g. html pages or pictures).

References

1. Dingledine, R., Mathewson, N., Syverson, P.: Tor: The second-generation onion router. In: Proceedings of the 13th USENIX Security Symposium, pp. 303–320 (2004)
2. Lenhard, J., Loesing, K., Wirtz, G.: Performance measurements of tor hidden services in low-bandwidth access networks. In: Abdalla, M., Pointcheval, D., Fouque, P.-A., Vergnaud, D. (eds.) ACNS 2009. LNCS, vol. 5536, pp. 324–341. Springer, Heidelberg (2009)
3. Bhavnani, S.K.: Information scattering. In: ELIS, pp. 1–8 (2009)
4. Mansor, S., Din, R., Samsudin, A.: Analysis of natural language steganography. International Journal of Computer Science and Security (IJCSS) 3(2), 113–125 (2009)
5. Desmedt, Y.G., Frankel, Y.: Threshold cryptosystems. In: Brassard, G. (ed.) CRYPTO 1989. LNCS, vol. 435, pp. 307–315. Springer, Heidelberg (1990)
6. Wayner, P.: Disappearing Cryptography: Information Hiding Steganography & Watermarking, 3rd edn. Morgan Kaufmann Publishers Inc., San Francisco (2008)

Censorship-Resilient Communications through Information Scattering (Transcript of Discussion)

Mauro Conti

Vrije Universiteit Amsterdam, The Netherlands

The problem that we are trying to address is to have an anonymous and censorship-resilient communication, and we know that these kinds of communications are important. We had different talks here yesterday about anonymity, for example, how to improve the anonymity of Tor[1], but anonymity is not the only the important factor, because in many scenarios what happens is that there is also a censorship authority that can ban the message; there is no point being anonymous if the message is not conveyed to the intended set of recipients. We have a different motivational example, of course there is nothing political around this example, but just to motivate that we know that in many situations it is necessary to have a mechanism to communicate in an anonymous way, and to have a mechanism to avoid that a censorship authority can then ban our message. Here we have a censorship authority that is basically a government, but I saw that there is another paper this afternoon[2] on censorship of eBooks, and in that example the censorship is not by a government. So in many scenarios what happens is that we need to communicate in an anonymous way, and we need to let the message reach the destination without being banned.

So here's what we want to do. We have a user, and we want the user to communicate a message to a set of potential receivers, without the user being identified as the source of the message, and without the message being banned by the censorship authority. So it's not a well-defined threat model, but at least we have a threat model; the adversary, which is this case is the censorship authority, can listen to all the natural communication, and can read all the published information, and also can ban a reasonably small fraction of the publishers. Of course, if you are able to switch off all Internet traffic, then there is no way you can convey a message using email. So we also talked yesterday about online protests[3], but if there is no Internet there is not even the possibility of that kind of protest.

What we consider to be the state of the art that we could leverage to solve these kinds of problems is basically to use Tor. But we know that Tor promises more on the anonymity. On the transmission of the message it is greater than the order of communication of the message, so the fact that the message actually reaches the destination, and in that case, for example, using hidden services in Tor, we would need the interested users to be within the Tor network. If you

---

[1] Mortier et al., these proceedings.

[2] Roe, these proceedings.

[3] Anderson, J., these proceedings.

B. Christianson and J. Malcolm (Eds.): Security Protocols 2010, LNCS 7061, pp. 90–97, 2014.

want to publish something on a website or blog service, you have to somehow own or manage that kind of server, and furthermore a service provider and server are able to identify a node, like a Tor node. What you want is a lightweight solution to convey a message that cannot be banned by a censorship authority, and a mechanism that is working on a machine without any fingerprint of that machine.

This is basically our starting idea. We have the message that we want to send, and we split this message into different chunks, and each one of these chunks is not directly published, we can use the blog example to write to this presentation. So each single chunk is not directly published as a blog comment, but it will be hidden using steganography technique into another message, so we will see how this step can be performed. And then each single different chunk will be published in a different repository.

At this point we need to let the intended receiver have the correct permission to retrieve all these message chunks, and to take out the message from the steganographic messages there. So intended receivers are provided with some guarded information to retrieve the overall message. As a simple case we can assume that we have some secure side channel to convey this message, like for example, just sending an email, or directly telling this information to the user. But optimisation of this can be done for example by sharing a secret then based on this secret we can choose the server where we are going to publish our information, because of course we can share the secret in advance, but we don't know, for example, the news that you want to communicate to the intended receiver. So if we pre-share a secret, and then we can use for example our pseudo random number generation function to determine what will be the set of publishers that we are going to use to publish our message chunks. So this can be a kind of optimisation. The kind of mechanism we need to implement to communicate this information to the intended receivers, what we need to communicate in the specific case, for example, of a blog post, so let's assume that the user wants to put a comment on a blog, and of course we do not want the user to be identified, and we do not want a censorship authority to ban this message. So what we do is split this message, use a steganography techniques for each chunk of the message, and then publish each message independently, say on a different blog. But what we want is that each single published message cannot be identified as a message that the censorship authority does not like.

So the kind of information that we have to send to the receiver is something like the link that is used in point-to-point systems like eMule. For example, let's say that we use two different publishers, the kind of information will look like this. For each single chunk we have to identify the URL of the publisher, the id of the message within that blog, and eventually we could have an encryption, a steganographic mechanism with a key, and then in that case we have to communicate also the key. So this will be the kind of information that we have to communicate to the intended receiver if we are using two publishers.

So this is how the overall architecture would look: we have a publishing client and a visiting client. The publishing client will divide the message into chunks.

Then we have to retrieve envelopes, so for example for a text message we can use as another text message, and what we can do for example is to retrieve the message from the Internet, from for example, Wikipedia, and we can retrieve an envelope that lets the message that we are hiding within that envelope not be suspicious. So we can use meta text of the same kind of text that we want to retrieve, to find that some text that is similar and on the same topic of the message chunk that we are going to hide within this text. And here we can use different steganography techniques, and so these are an open point, and we can optimise this part of the mechanism, so once we have a message chunk and the corresponding envelopes, we can use steganographic techniques to lose the blog comment that we are going to post. So we are going to post to these different blogs, and each post cannot be identified as a suspicious comment that the censorship authority would not like. Then we have to send that kind of information that I was talking about previously, and the visiting client will use this information to retrieve the message chunks, and take out the clear text from the steganographic message, and then reconstruct the overall message that was intended to send.

OK, I told you that the steganographic step is an open point; what we could do, for example, is to use encryption, so just encrypt the text, so once we have some encrypted code we can just forward this in text again, and then we can add this text with steganographic techniques within another place. But in this way what happens is that the encryption will look suspicious in a regular piece of text. Otherwise we can use some other steganographic techniques like, for example, where information is conveyed within text messages by shifting words from the UK site to the US site, shifting in this way can be representing 1, or 0 otherwise.

One other challenge would be to add these extensions, so we would like this mechanism also to be resilient on the integrity of the data, so if this is violated, it goes off message loss, message fail, transmission fail, or even if some of the publishers are colluding with a censorship authority, what we would like to add is that the intended receiver should be able to retrieve the original message, even if it doesn't receive all the publishers used. So we can use some sort of threshold cryptography mechanism to have a redundancy of the chunks, so we can publish for example, M chunks of the message, and let the intended receivers be available to retrieve the original message, even if they retrieve a smaller number of chunks than have been published.

James Malcolm: Isn't it more likely that censorship will take place at the person writing the message rather than the person trying to read the message.

Sandy Clark: Not necessarily — people in China trying to read western news.

Ross Anderson: I'm not convinced that this gives you much censorship resistance, because a necessary feature of censorship systems is that the censor is a subscriber. The censor is always a subscriber, because if you can exclude the censorship by means of a membership mechanism, you don't need a censorship resistance mechanism, right, if a document is only available to Freemasons, and no censor can ever become a member of the Masonic Lodge, there is no technical issue. So for such a system you have to assume that the censor is a subscriber, so the secret police always have a member in every free organisation. As soon as the censor knows that the forbidden content is hidden in blog posts 17, 34, and 36, he simply takes them down. So a steganographic model is the wrong mechanism here, surely.

Reply: But we get blogs that do not require registration of the users.

Ross Anderson: That's not the point. A censor is someone who has the power to delete content online, it's a record company which uses a DCMA notice to take down copyright infringing material, for example.

Saša Radomirović: Well I guess if you assume that there is a second channel where the actual spot where things are hidden is communicated, so even if you are reading the blogs, you're not directly aware of this information.

Reply: Yes, the censorship authority doesn't know where to retrieve the chunks of the original message.

Ross Anderson: Well we had a paper here 15 years ago[4],

the Eternity Service where we proposed a similar mechanism, but instead of using steganography for the fragmentation, redundancy and scattering, we used encryption plus the fetching of material via the peers themselves acting as anonymous re-mailers. Therefore as a result, nobody could know where any particular one of the fragments was held, therefore when the censor goes and retrieves the forbidden information, he has no idea where those shares were actually held, one of them could even have been on his own machine.

Reply: And in that case you have to use another mechanism to hide the source of that message?

Ross Anderson: Yes, I believe you would end up having to build a system like Tor into a mechanism like this, because the censor will always learn where the fragments are, and he will simply go to a machine and say, oi, take them down or go to jail.

Reply: Yes, but in this way you cannot identify someone, like the source of an embedded message, so an imposter may have a blog comment, and the censorship authority cannot attribute that comment.

Ross Anderson: OK, well if all you're worried about is imprisonment of the source, then mechanisms like this might produce some value, but the problem is, if you're worried about the availability of the forbidden content, if you want to see to it that the petition and affidavit remain available despite the efforts of the Scientologists to take it down, I doubt if this approach will suffice.

Reply: Yes, but I mean, anonymity of the sender that you guarantee, and there are some lightweight mechanisms so you can do this by scattering these chunks of messages that apparently look OK.

Paul Wernick: How do you get this from the point of view of the recent South Australian legislation, where, while the election campaign was on, the intention was not to allow anonymous blog posts about the election, every blog

---

[4] See LNCS 1361, pp 1–11, also Ross Anderson. The eternity service. In Proc. Pragocrypt 96, pages 242252, 1996.

post had to have the person's name and I believe a postcode. They rapidly retreated from that law, but it's still an issue. So seeing it from this point of view, I can see the advantage of being able to post anonymously, and without any back channel. What worries me is the need to provide the initial information, and the emails going through the system, which are probably also visible, to some destination somewhere saying what the keys, etc, are. Is there a weakness there that it provides a route for the censor to trace back?

Reply: One weakness is the fact that I still need to send some information to the receiver. But look, what we can do for example is pre-share a secret, then if I have to publish the news today, we can use some pseudo-random number generation or hash function to determine where today I will post my scattered messages.

Paul Wernick: But the mere fact of sending, I'm sending a message to my blog site that I want to post anonymously, however long in advance I send it, the spooks will have a copy of that email, so really it's the emails that seems to be the crowbar in a sense.

Reply: Yes, but if we pre-share a secret before, and we do not use any more the emails; what you need to redeem the news today is to know where you are going to publish the end channels today, right. So you have the pre-shared secret with me; based on that you can determine, OK, we have three thousand blogs, today I will use these ten blogs. So you know that you want exactly these blogs without me sending any mail to you today, then you can retrieve today's news.

Paul Wernick: So all the spooks will know is that a certain number of people have sent messages to this destination saying, I will at some point in the future send you anonymous stuff by various routes, and when they see the entry they want to trace back, they don't know who of the three thousand who sent the emails actually did it, is that the idea?

Reply: Yes. These are just options that we are thinking and trying to see what are the best ones. But perhaps I can tell you these passwords so there is no email, but I cannot tell you today the news of next week, but I can tell you today the password, to all the secret, to know where to retrieve the news the next week, so the censorship authority isn't able to know ...

Paul Wernick: ... to know who's going to be sending messages in the future?

Reply: Yes. So just to sketch the evaluation of this approach, what happens is that, OK, the intended message is not posted as it is so there is no way that M can be directly banned by the censorship authority. This chunk also is not possible, it is there, but it is hidden with steganographic techniques. And if we use text to text encryption we choose a message, a piece of text, that is related in topic to the chunks that we are going to hide within that text, so the overall message that is posted will not look suspicious. And the information required by the intended receivers to retrieve all the information is shared by the sender through a secure channel, or with another mechanism which we are discussing. One other interesting point is that these are lightweight solutions, so I was telling you that it doesn't require things like Tor, it doesn't require to be part of the Tor network, and things that can be identified with certain analysis or other techniques. So you can, for example, go in an Internet café, just use some outlet without any protection, and go to the blogs that you have to use today if you want to publish something, and then send that information. And also, compared with Tor, for example, it doesn't have a firewall problem.

Concluding, we propose this anonymous and censor resilient communication system, but we are still working on this solution, so we have to better understand how much this solution will be effective and efficient also based on these kind of steganographic techniques that we are going to do, so how many chunks we need, how much information can we convey with a given the number of chunks, and things like that. So if you have questions about this, suggestions, weakness, things that we can leverage to optimise the solution, . . .

Audience: How big is the set of the intended recipients, and what is your level of trust for the recipient of the message?

The reason I'm asking is that if you want to publish to a wide set of recipients then expect that the censor, say the government, will also get that link, and will also get to know where the information is hidden. Otherwise if the set of recipients is small, say you were only posting for your friends, or for your own small political party, you could just as well use cryptography and send them an email, because you have to send a URL anyway. So I'm just wondering, what is the use scenario in this case?

Reply: If I have to send something to a small set, I use communication, you can see that I was sending it before, but you can optimise this kind of information by pre-sharing a secret, and then determine where we publish by using the pre-shared secret.

Audience: So if I understand correctly, you are publishing for a small set of recipients with whom you have a pre-shared secret?

Reply: Yes.

Ross Anderson: If what you want to do is publish information, say you were a guy in China and you want to publish something about the Dalai Lama that the Chinese secret police don't like, and you want this to be visible to as many Chinese citizens as possible, for as long as possible, provided you tell them where to look, then rather than using steganography you might be better off using a choice of a very wide diversity of forums. Because there are millions of forums where people can post comments, comments of news articles, book reviews on Amazon, there are millions of websites that let you as an anonymous user, in effect, post stuff. Now from the point of view of the censorship authorities, they have got considerable bureaucratic costs in maintaining, for example, their great firewall, so on Monday when you want to publish your comments about the Dalai Lama, you publish it on seven different randomly selected websites out of millions worldwide, you then send out a message saying initially, for example, here are three websites in which there is the Dalai Lama's latest news. The authorities rush to censor those, so they turn off Amazon for the whole of China while they work out how to censor that particular book, then perhaps something on eBay and so on, then after a few hours you say, the comment is also available on these two, and after a few hours you say, it's also available on these two.

My suggestion is that for this kind of application what we need is not so much the steganography but the agility which enables you to use the opponents weight and inertia against them.

Reply: OK, one sort of weakness that I see here is that I'm asking still that you need to anonymise the sender of the message, because otherwise you can trace back.

Ross Anderson: Well that's a separate problem.

Reply: Yes, but what if you want another solution that allows you to publish anonymously.

Ross Anderson: Well in that case you have to understand where to put stuff on the web without leaving a trace of your IP address. That means, at the very simplest you use a proxy, those kids in Iran do, there are many proxies to use. Or if you want to be really paranoid you use something like Tor.

Reply: Yes, and you will be identified like a Tor user.

Ross Anderson: Only if you're careless and leave things at the application layer.

Reply: And you need to leave some fingerprint on the machine you use for Tor.

Ross Anderson: Well if the machine that you're using is in a Chinese Internet café and it's got a government key logger on it, a CCTV camera over your shoulder, and you have to show your photo ID in order to buy service at the café, then you're dead meat no matter what you do.

Reply: Yes, also if you are in prison or the government is able to control everything or block, or switch off even.

Joseph Bonneau: You made this claim that you can do this software in JavaScript, or in Flash, or whatever, and in a web café you have no control over the platform, but you have to make it hard for people who run the web café (either the government, or heavily monitored by the government), to not block yourself. Unless there's some non censorship resistant use for it, they can just block the website where you host the applets that go and find all of these posts.

Reply: You're talking in terms of the sender or receiver?

Joseph Bonneau: Receiver, the person browsing the web, and who has to go to a web café, and load your software in Flash or in JavaScript.

Reply: What you will see is that it is just from typing on blogs.

Joseph Bonneau: They have to fetch your software that parses these different URLs, and contacts all the different sites and compiles data.

Reply: You implement this software with a low level interface for the user, and just around the application you put the secret, the application then ...

Joseph Bonneau: Yes, I mean, I guess in a web café you can't run your own applications though.

James Malcolm: It could be on dozens of blog posts, the same as the Dalai Lama.

Bruce Christianson: Well you could have a situation, for example, where I send a message saying, if you go to these five places and get these five posts, and Xor all five of them together, a message about the Dalai Lama will magically appear, and the thing is, I don't need to have control over all of those five posts, there's enough redundancy that three of them might be completely innocent.

Joseph Bonneau: Yes, so I'm concerned about the software of it, even doing Xor, like people can't Xor 10K in their head.

Jonathan Anderson: Yes, but you don't need to go to a central repository for the JavaScript if there's like a word-press plugin, or something, that everybody has on their own blog server.

Bruce Christianson: Yes exactly, and that's on the client side anyway.

Paul Wernick: But there's still you saying, go there and do that, and the spooks will see you saying something, it's making sure that you isn't identifiable as you, just somebody.

Bruce Christianson: You know, each one can say where to go for the next one, unless they were in at the beginning, they can follow it but they don't know where it came from.

Paul Wernick: But the source of the message saying where to go is still ...

Ross Anderson: At some layer you have to try and specify what the threat model is. One case is you are talking about someone who can do anonymous broadcast to an audience which includes a secret policeman who has got the power to take down websites, and the question is then, how do you keep information available for the longest possible time, then you're led to something like the eternity service, or to the more agile version that I just mentioned a few moments ago.

Bruce Christianson: Another case is that you want to ensure that if the secret police weren't in at the beginning, then getting in later on doesn't help them work out who's actually doing it.

Ross Anderson: But then you probably have to think of the total life-cycle: that even if you start off clean, spooks come in once you become powerful, your founders get arrested and taken off to the uranium mines, and the equilibrium at some time in the future may have nobody as a member of your organisation who joined before the first spook joined, and there's a more interesting resilience problem.

On Storing Private Keys in the Cloud

Jonathan Anderson and Frank Stajano

University of Cambridge
Computer Laboratory
15 JJ Thomson Avenue, Cambridge, UK
{jonathan.anderson,frank.stajano}@cl.cam.ac.uk

Abstract. Many future applications, such as distributed social networks, will rely on public-key cryptography, and users will want to access them from many locations. Currently, there is no way to store private keys "in the cloud" without placing complete faith in a centralised operator. We propose a protocol that can be used to share secrets such as private keys among several key recovery agents, using a weak password, in a way that prevents insiders from recovering either the private key or the password without significant collusion. This protocol will enable the safe storage of private keys online, which will facilitate the advent of secure, decentralized, globally-accessible systems.

1 Introduction

Today, online services such as social networks can rely on passwords for authentication because they are provisioned in a centralised way: user passwords, or hashes thereof, can be tested against values stored on the provider's servers. The integrity of the personal information stored in these networks is attested to by the service provider, which implicitly asserts that "you should believe that Alice said this because I know that the person who typed it in knew Alice's password."

We have proposed that in the future, distributed social networks will provide such attribution via public-key cryptography, taking centralised providers out of the identity verification game [1]. The trouble is, public-key cryptography requires the secure storage of private keys, and a system that requires users to carry a Trusted Computer Base (TCB) in order to post status updates is unlikely to compete well with traditional, familiar, token-less authentication via password.

Other online services have a similar problem. Webmail providers may typically be trustworthy, but as Chinese dissidents have discovered, they sometimes co-operate "regularly and efficiently" with authorities [2] in order to operate in nations with widely varying standards of free speech and tolerance for political diversity. Many online services allow or require users to register an e-mail address as a backup authentication channel in case they lose their password, but acquiring access to this e-mail account gives an adversary the keys to the proverbial kingdom: if she can read your e-mail, she can reset all of your other passwords. Online services could use stronger means of authenticating users, e.g.

B. Christianson and J. Malcolm (Eds.): Security Protocols 2010, LNCS 7061, pp. 98–106, 2014.
© Springer-Verlag Berlin Heidelberg 2014

SSH keys or client certificates, but the problem is, again, that forcing users to carry a TCB for authentication is likely not a smart business strategy.

One could propose a system in which private keys are stored encrypted on a server, but this only solves the problem if the user can remember a cryptographically strong key with which to decrypt their private key.

The problems that we wish to solve are:

Problem 1. We wish to allow users to recover very sensitive information, such as private keys, from an untrusted online service without needing to remember cryptographically strong secrets.

We discuss the authentication properties of this problem in Section 2, in particular justifying the use of weak passwords in a system that uses public keys. We propose a concrete threat model in Section 3 in the context of a distributed social network, describing security threats from both insiders and outsiders.

A related problem is *plausible deniability*:

Problem 2. We wish for the key recovery service to provide outsiders and malicious insiders with as little information as possible about the users of the service, including their identities and knowledge of whose keys are stored where.

We propose a series of cryptographic protocols in Section 4 which answer Problem 1, allowing our user to recover his private key from untrusted sources, and move towards answering Problem 2, requiring progressively less trust in the other principals involved.

2   Passwords

The most widely-deployed authentication system for online services is also the least expensive: "something you know", typically a username and (likely weak) password. Authentication credentials are revealed to the computer that they are typed on and the centralised service's provider, both of which have the ability to violate the user's security expectations and must thus be trusted absolutely.

Since we propose using public-key cryptography for message integrity, it is tempting to require users to carry some form of Trusted Computing Base, perhaps storing private keys on a mobile phone. If, however, we want to enable the use case, "Alice wants to use an online service on a friend's computer with a proper screen," then either:

1. the computer and Alice's phone must be tethered e.g. via Bluetooth, or
2. Alice's private key must be made available to the computer.

The first of these options may be acceptable for services such as online banking, but for photo sharing or other social applications, only the second, with its uninterrupted workflow, is likely to encourage widespread adoption. Alice is going to supply the local machine with her private key, so there is little reason for her to carry it around with her. Rather, she should be able to retrieve it from "the cloud," using nothing but what she knows to authenticate herself, and what she knows is likely to be a very weak password.

It is true, then, that we require Alice to gauge the trustworthiness of the computer that she is sitting in front of. This is, on the face of it, a ludicrous requirement, but it is a requirement which is currently accepted by many, many users: despite the existence of key-loggers and other malware, people use online services via computers owned by friends, airport lounges and other Internet cafés. This decision is made, implicitly or explicitly, based on the user's perception of the computing environment, sensitivity to risk, education in security issues, etc.

In short, to use computers is to trust computers. We do not attempt to solve this problem, but we do reduce the number of principals which the user must trust. In the current model, there is an implicitly trusted service provider at the other end of the TLS tunnel whose security practices may be unknown. We replace absolute faith in this single principal with limited trust in a number of principals, reducing the trust that we are required to place in any one.

3   Principals

Bob, B, is a user of a distributed online social network. This network has no central, trusted authority to map Bob's digital identity onto his real-world one, so his client software proves who he is using Bob's private key.

Wishing to access the network from abroad without carrying any hardware, Bob prepares a private key K_B^{-1}, which he advertises to his peers along with a set of constraints[1]. He then enlists friends Alice, Alexa, Alicia, etc. $(A_0, A_1, A_2, \dots)$ to act as "key recovery agents" on his behalf: each will run code on their computers that stores some portion of the private key, which will only be given out to Bob later if he authenticates himself with the weak password k_B [2].

3.1   Insiders

We assume that Alice, Alexa, etc. are not particularly malicious — they will try to guard secret information that they are entrusted with and they will not collude *en masse* — but they not particularly trustworthy either. In particular, any or all of these key recovery agents may be susceptible to curiosity or malware.

---

[1] For instance, Bob could prepare one key per calendar week and declare them valid for signing instant messages but not sharing photos. This would ensure that, if a key is compromised by an untrustworthy computer, the damage which can be done is limited.

[2] We assume that Bob is able to recover his public key, K_B, and those of his agents ($K_{A_0}, K_{A_1}, \dots$) from a public source, but that the only secret information which can be used for authentication across sessions, computers, etc. is k_B. This means that the public keys which Bob recovers can be used to provide confidentiality of communications, but not authentication of principals.

Curiosity. We assume that, if Bob gives his private key and/or password to Alice in the clear, she might look at it out of sheer curiosity. In fact, Alice might even be willing to mount a dictionary attack if it is easy enough to do. This definition of curiosity is different from the classical sense of "honest-but-curious:" an honest-but-curious participant will complete a protocol faithfully, but may gossip with the other participants after the protocol run in order to learn additional information [3]. We assume that an agent will not collude with $k - 1$ of n others in order to learn additional secrets such as Bob's private key or password.

Malware. We assume that many, or even all, agents may be infected with malware that can read any stored information and eavesdrop on any network communication. In our favour, however, we assume that the malware which infects the various agents is not capable of collusion.

Malice. We assume that, without resorting to large-scale collusion, one agent may attempt impersonating Bob to another agent in order to learn secrets such as Bob's private key K_B^{-1} or password k_B.

3.2 Outsiders

We assume that there is a malicious outsider, Eve, who can observe all communication between Bob and his agents, and that she might attempt to impersonate either Bob or a subset of agents. Her goal may include learning Bob's password and/or private key or ascertaining which agents Bob has stored his key with, or even simply whether or not Bob uses the system.

4 Protocols

We present several protocols, beginning with a "straw man" and building incrementally towards the final goal of key recovery (Problem 1) which thwarts attacks from both insiders and outsiders (Problem 2). Each protocol is more complex than its predecessor, but also mitigates more attacks.

4.1 Trusted Storage

The first, essentially trivial protocol we consider is to store the private key on a trusted server in the clear. This is analogous to a common practice in backup authentication: if Bob loses his Flickr password, he can have a reset token sent to his webmail account, which is hosted by a trusted provider. Since Bob is able to download Alice's public key from a public source, the protocol is simply:

$$B \rightarrow A : \{B, K_t\}_{K_A}$$
$$A \rightarrow B : \{n\}_{K_t}$$
$$B \rightarrow A : \{k_B, n\}_{K_A}$$
$$A \rightarrow B : \{K_B^{-1}\}_{K_t}$$

in which K_t is a temporary key used by Bob to provide confidentiality until he recovers his private key K_B^{-1}, and n is a nonce selected by Alice, which prevents Eve from performing a replay attack should she later learn the value of K_t.

Attacks. This protocol prevents outsiders from conducting successful dictionary attacks, since Alice can simply limit the rate of incoming password guesses. Eve's dictionary attack must be performed online, so Bob's password can be as weak as an English word.

There are, however, two very obvious attacks against the system: firstly, insider Alice can simply read Bob's private key and password in the clear, and secondly, outsider Eve can impersonate Alice to Bob in order to learn Bob's password—Bob can download a K_A which is attributed to Alice, but without a shared secret, he has no way to verify that it is actually Alice's key.

4.2 Semi-trusted Storage

A slight improvement on the previous scheme is the "semi-trusted storage" scheme, in which Alice does not hold Bob's password and private key in the clear, but rather a cryptographic hash of the password with her own public key, $h\left(K_A|k_B\right)$, and the private key encrypted using the weak password, $\left\{K_B^{-1}\right\}_{k_B}$. The protocol is very similar to that of the trusted storage scheme:

$$B \rightarrow A : \{B, K_t\}_{K_A}$$
$$A \rightarrow B : \{n\}_{K_t}$$
$$B \rightarrow A : \{h\left(K_A|k_B\right), n\}_{K_A}$$
$$A \rightarrow B : \left\{\left\{K_B^{-1}\right\}_{k_B}\right\}_{K_t}$$

After receiving message 3, then, Alice verifies that $h\left(K_A|k_B\right)$ matches her stored copy, and returns $\left\{K_B^{-1}\right\}_{k_B}$ to him in message 4.

Attacks. This protocol prevents a truly disinterested Alice from reading Bob's password and key, but it does little to stop a curious Alice or a clever Eve: either can mount an offline dictionary attack, against either the private key (Alice) or the password hash (Alice or Eve). Since the password is assumed to be weak, we expect that such an attack would succeed without very much effort.

4.3 Threshold Encryption

A logical extension to this protocol is for Bob to spread his private key across several agents, Alice, Alexa, Alicia, etc. using a standard k of n secret sharing scheme [4]. In this case, Alice stores $h\left(K_{A_i}|k_B\right)$, which is a version of $h\left(K_A|k_B\right)$ above, but personalized to her, and instead of the private key K_B^{-1} she stores D_i, which is one portion of the key K_B shared according to the thresholding scheme. The protocol between Bob and any of his agents is now:

$$B \rightarrow A_i : \{B, K_t\}_{K_{A_i}}$$
$$A_i \rightarrow B : \{n\}_{K_t}$$
$$B \rightarrow A_i : \{h\,(K_{A_i}|k_B)\,, n\}_{K_{A_i}}$$
$$A_i \rightarrow B : \{D_i\}_{K_t}$$

Attacks. This addition to the protocol prevents Alice (or Alexa, Alicia, etc.) from reading Bob's private key or performing a dictionary attack against its encrypted form, but there is nothing to prevent her or impostor Eve from attacking the weak password by brute force and, once successful, impersonating Bob to other key recovery agents in order to assemble Bob's public key.

4.4   Collision-Rich Password Hashing

We can improve on this protocol further by using collision-rich functions [5]. In this case, Bob authenticates to Alice via a hash function that intentionally has many collisions. This means that Bob's authentication to Alice is weaker, but two important purposes have been served:

1. Alice does not need to know k_B or even $h\,(K_{A_i}|\,k_B)$, but merely (see the Insider Dictionary Attack, below) $h\,(K_{A_i}|\,k_B) \bmod N$, and
2. Eve, should she impersonate Alice, will not be able to perform a successful offline dictionary attack[3] (see the Outsider Dictionary Attack, below).

The protocol is now:

$$B \rightarrow A_i : \{B, K_t\}_{K_{A_i}}$$
$$A_i \rightarrow B : \{n\}_{K_t}$$
$$B \rightarrow A_i : \{h\,(K_A\,|\,k_B)\ \bmod N, h\,(n)\}_{K_{A_i}}$$
$$A_i \rightarrow B : \{D_i\}_{K_t}$$

where N is a number chosen by Bob when he enlists Alice's help as a key recovery agent.

Attacks. Having eliminated the most straightforward attacks, we introduce more interesting ones.

---

[3] Collision-rich hash functions frustrate dictionary attack because the input can be grouped into equivalence classes, any member of which will produce the same output as any other member. Which member is actually the correct password must be determined by online dictionary search, which will be expected to fail if the classes are large.

Insider Dictionary Attack. Using this protocol makes it more difficult for Alice to obtain Bob's password via offline dictionary attack, since many passwords generate the same hash. If the number of possible passwords is x, then the number of password candidates that Alice will be able to learn from an offline dictionary attack is:

$$\begin{cases} x & N \geq x \\ \frac{x}{N} & N < x \end{cases}.$$

Since Alice's hash takes both Bob's password and Alice's identity and input, the hashes stored at each key recovery agent are independent. Thus, if Alice attempts to impersonate Bob to Alicia, she will have no likelihood information about the $\frac{x}{N}$ candidate passwords.

Still, there are $n - 1$ other agents that Alice can go to and try to confirm Bob's password. If we allow Alice α guesses at each, she will expect to guess Bob's password if

$$\alpha \cdot (n - 1) \geq \frac{x}{2N}$$

$$N \geq \frac{x}{2\alpha \cdot (n - 1)}.$$

If we assume that Bob uses $n = 9$ recovery agents with $\alpha = 5$ attempts allowed and a dictionary of 10,000 equally-probable passwords[4], then Alice would expect to be able to guess his password if $N \geq 125$.

Large-N Attack. If Eve impersonates Alice, she could send a large value of N to Bob. He should ignore values which lie outside of some reasonable range related to the strength of his password.

Outsider Dictionary Attack. If N is small—in order to minimize the success probability of insider attack—there is a non-trivial chance that Eve may be able to obtain Alice's portion of the shared secret by impersonating Bob and authenticating to Alice with a randomly-selected $x \leq N$. This does not give Eve access to Bob's key, however, only one portion of it. In order to recover Bob's key, she needs k portions of the secret. This is still difficult, because having successfully guessed $x \leq N$, Eve is now effectively in the same position as Alice, attempting to employ the Insider Dictionary Attack.

Impostor Identity Disclosure Attack. If Eve impersonates Alice, she will not be able to learn Bob's password easily, for the reasons given in the section on

---

[4] Of course, in a natural-language or chosen-password dictionary, all words are not equally probable. If the dictionary is small, however (e.g. 10,000 words / 4-digit PINs), random assignment is possible. If user-chosen passwords are essential for memorability reasons, password strengthening techniques might be of use, even if they are of little help against a conventional offline dictionary attack.

the Insider Dictionary Attack. Neither will she be able to perform a completely successful middle-person attack, since the hash $h(K_A|k_B)$ is bound to Alice's public key. She would, however, learn that Bob has stored his private key with Alice by virtue of the fact that he has attempted authentication, so Problem 2 is still not satisfied.

4.5   Collision-Rich Identity Hashing

In order to prevent identity disclosure in the face of the Impostor Identity Disclosure Attack, we can add one more layer of complexity: collision-rich hashing of Bob's identity. To prevent such hashes from acting as *de facto* persistent identifiers while allowing agents to perform their service for many clients, Bob should first send Alice a collision-rich hash which takes both his identity and Alice's as input, using a very low modulus of his choice. If Alice cannot disambiguate him using this hash, he can try again using a different modulus, reducing the size of the set of possible client identities to one (possibly after several iterations).

$$B \to A_i : \{h(A_i|B) \bmod N, N, K_t\}_{K_{A_i}}$$
$$A_i \to B : \text{try again}$$
$$B \to A_i : \{h(A_i|B) \bmod N', N', K_t\}_{K_{A_i}}$$
$$A_i \to B : \{n\}_{K_t}$$
$$B \to A_i : \{h(k_B|A) \bmod N'', h(n)\}_{K_{A_i}}$$
$$A_i \to B : \{D_i\}_{K_t}$$

Attacks. This protocol gives the same (low) probability of successful dictionary attack by insider or outsider, and it also counters the Impostor Identity Disclosure Attack, for the same reasons. It does not, however, mitigate the potential for traffic analysis: a technically competent adversary could observe that Bob has connected to Alice.

5   Related Work

Lomas and Christianson [5] have used collision-rich hash functions to provide assurance of OS kernel integrity when booting across an untrusted network.

SRP [6] is a protocol which allows clients to authenticate to servers using zero-knowledge proofs, but it provides little protection against a malicious server unless the user's password is strong enough to resist an offline dictionary attack.

6   Conclusion

We have developed a protocol which allows a user to store a private key "in the cloud," using the services of several key recovery "agents" who are expected to be curious and perhaps even malicious, but who are trusted not to collude *en masse*. The user is able to authenticate himself to these agents using a very weak password, yet the agents are unable to learn what the password is, and malicious outsiders are unable to even verify that a particular user avails himself of the recovery service.

Using such a key storage service enables the development of online services that rely on public key cryptography without requiring users to carry key material with them. We hope that these future services, such as distributed social networks, will allow people to do the things that they want to do online without needing to place absolute faith in any one software developer or service provider.

Acknowledgements. We would like to thank Joseph Bonneau, Bruce Christianson and Michael Roe for their helpful review of this work.

References

1. Anderson, J., Diaz, C., Bonneau, J., Stajano, F.: Privacy-Enabling Social Networking Over Untrusted Networks. In: The Second ACM SIGCOMM Workshop on Social Network Systems (WOSN 2009), pp. 1–6 (May 2009)
2. Blakeley, R.: Yahoo in second Chinese blogger row. TimesOnline (January 2006)
3. Beimel, A., Chor, B.: Secret Sharing with Public Reconstruction. In: Coppersmith, D. (ed.) CRYPTO 1995. LNCS, vol. 963, pp. 353–366. Springer, Heidelberg (1995)
4. Shamir, A.: How to share a secret. Communications of the ACM 22 (November 1979)
5. Lomas, M., Christianson, B.: Remote Booting in a Hostile World: To Whom Am I Speaking? IEEE Computer, 50–54 (1995)
6. Wu, T.: The Secure Remote Password Protocol. In: The 1998 Internet Society Network and Distributed System Security Symposium, pp. 97–111 (1998)

On Storing Private Keys in the Cloud
(Transcript of Discussion)

Jonathan Anderson

University of Cambridge

Hello, I'm Jonathan Anderson, a PhD student here in the security group in Cambridge, and these are some thoughts I've been having with my supervisor Frank, who couldn't be here today. Since it seems to be very much à la mode to have disclaimers at the beginning of the Protocols Workshop talks this year, well I disclaim you have no right to quiet enjoyment of the work I'm presenting. This is a work in progress, ideas, there's no implementation, and you may very well find some points we haven't thought of, so let's have some hearty discussion.

I am interested in the distributed authentication problem. In the current set-up with social networking, email, etc., Bob provides a user name and some proof of knowledge of a password to a server, and then he can send messages to Alice. You have integrity provided by this implicitly trusted centralised service: the server tells Alice, "you ought to believe that Bob sent this because somebody who knew Bob's password was talking to me". This provides us with some convenient properties, like the fact that Bob can login from a public library. What is less convenient is the fact that, as far as social networks go, these guys in the middle are often absolute scoundrels, they can't be trusted, and the people who write their applications are even worse scoundrels: they really, really can't be trusted. A little while ago I think MySpace decided they were actually going to start selling user data: not to pretend anymore that they're doing it through advertising, they're just going to say, "here's a DVD, would you like to buy it". So we don't like this, and so for lots of reasons, some of which I touched on last year[1], I want to move to a different model where we have some kind of decentralised or distributed social networking set-up.

Now, this means that we're no longer able to rely on the very convenient, and yet rather inconvenient, centralised third party, so we have to do things like public key crypto. It's very obvious that Bob can sign messages, and he can encrypt, and that's fine. But the use case that I'm interested in, that motivates the thinking behind the protocols I'll talk about today, is Bob at the library using a shared computer. People really like to be able to do social networking from other people's computers, from friends' computers, from wherever they happen to be. So how do we do this?

We could force Bob to carry around keys with him on a physical device like this online banking token, but who wants to do digital signatures by manually typing in codes on a calculator? Nobody. Well hang on, we can actually do something a little bit more sophisticated than that: lots of people are carrying smartphones, and so you could imagine a world in which in order to do your social networking

---

[1] See LNCS 7028, pp 343–364.

B. Christianson and J. Malcolm (Eds.): Security Protocols 2010, LNCS 7061, pp. 107–114, 2014.

you have Bluetooth tethered to your smartphone, and whenever you want to sign something it asks, "is this really what you want to say"?

Well, we've cheated here because we're not actually enabling the use case that I care about at all: if we're saying you require a smartphone in order to do your social networking from an untrusted computer, then why not just do your social networking on a smartphone? Frankly this is also a little bit boring, it doesn't provide us with the opportunity to try and think up new protocols, and do things in a new and interesting way. So why don't we try doing something a little bit different.

So here's an illustration of a user Bob in this social networking world, surrounded by a big cloud of people, some of whom are who they pretend to be, and some of whom aren't, and Bob has something that he knows for authentication purposes: a username and password. We're going to assume, of course, that the user name is public, and the password is garbage, it's useless, it's a very, very weak password, and this is probably a reasonable assumption to make in many cases. We're going to assume that no biometrics are required for Bob to log into his social network using his friend's laptop, so we really only have something Bob knows. We don't actually have a whole lot: Bob wants to somehow protect private keys using really, really weak secrets. This seems insurmountable, but maybe not... if it were insurmountable then I wouldn't be talking about new protocols today!

What Bob does have is other people. Now, I'm going to talk about authentication agents Alice, Alicia, and Alanas, and these might be real people, Bob's friends running a bit of code for him, but they might be VMs running on various cloud providers. And if Bob can convince these various authentication agents that he is Bob, then he can get access to his key again. OK, so that still sounds pretty straightforward, so let's introduce a new complexity. The problem is that these agents also can't be trusted because perhaps your friend isn't very good at keeping malware off of his computer, or perhaps your friend wears a black hat. Or they may not be malicious, but if there was a button that said, "would you like to read all of Bob's messages", they would probably click on it: a little bit curious, but not necessarily malicious.

So our goals are: we want Bob to be store this private key out there somewhere in this cloud, and we want him to protect it using nothing but a weak secret, and we want to use untrusted peers, so they can't know what the secret is. We are going to assume that there is some kind of public key directory, but not that it provides integrity properties — the directory could return an imposter's key. If that's not hard enough, then we're also going to say, we want Bob to be able to use a weak secret to assert his identity, to get a private key which gives him a stronger identity *without* revealing his identity.

Next, problems I don't care about. If you're sitting in front of a computer which has key loggers and all kinds of bad things installed, if it wants to mess with your social networking session while you're logged in, or wants to remember your password and re-use it later, there's nothing we can do to stop that. We can mitigate risk by only exposing limited-validity keys through this protocol, but there's no getting around the fact that using a computer requires a certain amount of trust in the computer. What we can do is deprecate all of the trust that's required in these backend systems written by scoundrels and untrustworthy people in order to reduce the trust decision to, "do I trust this computer sitting here in front of me". While most people may not be able to answer that question, at least they have some kind of a hope of being able to answer it. I'm also not trying to solve the conspiracy problem. If Bob does this distributed authentication thing with his friends and his friends all conspire against him, then Bob needs new friends, there's no technical solution for that.

So, to the protocols, hurrah. We're going to run through kind of a series of these, start with something that's awfully trivial, and then introduce new little bits of complexity, so if your criticism of the first protocol is that it's trivially broken, well yes, because it's not actually *the* protocol, it's a starting point. But as we introduce new things, as you see little yellow circles appear that say, this is new, if you think, "that's a crap assumption", then please speak up.

So the first thing you can do is kind of a webmail model that people use today implicitly. This is where you take one authentication agent, and I'm going to call her Alice, and she stores Bob's identity, and that identity is used to look up his password, and the private key, and this is not altogether different from webmail-based route of trust kind of stuff, where if you get locked out of an online service they send a password to your email account, at which point GMail is the ultimate trusted authority for everything in the whole world. The protocol is very simple: Bob sends Alice a temporary key to use to talk to him for the time being — this could be a negotiated session key, just to say, there's confidentiality we assume here. Alice says, "let's get some freshness out of you", and Bob says, "here is my password", and Alice says, "here is your private key". OK, so far so good. Attacks are obviously trivial because Alice has access to Bob's password and private key, so she can do whatever she wants, so that's kind of obvious. However, other problems include impersonations: there's no way for Bob to be sure that he's actually talking to Alice, and he's sending his password out in the clear to somebody, and he hopes it's Alice, but maybe it isn't. People like VeriSign try to deal with this in the webmail trust model, but they don't always get it right either, especially if you're living in Turkey (I think). And then of course there is the dictionary attack, where an attacker goes to Alice and tries various passwords.

Now, the nice thing is, because there's no password file that this outside attacker has access to, the dictionary attack, has to be online, which means the password doesn't have to be very strong. So what we want to do is to force the attacker into an online dictionary attack, but in some kind of distributed way that takes this massive amount of trust out of the one authentication agent. So we can take a very small baby step and say, Bob's no longer going to send his password in the clear, he's going to send a hash that was composed from things including his password, and Alice no longer stores the private key directly, she stores it encrypted under a key that's derived from this weak password. This sends a social signal in a sense: it says, I would prefer you not read my password, but there's no technical enforcement, because it would be very, very easy to brute-force these weak passwords that we're making assumptions about, and furthermore if there was an app that said, "would you like to read your friend's password", then again, many people would just click "yes".

So can we do a little bit better? Well, perhaps we can. Given that we're talking about multiple people, you might immediately think of a threshold encryption scheme: instead of giving Alice access to Bob's private key, she just has one chunk of it, and Bob has to go and convince n of k people that he is Bob, and then he can reassemble his private key. This is an obvious step, but it actually provides zero additional security, because in order for Bob to prove his identity to Alice, Alicia and Alanas, all of these agents still have to hold this hash, and the only secret that can possibly be in this hash is the weak password. So doing this thresholding scheme actually doesn't give you any additional security properties on its own because this can still be brute-forced, and once Alice has this, she can go to Alicia, she can go to Alanas, whoever, and she can say, "here's the password, please give me your chunk of the key", and reassemble Bob's key. Again, it's a slightly higher social barrier, because it's a little bit more of an active attack, but again, there's nothing to actually stop people from doing it.

So here is where we try to do something a little bit more creative, and a little more interesting, and when I say creative, I mean taking inspiration from the 15 year old paper that Bruce Christianson and Mark Lomas wrote[2], in which they were authenticating kernels moving around on a network. What if we intentionally introduce collusions into the hashes? Instead of Alice holding this hash, she holds this hash mod N, where N could be something like 256: she doesn't have a hash of Bob's password, she has several bytes of the hash of Bob's password. Now you might say, "whoa, whoa, whoa, this makes the authentication much weaker because it's easier to brute force". That's true, it does weaken the authentication with each individual agent, but also greatly weakens the attacks that can be performed by a malicious agent. This comes from the fact that now passwords become equivalent: "biscuit" and "cat", SHA-1 mod 256, both hash to the same value. An insider with several bytes of Bob's password hash can brute-force it, but the result isn't a password, it's a whole set of passwords; the insider becomes an outsider running online dictionary attacks against the other agents, just with a little extra information to start with.

If we do some sums, we expect that Alice will be able to guess Bob's password via a successful dictionary attack if this inequality is satisfied, where α is the number of guesses that you get per agent, small n is the number of agents Bob uses, x is the size of the dictionary — we'll talk about the assumptions on the dictionary in a second — and N is this value that you're hashing modulo to. And so for different parameters you can see α gives you different values of N.

Now let's talk about some of the assumptions that go into this. This only works if the the dictionary is composed of equally-likely passwords. Now you might say, "whoa, people don't choose equally likely passwords" and you'd be right, so we can't let people choose their own passwords. That's a bit of a downside. However,

---

[2] Reference [5] in the position paper.

look at the size of the dictionary: 10,000. Can we expect to remember a 4-digit PIN? Maybe. A dictionary of 10,000 words includes words like cat and dog, a dictionary of size 100,000 includes things like monkey7, so we're talking about pretty weak passwords, and the hope is that, even though they're chosen for you by the computer, if they're really, really easy then you might be able to remember them. And of course, if you start doing traditional stronger passwords then you get much better protection, so this dictionary explodes. This slide shows, for various assumptions of the number of authentication agents, and how many guesses they let you have. If you're allowing passwords like monkey7 or fish2, then if N is greater than 5,000, then you'd expect Alice to be able to conduct this attack successfully. So you set $\alpha = 1024$ or something, and that means that the probability of an outsider guessing correctly when they go to Alice is very, very low.

So that's the insider guessing attack. An outsider can come and do the dictionary attack, but again, in order to do so, the first thing they do is they go to one agent, or they go to all the agents, they try to find a password, or a bit of hash that works, and that's α times little n over big N probability of succeeding, and once they have that then they become an insider, and then they have to run this attack. So in fact we can still have some pretty strong properties, even though the authentication with each agent is weak. So we say, OK, that's pretty cool, at this point let's declare victory, hurrah, we've won, Bob was able to store a private key out there somewhere, he is able to protect it with nothing but a really, really weak password, he's able to recover it, he's able to prevent insider and outsider attacks, this is great.

But we still have the problem of an impostor doing an identity disclosure attack. In some cases Bob might not want anybody in the world to know that he's using this service, and he's stored his password with Alice: maybe that means Alice gets her door kicked down and that's very inconvenient for everybody. So if we apply a very similar kind of technique then we can in fact do identity hashing as well. The N in this modular operation can be truly, truly small. We could start with N_I as 2, and then move to 4, and then move to 8, asking "now can you uniquely identify me in the set of people that you are performing this service for?". If you're only acting as an authentication agent for ten of your friends, or if your computer is only running authentication agent code for tens of friends, you actually should be able to uniquely identify people with an NI that's very small. The "try again" message is because you do in fact want to uniquely identify which person you're authenticating as, because once you start saying, "this bit of hash is valid for somebody that Alice authenticates", we might start to get into trouble if she in fact authenticates many clients.

The "try again" message seems a little scary, like a chosen protocol attack, but it's not really: if Alice is in fact being a very bad person, and she's just sending lots of "try again" messages until she can get a really, really large chunk of hash out of Bob's identity, by the time she gets to the third or the fourth "try again" message, Bob's already successfully authenticated with everybody else. And of course, there could be a general or user-specific limit on this N. Exactly how to deal with that is perhaps the weakest bit of what I'm talking about here, but I do think this is a viable approach to let Bob to get his key out with a very weak secret. I do mean really, really weak: cat, dog, these are not the kinds of passwords that we encourage people to use, but they could be just fine in this system as long as it's assigned by the machine. Using peers who are hopefully not conspiring against you but are otherwise untrustworthy, and we can even let Bob assert his identity without revealing his identity, which I think is kind of cool. So that's all. Any questions?

Malte Schwarzkopf: So you've outlined all of this for authentication and obviously that's the viable use case, but if you're saying, as you said at the beginning, all the social network providers are scoundrels who want to sell all your personal data, then you also need to protect all the message exchanges. So are you suggesting that you use this for authentication, then devise some sort of encryption scheme, and then use that to encrypt your messages, because your data is still being stored somewhere, and they still have access, and my question I guess is, do they actually care that much about your password if they don't actually need your password in order to get to your data?

Reply: So this all kind of comes out of work that I want to do for distributed social networking, where in fact there is no centralised provider who stores all of your data in the clear. And one of the barriers to that is the fear that people will have to carry their private keys around, so I thought about how we can do something a bit more interesting. So the assumption is that you might use a centralised provider for availability reasons, but you don't trust them with your confidentiality or integrity, they're a CDN that stores encrypted blobs of stuff, and the clients have to interpret what those blobs mean.

Ross Anderson: The collision for hash function stuff that a number of us played with 15 yeas ago, Mark Lomas, me, Bruce, etc., was kind of a response to Steve Bellovin's EKE paper. That was an attempt to set up a protocol providing the user password to authenticate to a website by authenticating the set-up of a different known key in such a way that if you didn't know the password you couldn't extract it from the protocol. Now there were several dozen variants on that theme produced using different mechanisms, and in the end none of them got deployed because Lucent, the successor of Bell Labs, where Steve Bellovin worked, took the dog in the manger attitude to patents: they just waited and hoped that Microsoft would put this in browsers so that they could sue Microsoft for $100m. And so Microsoft of course didn't put it in the browser. But it happened in a few years, so it's perhaps opportune to start thinking about this type of protocol again.

Reply: So one of the results of Olivetti cryptic key exchange stuff was the SRP protocol, which Joe pointed me at, which again does secure remote passwords, but the problem with protocols like that is, you can't extract the password by observing a run of it, but the person that you're authenticating to does have to have some kind of information that they could use to get your password if your password is as weak as we're assuming it is. So they have to store something, and they can brute your force your password out of the information that they have. If they're compromised or they're wicked then they can get your password, and then they can impersonate you, and so that's the motivation for why I did the collision-rich hash stuff, again because that sort of a model doesn't really give you the property that I want, it's still basically requires you to fully trust an authentication agent.

Malte Schwarzkopf: One comment about the last bit where you said, OK, with the "try again" thing you're kind of protected against a malicious authentication if you are already authenticated with everyone else, so at some point you just don't care about that anymore. So that's obviously true, however the assumption there is that your connectivity to all of them is the same, and that your adversary cannot engineer the connectivity, which might be a perfectly reasonable assumption. But this only fails under the assumption that you don't have one malicious authentication agent who can send you messages very quickly, much quicker than everyone else, and thereby get access to your key.

Reply: So that's true, and that's why it would be nice if Bob could know my N_I, I have a maximum value that I'm going to let that go to, and I'm never going to reveal more than eight bytes of this identity hash, because nobody ever needs that, for instance. This is one of those things where earlier I said we assume that there is a directory where you can look up public keys, we make no assumptions about integrity. It would be nice if there was some kind of visual fingerprinting or something, Bob could at least say, yes, I think this is my public key, so Bob could read a self-signed message saying "my maximum N_I is this, and I will never respond to messages greater than that", so Bob can cache that information for himself. But again, that could just be in a lot of cases a software default sort of thing.

Malte Schwarzkopf: And the second question, so how would you go about bootstrapping this model? You still have to start off with a small number of authentication agents, you can't just join this social network and immediately have 20 friends that I can use as my authentication agents. Now they don't necessarily have to be a friend, there are other models as well, but if we assume that they are your friends on the social network, you are at some point going to start off with one, and you have full trust in them, you then distribute later, and I was just wondering if you have at all thought about how you would actually do this redistribution once you get more authentication agents, how it would scale, how you bootstrap it?

Reply: So part of what I want to say to that is that this stuff only applies when you are to the point where you want to be able to use other computers, so when you're first getting started, you have client software on your computer, you generate a master signing key for yourself, which probably gets stored on your computer, or if you're really paranoid, only on your Android phone, or if you're super-paranoid only on your iPhone. And so you set up your key, you do mutual identity verification, you do stuff like the MANA-III protocol, which allows you in a very lightweight way to figure out that the person you're talking to online is in fact the person that you talk to in real life, you could do all these things. Once you're ready to set this up, and this could be after you've identified friends, after you've purchased virtual machine time ahead of time, then you set this stuff up, and you just do some kind of secret sharing scheme, so if you add new people, it's kind of a matter of just recreating this stuff. And this thing doesn't need to change, if you want to change your password you can, but adding new people to the scheme, they can all keep what they already have here, and just new people have, instead of Alice here in the hash, it's Alicia, it's whoever, and this is the thing that has to change.

Joseph Bonneau: Just an observation, the uneasiness about the second message is simply the fact that there's no authentication on it at all, so you don't know who is telling you try again.

Reply: Right, and it's at this point kind of impossible to have the authentication because we're assuming that Bob can't tell Alice from Eve.

Joseph Bonneau: So going back to the SRP thing, I buy the reason you're doing a collision-rich hashing is that you don't actually have to give any of these Alices an actual password, you map it down so they have a set of passwords. But it seems like you could layer that on top of some other protocol, SRP, or whatever, where at the point in SRP when Bob is supposed compute things based on an actual password they just compute it based on this collisionable hash of the password. But since you're running high-end software anyway you could do that.

Reply: And that, yes, might be a very reasonable way to proceed. What I've got here is an outline of what a protocol could look like, and I said things like, "maybe this is actually TLS", but I just don't want to have a protocol notation for TLS. The contribution here is doing the collision-rich hash and the association with the n of k secret sharing. And if you want to base this on some well-known standardised protocol that has a user base, that's fine.

More Security or Less Insecurity

Partha Das Chowdhury[1] and Bruce Christianson[2]

[1] Emotions Infomedia
partha.dc@gmail.com
[2] University of Hertfordshire
b.christianson@herts.ac.uk

Abstract. We depart from the conventional quest for 'Completely Se-cure Systems' and ask 'How can we be more Secure'. We draw heavily from the evolution of the Theory of Justice and the arguments against the institutional approach to Justice. Central to our argument is the identification of redressable insecurity, or weak links. Our contention is that secure systems engineering is not really about building perfectly secure systems but about redressing manifest insecurities.

1 Introduction

The purpose of authentication is to verify that a user is who he/she is claiming to be. The goal of authorization is to provide access for certain users to certain resources based usually on predefined rules. An audit trail links actions to prin-cipals retrospectively. Authentication, authorization and audit trail are three traditional concerns in building a privilege management infrastructure (PMI). Traditionally, authentication is strong (based on long term credentials linked to a stable identity) and authorization is linked to audit via the authentication mechanism (explicitly using the same long term credential and identity).

The traditional approach to PMI has variously been institutionalised in the form of PKI [17] or trust management engines [6] or Role Based Access Controls [14, 19] or ticket based access management services [18]. We observe the same trend of institutionalisation even by the proponents of privacy enhancing tech-nologies [8–10, 7]. The temptation has always been to identify 'completely secure' systems without consideration of the actual societies and groups that would use such systems, i.e. the design process discounts[1] behavioural transgressions.

2 Case for Departure

We present a case for departure from the conventional theory of 'wholly secure' systems in this paper. We draw from the debate on 'Justice' where we see a clear conflict between a 'Wholly Just' approach based on Transcendental Insti-tutionalism, and realization-based approaches which focus on the advancement or retreat of Justice [20].

---

[1] For example, by assuming them away, or by classifying them simply as attacks.

B. Christianson and J. Malcolm (Eds.): Security Protocols 2010, LNCS 7061, pp. 115–119, 2014.

The thesis of this paper is that the pertinent question for systems engineering is not 'What would make our Security Perfect', but 'How can we be more Secure' in the context of our strong perceptions of manifest insecurities in our daily lives [3, 2, 5]. The identification of redressable insecurity is central to this thesis.

We first argue that institutionalism (in particular, the discounting of behavioural transgressions) often leads to weak links, which render the entire system more vulnerable; then we argue that just as institutions often tend to be indifferent to liberty and life, so institutionalism tends to give rise to systems which do badly at meeting legitimate aspirations of users.

2.1   Building in Weak Links

It has been reported widely in the literature that investigations into most frauds in the banking systems lead to an insider who has legitimate access to the system, and who knows his way around it [3, 2, 1]. In [1] the author clearly points out

> "Designers of cryptographic systems have suffered from a lack of information about how their products fail in practice, as opposed to how they might fail in theory. This lack of feedback has led to a false threat model being accepted. Designers focused on what could possibly go wrong, rather than on what was likely to; and many of their products are so complex and tricky to use that they are rarely used properly."

We can observe a clear similarity between this observation in [1] and the conflict between "institutional-focused' [20] approaches to Justice (initiated by Thomas Hobbe's social contract model and pursued by Jean Jacques Rosseau, Immanuel Kant and John Rawls) which presume a well-ordered society; versus the "realization-based" comparisons which are required to include the actual behaviour of people rather than presuming ideal behavior. It is our contention that systems engineering should take into account the realised actuality rather than assuming compliance by all the stakeholders of the system.

Our case for taking realised actuality into account can be illustrated by the work in [11]. Presumption of ideal behavior would seduce us to think if A trusts B to be honest and competent and B trusts C to be honest and competent then A can behave as if A trusts C to be honest and competent. However it is argued in [11] and [15, 12] that such spontaneously transitive trust relationships can have negative consequences and are not always desirable. And yet institutionalised PKI forces exactly this assumption of transitivity upon the user[2].

The realised actuality in the case of banking systems can be users who are entrusted with protecting the system but do not have the incentives to do so [3], or for legislation like RIPA can be behavioural transgressions by errant officers [4]. We emphasise the fact that in [11, 1, 3, 2, 4] the authors were engaged in redressing manifest weak links (e.g. arguing for elimination of transitive trust relationships) which they, reasonably enough, thought could be overcome.

---

[2] This type of involuntary trust relationship is called 'Compulsive Trust' in [12].

2.2   Examining Realised Effects

Human life is as much about freedom as about utility [20]. The case for realisation-based understanding can be further strengthened by the observation that institutions tend to be indifferent to the lives of people [4, 5, 1, 3, 2].

Instances of *Matsyanyay*[3] are pretty common in applications such as banking security systems [2, 3] where users are helpless against big corporations [3, 2], and with laws such as RIPA [4].

As argued before [12, 11, 13, 15], institutionalised approaches to security often compel users to enter unwillingly into a trust relationship with large parts of the system infrastructure. In consequence, the user is left without any means to control the risks to which they are exposed. A realisation-based understanding would make it easier to identify redressable insecurities. For example in the practical world of law enforcement we observe century-old "orthodox" institutions adopting a feedback mechanism (exactly as argued in [1]) to obtain a better understanding of the realised actuality. In the recent initiatives by Kolkata Police[4] the focus is more on the realised actuality [21] of various policies and mechanisms. The intention is to identify instances of redressable insecurities and inequalities, and to build upon this realised actuality, rather than imposing a set of 'Principles and Mechanisms' on citizens in a manner which is effectively oblivious to the actual impact of these mechanisms on lives and liberty. Similarly campaigners against ID cards and crypto laws in the UK have been animated by the identification of the impact those systems or laws would have on life and liberty [16, 4].

We advocate an explicitly realisation-based approach to secure systems engineering which builds upon an identification of such redressable insecurities. The institutionalised approach effectively regards security policy as an input-only parameter to the design process, and asserts a single threat model which must be accepted by all stakeholders, thus forcing a rigid distinction between stakeholders and attackers. We advocate rather to look at the effects which a given system realisation will have upon the behaviour of its users, and the incentives which it provides for that behaviour. We can then identify and redress the weak links, i.e. the manifest insecurities which emerge, and allow for the effect of feedback on the security policies themselves.

3   Summary

The motion before this house is that when it comes to security the best is the enemy of the good. We endeavour to learn from the debates in the formulation

---

[3] The classical distinction in Indian Jurisprudence is between *Niti* and *Nyay*, two Sanskrit words for Justice. *Niti* stands for organizational propriety and behavioral correctness, *Nyay* stands for realised justice [20]. *Matsyanyay* (literally 'Fish Justice') refers to the default case, where small fish have little redress against being eaten by big fish.

[4] Formerly Calcutta Police; Calcutta was the capital city of British India before Delhi.

of principles of Justice, and to draw an exploitable analogy to the world of security. The situation where a mentally ill man is subjected to injustice due to the incompetence of institutions is redressable. We advocate building on identification of redressable insecurities to address the question 'How can we be more secure'. Discounting social realizations as narrowly consequentialist (which is the current tendency in secure systems design) would lead us into developing mechanisms and institutions whose very insulation from the practical world makes them vulnerable.

References

1. Anderson, R.: Why cryptosystems fail. In: ACM Proceedings of the First Conference on Computer and Communications Security (1993)
2. Anderson, R.: Security Engineering. Wiley, Inc. (2001)
3. Anderson, R.: Why Information Security is Hard — An Economic Perspective. In: Proceedings of the 17th Annual Computer Security Applications Conference, p. 358 (2001)
4. Anderson, R.: RIPA III: A legislative turkey comes home to roost. The tragic consequences of anti-crypto law. The Register (2009)
5. BBC. Tax Records for Sale (2003),
   http://news.bbc.co.uk/1/hi/business/2662491.stm
6. Blaze, M., Feigenbaum, J., Strauss, M.: Compliance Checking in the PolicyMaker Trust Management System. In: Hirschfeld, R. (ed.) FC 1998. LNCS, vol. 1465, pp. 254–274. Springer, Heidelberg (1998)
7. Camenisch, J., Van Herreweghen, E.: Design and Implementation of the idemix Anonymous Credential System. In: Proceedings of the 9th ACM Conference on Computer and Communications Security, pp. 21–30 (2002)
8. Chaum, D.: Untraceable Electronic Mail, Return Addresses and Digital Pseudonyms. Communications of the ACM 24(2), 84–90 (1981)
9. Chaum, D.: Security without Identification: Transaction Systems to Make Big Brother Obsolete. Communications of the ACM 28(10), 1030–1044 (1985)
10. Chaum, D.: Achieving Electronic Privacy. Scientific American, 96–101 (August 1992)
11. Christianson, B., Harbison, W.: Why Isn't Trust Transitive. In: Crispo, B. (ed.) Security Protocols 1996. LNCS, vol. 1189, pp. 171–176. Springer, Heidelberg (1997)
12. Chowdhury, P.D.: Anonymity and Trust in the Electronic World. PhD thesis, University of Hertfordshire (2005)
13. Das Chowdhury, P., Christianson, B., Malcolm, J.A.: Anonymous Context Based Role Activation Mechanism. In: Christianson, B., Crispo, B., Malcolm, J.A., Roe, M. (eds.) Security Protocols 2005. LNCS, vol. 4631, pp. 315–321. Springer, Heidelberg (2007)
14. Ferraiolo, D., Sandhu, R., Gavrilla, S., Kuhn, R., Chandramouli, R.: Proposed NIST Standard For Role Based Access Control. ACM Transactions on Information and Systems Security 4(3), 224–274
15. Harbison, W.: Trusting in computer systems. Technical Report 437, University of Cambridge (1997)
16. Minutes of Evidence Taken Before Home Affairs Committee House of Commons. Inquiry into identity cards (2004), http://www.publications.parliament.uk/pa/cm200304/cmselect/cmhaff/130/13002.htm

17. KohnFelder, L.M.: Towards a practical public key cryptosystem. BS thesis, M.I.T (1978)
18. Clifford Neuman, B.: Theodore T'so. Kerberos: An Authentication Service for Computer Networks. IEEE Communications 32(9), 33–38
19. Sandhu, R.: Lattice Based Access Control Models. IEEE Computer 26(2), 9–19 (1993)
20. Sen, A.: The Idea of Justice. Penguin (2009)
21. Times News Service. Kolkata police set up blog for popular feedback (2009), http://timesofindia.indiatimes.com/city/kolkata/Kolkata-Police-set-up-blog-for-popular-feedback/articleshow/5034239.cms

More Security or Less Insecurity
(Transcript of Discussion)

Bruce Christianson

University of Hertfordshire

This is actually work done by Partha, it's his talk, but the UKBA[1] decided we could do without him, which is why it's me talking rather than him. The purpose of this talk is to explore the possibility of an exploitable analogy between approaches to secure system design and theories of jurisprudence. The prevailing theory of jurisprudence in the West at the moment goes back to Hobbes. It was developed by Immanuel Kant and later by Rousseau, and is sometimes called the contractarian model after Rousseau's idea of the social contract. It's not the sort of contract that you look at and think, oh gosh, that might be nice, I might think about opting in to that, it's more like a pop up licence agreement that says, do you want to comply with this contract, or would you rather be an outlaw. So you don't get a lot of choice about it. Sometimes the same theory, flying the flag of Immanuel Kant, is called transcendental institutionalism, because the basic approach says, you identify the legal institutions that in a perfect world would govern society, and then you look at the processes and procedures, the protocols that everyone should follow in order to enable those institutions to work, and then you say, right, that can't be transcended, so therefore there's a moral imperative for everyone to do it. So this model doesn't pay any attention to the actual society that emerges, or to the incentives that these processes actually place on various people to act in a particular way. It doesn't look at any interaction effects, it simply says, well you have to behave in this particular way because that's what the law says you have to do, and the law is the law, and anybody who doesn't behave in that way is a criminal, or (in our terms) is an attacker.

In the vanilla model of secure systems design that we find in books for children, we advocate the same kind of approach; you have a security policy, you identify the institutions and protocols that are going to implement this policy, and you say, well people have to behave in accordance with the security policy because otherwise they are policy breakers, and that's the definition of an attacker. And the problem with these assumptions is not only do they make systems hard to use, and unpleasant, but they also have the effect of building in the weak links to the system.

Paulo Verissimo: Would you say that those weak links are proportional to what we might call the realism of the assumptions, meaning you want it to be, that's why it's not possible?

Reply: Precisely so, that is where the tension comes from. We put the assumption in because we need to do a proof, but that assumption means that we

---

[1] United Kingdom Border Authority.

B. Christianson and J. Malcolm (Eds.): Security Protocols 2010, LNCS 7061, pp. 120–126, 2014.
© Springer-Verlag Berlin Heidelberg 2014

are not considering that attack, because we have defined it away. So precisely your point.

We don't look at the incentives that our implementation places on people. Most security breaches happen due to insiders being dishonest or incompetent, and because we made assumptions about ideal behaviour these weaknesses spread. For example, we assume that trust is transitive, and the consequence of that is that users now are compelled to enter into a non-negotiable trust relationship with large parts of the system infrastructure, so the individual client has no control over the risks that they are exposed to. Public key infrastructure is a classic example of that, where you have these innocuous looking assumptions, that even look as if they ought to be true for an ideal world, and yet they expose you to all these risks. Ross Anderson's "Why cryptosystems fail" comes back to exactly this point: designers know a lot about how their products might fail in theory, but they don't have the experience to know how they would fail in practice, and they don't really have a way of getting feedback into their model of policy. So they've got a particular threat model, and instead of saying when the system fails, oh the problem is with the threat model, they either say, oh the problem is with the protocol, we need more countermeasures, or they say, oh the problem is people didn't use the system properly, people didn't understand the licence before they clicked agree.

Now this brings me back nicely to a point that Sandy raised yesterday[2], which is, to what extent there's an analogy between bugs in ordinary systems where users just want performance and usability and things like that, and security violations in systems where we have some sort of anti-requirement; the things that we want the system not to do are just as important as what we do want it to do. It's almost a definition of maturity; a system is mature when most of your bugs come from fixes that you have put in to correct bugs that were there before. But there are two important differences. The first is, bugs don't get fixed unless they actually caused a problem, right, there's no notion of prophylactic fixing, if it doesn't cause a problem, it's not a bug yet. And the second thing is that after any piece of code has been in the field for a certain length of time, the fix is to document the bug carefully and propose a work-round. In other words, you change the behaviour of the client so as not to get the system to mis-behave, because that's got a good chance of working, whereas any bug that's been out there for that long that hasn't been fixed yet, either it's not really a problem, or it's not easy to fix.

Now in the security world there's an argument that says, in a mature system most security failures are enabled by countermeasures that we put in to counteract other threats. And the problem is that we have real genuine security threats coming from countermeasures that are there because of pretend threats. OK, we have a threat, and I don't think it's real, I'm not bothered about it, the world I live in is horribly insecure, I'm quite willing to take risks that are much bigger than this everyday, but the designer of the system thinks that it is a threat, and so they put in this countermeasure, and the countermeasure is what's giving me

---

[2] Clark, these proceedings.

the grief, because the counter-threat is real. In order to prove perfect security we have to make behavioural assumptions, and the assumptions have the effect of masking the real threats. For example, I don't have a choice but to trust my bank, it's that or nothing. I don't have a choice but to trust the doctor or the boss. What's their incentive to be honest and competent? Well their incentive is that the policy says they have to be, yes, the law is the law, and it applies to everyone, so that's your guarantee. So what will be our Enlightenment? We're actually working with a medieval model of secure systems design, and so the argument is that this Holy Roman Emperor approach to system security[3] is not just a bad deal for users, it's actually a bad deal for system security as well.

The second part of the argument is to say that there are alternative approaches to jurisprudence, there are actually a couple of alternative theories about how judicial systems should be built. In the West, the opponents of Hobbes never really got their act together, so you've got all these guys like Woolston, Croft, and Bentham, and so forth, they never quite managed to agree on an alternative. But in Indian jurisprudence (my Sanskrit is even worse than my Latin, I'm sure that some of these should have a vowel on the end) there are essentially two Sanskrit terms for justice in Indian jurisprudence, one of which corresponds pretty much to the Western mainstream institutional transcendentalism, which says, well you have correct organisations, and people do what the protocols say they should do. And then you have this idea of Nyay, which is looking at what actually occurs, and coming to a view about whether or not justice has been done, and there's plenty of examples of what's called Fish Justice. The justice of Fish is that big fish eat little fish, and the little fish have no redress, right, and that's generally regarded as being a bad outcome. And there's all sorts of examples that you can think of where the key point is that according to the transcendental institutionalist view of justice, no injustice has been done. Institutions that have been constituted for that purpose have done things the protocol says they ought to do, and what has happened is exactly and perfectly correct. And yet it's very clear that the outcome isn't right, and something else ought to happen.

We have a very narrow view of what the system is there to do, but in fact people build systems because they believe that that system will enable them to interact socially in some way that they couldn't without it. So the idea is to look at one of these other systems of jurisprudence, obviously Partha's used Nyay because it's a concept that he's familiar with, I might have wanted to run with Bentham or Rawls and Croft, but the focus shifts from saying, well we must have absolute justice, or absolute injustice, you know, absolute security, or no security at all, to saying, well there's a continual retreat and advance, and the trick isn't whether a system is secure or not, it's whether the insecurity manifests itself,

---

[3] *Fiat justitia, et pereat mundus*: "follow the security policy though the world be destroyed" was the motto of Ferdinand I, Holy Roman Emporor, 1558-1564. This phrase was also used by Kant in his "Perpetual Peace" (1795) to emphasise the counter-utilitarian aspect of his moral philosophy.

and if it does, is it redressable? What do you pay attention to, and what do you do about it? So it's actually much more like the bug fixing function.

The point is that we want to conform the system to what users want it to do, rather than saying, well the reason you have that login and password is so that you can comply with the security policy, that's what you were given those credentials for. So the consequence of that is, we have to build in some way of allowing manifest behaviour to feed back into the security policy. This is I guess the slightly heretical part that I'm putting forward, that we shouldn't take security policy as an input and read-only parameter for the design process. The design of the system shouldn't simply model incompetence and dishonesty as an attack, but should model it as motivated behaviour, and look to see what gives rise to it. So if you've got a problem with giving people the wrong incentives, then build the system in a way that gives different incentives, or move the weak links to somewhere where you believe you can redress them. The second slightly heretical suggestion is that, contra Mansfield[4], it is a very good idea if you're trying to take somebody's liberty away, or to restrict the freedom with which they can exercise the system, to explain to them as part of the design process exactly why you want to impose that restriction. Because quite often the provision of the reasons allows the right debate to take place, instead of falling back on the approach that says, well you've got to have an identity card because otherwise the security policy won't work.

The other point is that there's a very consequentialist view of behavioural transgressions that emerges in the current approach, which says well they did something wrong, and that had bad consequences, whereas actually this is an opportunity to allow the implementation to feed back into the policy. So we shouldn't just look at low-level details and say, well that's implementation, we specified what you have to do, and you do it, it doesn't really matter how you do it, just make sure you meet the specification at the higher level and you're fine. It's important to look at the impact of choosing one mechanism rather than another and to be willing not just to change the mechanism, but to go back up a level, reconfigure the user, and change the policy in such a way that when you re-implement it, it will manifest itself differently.

"The best is the enemy of the good", that one's Voltaire. There's still debate about which way round he meant it. But certainly in security there's an argument that pursuit of excellence is pernicious, and rather than pretend to be able to get it right, we need to accept that as soon as we release the system there will be a honeymoon period where people will start finding out the things that are wrong, and the question is, how can we redress an insecurity that emerges once it manifests itself. Part of that involves accepting that there isn't a unique Platonic threat model that we just haven't guessed right yet, instead we do have to cope with multiple intersecting views. And configuring the users is a perfectly

---

[4] "Tut, man, decide promptly, but never give any reasons for your decisions. Your decisions may be right, but your reasons are sure to be wrong." William Murray, 1st Earl of Mansfield, 1705–1793, quoted by John Cordy Jeaffreson in "A Book about Lawyers", Volume 1, page 85 (1867).

legitimate thing to do, we tend to try and do it by coercion and re-education at the moment, doing it by providing reasons and matching the incentives would probably be a better approach. And we have to allow for the effects that these mechanisms should have on the security policy.

Sandy Clark: The problem with configuring the users and the idea of using different motivations is that users aren't rational, they don't think logically, they don't make decisions logically, they make them emotionally.

Reply: Absolutely.

Sandy Clark: And so trying to reason with them, it just wouldn't work.

Reply: Ah yes, I should distinguish very carefully between reasoning with people and offering them an incentive, OK. So offering an incentive, for example might be, vote for the Healthcare Bill because it will bring the Rapture closer, that's a perfectly reasonable incentive, and it's the deep South mostly that's not got the healthcare anyway.

We've only got to do better than the techniques that systems are using at the moment. But I think you've made a very good point about the fact that people's responses to incentives are not necessarily rational, and thinking about it all in a remorselessly Benthamite way isn't necessarily a good approach. But even when people are behaving completely rationally, they don't make decisions based on what is true and what isn't, they make decisions based on what they believe to be true, which in turn is based on their perception, and even if you're dealing with perfectly rational people, that's a real stumbling block that the current approach can't cope with, or at least doesn't.

Paul Wernick: And not just when dealing with rational people. How many times have you gone onto a website, it demands a password, they're not going to come here again, I don't want it, chuck in something so the wretched thing will allow me access. And you know, the model that the designer of the website had was, this has got to be secure, a secure network will have passwords, if you have a password you will be secure, and people are saying, stuff this, I just want to get this one thing and go away.

Jonathan Anderson: But that is rational behaviour, for me to say, I don't care about your security policy, I just want to read the New York Times.

Reply: The irrational behaviour there is on the part of the designer. What they've effectively done is to pop up a box that says, do you really want to use this website, and you type yes in as your password, and away you go. That isn't what they had in mind, partly because they never explained their reason, so there was never any discussion about whether this was a reasonable thing to do or not, and partly because of the incentive that they've offered you, enter a password and win a chocolate fish right now.

Paul Wernick: And there is also a reluctance to learn from safety engineering; I've seen in the past a paper on security protocols that seemed to say, we have a generally single track railway, but we might slow down for the threat of these two trains coming towards each other on that track. If you take a holistic view of the entire thing, you can't design out of it some particular threats, you just need to accept that the real world is the message.

Reply: Well it's our policy that we don't, and from the software point of view, it's a sort of a looking glass game: if somebody says, well in our policy we assume we have tamper-proof hardware, that sounds really secure, you know, tamper-proof hardware, brilliant, but what they're actually saying is, we are not going to consider the threat of somebody getting the secret out of the box, we're defining it away. It's the same again: wouldn't it be better to look at the consequences of what we assume?

Paul Wernick: And perhaps treating people as human beings rather than as rational creatures?

Reply: Well we have this idea, as I said, in the books for children, that says, come up with the perfect threat model, then design the transcendental countermeasures, and then implement. Whereas to do something that's more or less right, and stand by it with a mallet, and play whack the mole when they start appearing, that's a terrible and wicked thing to do.

What I'm trying to say is, actually if you do that properly it's not such a bad approach[5].

Paul Wernick: Doesn't that also suggest the idea of redundancy: the mechanism is connected together by three bolts in case some goon forgets to put one of them in; it will continue to work with only two until somebody comes along and notices the hole.

Reply: That's the other problem with the current approach to formal proof, it just gives you true or false.

Paul Wernick: It's not resilient.

Reply: It doesn't tell you how redundantly true it is. It's not very good, because where you end up is that, even when you do have a system that's workable and secure, it's very fragile, because it relies on some very tendentious assumption that's right out on the edge of what you can comprehend: change slightly, and suddenly you've gone from one to zero (although it takes people a little while to work out how to exploit it).

Saša Radomirović: I think the problem we have here is the problem of trade-offs, we try to design security to be perfect, and then it isn't, and then we have a mess. So now we're saying, well maybe we want to design something that we acknowledge is not perfectly secure, and start squashing bugs. But eventually you will have this one bug that won't squash, and hitting that mole will cause terrible other consequences, and not quite get rid of it. Not knocking it out will have other bad consequences. So it might be that no-one should choose perfect security, but the problem is these trade-offs.

Reply: Yes exactly, but the point is that security is a trade-off, it's not an absolute. Shopkeepers all understand that shoplifting is a cost of doing business, they understand that they could reduce shoplifting to zero by using simple

---

[5] This talk was given in 2010. The following year saw the publication of David Deutsch's book "The Beginning of Infinity" which makes a very similar point about social institutions as well as science, see especially the chapter "Unsustainable"; designing the perfect system is a non-goal, a good system is one where the problems are easy to identify and the system is easy to change.

measures involving dogs and armed guards, but that will also cost them all their business. So they say, well I would rather have shoplifting so long as it's below three percent of my turnover. Banks do have that approach to security, but not in a good way.

Paul Wernick: Exactly, they pass it onto their customers.

Reply: Yes, they pass it onto their customers, but the point is the customers have no choice. But if I'm a small grocer and I pass it onto my customers, if I'm bad at it they'll go and shop somewhere else. But our clients don't even have a choice.

Joseph Bonneau: Yes, I guess the question can be, can you point to a real world example of something, some system that's been vaguely designed in this way successfully?

Sandy Clark: Joseph, your immune system is a vital defence, it's not perfect, but it moderates itself as needed for attacks the best way it can.

Joseph Bonneau: I'm going to rephrase, something designed by people. Because it seems like some dispensables that banks actually took when designing EMV is that there's a million different options, and they can put leverage theoretically, if certain movements start happening, and they can check for this, and they can stop accepting that, and I think we'd all say that hasn't worked out well.

Reply: No, but people have said about some of the IPSec protocols that it's almost as if they were holding back on a release because they wanted to see the old holes exploited before they deployed the next set of features. So there is an underground view that they are already playing this game, possibly covertly, or possibly even subconsciously.

Jonathan Anderson: This is also an argument for defence-in-depth things, because all of a sudden it doesn't matter too much if there's a buffer overflow in your jpeg library as long as it's being run inside a chromium sandbox, then it gives you a little bit of time to try and whack that particular mole.

Reply: Yes, so the fact that you have to hold off on whacking a particular mole doesn't mean you've got no security at all.

It's the Anthropology, Stupid!

Ross Anderson and Frank Stajano

University of Cambridge

Imagine a world five or ten years from now where virtualisation has become pervasive. Rather than doing your work on a personal computer, you have a laptop (or a tablet or a virtual reality headset) with a number of virtual machines — say one for work, one for play, one for serious personal things like banking, and one for the classified work on the defence contract your employer picked up.

These virtual machines communicate in turn with a number of virtual servers in various clouds. Your work machine talks to a corporate cloud and to services run by subcontractors such as `salesforce.com`. Your play machine might, according to taste, talk to an assortment of game servers, porn servers or bridge clubs. Your serious personal machine will talk to your bank; you might have other machines to talk to other banks, or to your broker, or to your oncologist, but for the sake of argument let's just consider one of them for now. And your classified machine will talk to a dark green box somewhere in the government cloud. What's more, many of these servers will not be single VMs but will be replicated over several machines — maybe in more than one country for resilience.

This brave new world is the direction in which both hardware design and service delivery appear to be travelling. What extra work will it create for the security engineer? Well, there are some matters of functionality and assurance at the operating system level. First, we need better separation between virtual machines, so that different VMs on the same physical machine can't attack each other. Second, high-assurance service providers will want ways to tie down particular services to particular sets of boxes; and third, they will want robust ways to get key material into VMs. Whether these two problems are solved using administration or some kind of hardware cryptoprocessor is really a detail. Surely the virtualisation vendors can harden up their product, and surely service firms will work out ways to manage keys. And whether communications with client VMs are handled using TLS, or SSH, or Kerberos, or something new, is really not that exciting. Of course there will be plenty bugs and blunders, but basic protocols are no longer rocket science.

When we contemplate the client end, things get harder. The modern laptop or desktop PC is a much more complicated beast than a typical server, and providing high-grade technical separation between VMs is not at all trivial. For example, how do you assure yourself that only you have access to the microphone and camera right now? And what about covert channels in the graphics card? There is some red meat here. Presumably the services with most to lose by being excluded from using commodity platforms — yes, the military — will fund the necessary research, as they have in the past.

B. Christianson and J. Malcolm (Eds.): Security Protocols 2010, LNCS 7061, pp. 127–130, 2014.
© Springer-Verlag Berlin Heidelberg 2014

But perhaps the biggest problem of all will not be the cryptographic protocols that tie one virtual machine to another, but the human protocols that enable the right user to deal with the right virtual machine.

To Whom am I Speaking?

Once our typical user has multiple virtual machines in her laptop — `alice.work`, `alice.play`, `alice.bank` and `alice.mil` — the traditional view is that she needs a trusted selection mechanism to help her invoke the right VM for the job. The enemy intelligence agent, Charlie, will try to trick her into mistaking a mil-like simulation in his game site in `alice.play` for the genuine `alice.mil`. So we will engineer a secure attention sequence, control-alt-delete or whatever, to take Alice dependably to a hypervisor where she can select from among these four machines. We will then train her to never enter classified information without going through this ritual first.

So far so good. But what about her brother Bob, who has no clearance? As a result, he's untrained in the holy doctrine of trusted path and has not been indoctrinated into the ceremony (indeed the reflex) of the secure attention sequence. There's no `bob.mil`; in his case the fraudster David is trying to trick him into mistaking a bank simulation in `bob.play` for `bob.bank`.

And what about mistakes? They matter much more than targeted attacks. To a first approximation all attacks are by insiders, and most of them spring (initially at least) from errors rather than malice. The main practical benefit of mandatory access control is that it prevents Alice entering High information into a Low system by accident. Accidents also cause much expense and embarrassment to civilian users. (One of the first writer's most embarrassing moments in recent years came while using a PC at a friend's house to check email, and — on an unfamiliar browser — deleting the host's cookies, passwords and browsing history, while trying to unjam gmail.) Mistakes are often caused by getting the context wrong, so if we're going to make them less likely, our designs should be better at synchronising the user's mental model better with that of the machine.

This brings us to the central idea of this paper. It's not just computers that operate a number of virtual machines; people do as well. The human-computer authentication problem isn't one-way, but two-way. It's not enough to tell Alice or Bob "hereafter you will be in `machine.work`"; a robust system must also assure the machine "the user sitting in front of you is in the mindset `.work`".

In other words, secure virtualisation isn't just about ensuring that the right VM in the laptop talks to the right VM in the cloud. It's about ensuring that the right VM in the laptop (or the cloud) talks to the right VM in the user's brain. It's not primarily about the outside attacker, but the insider: and the critical question is which insider.

Psychologists have written about how our different personae fail to anticipate each others' likely reactions. For example, Dan Ariely and George Loewenstein showed that when we are in a rational or "cold" state we underestimate how we will react when in an aroused or "hot" condition; with experience, we learn to avoid circumstances in which we might fall into temptation and lose our temper, drink too much, or spend more than we should [1]. But the strategies people develop to cope with this "hot-cold empathy gap" don't always translate so well online. As another example, Joe Bonneau and Sören Preibusch remark that Facebook might make people more vulnerable to scams, because it encourages rapid browsing and instant interaction in a noisy, distracting environment while often in a state of partial arousal [2]. This has clear hazards if Facebook users operate payment mechanisms, or authenticate themselves to other websites, while in a careless mode — in other words, if `alice.play` talks to `machine.work` or `machine.bank`.

The traditional solution to the "human VM" problem involves the empathic synchronisation we achieve via nonverbal communication, to which cultures add manners, rituals and dress codes. Soldiers wear uniforms, and the parade-ground ritual of calling them to "attention!" literally gets their attention for the orders of the day. (It's the military equivalent of control-alt-delete.) The banker's suit, and the dentist's white coat, condition the behaviour of the wearer as well as his customers or patients.

How then can we bridge the gap between the mechanisms that we can use to order human VMs, and the quite different mechanisms that work with the technical variety?

A Modest Proposal

Matt Blaze noted how many real-world ceremonies, such as the ritual of ordering and sampling wine in a restaurant, are actually security protocols [3]; and Carl Ellison argued that human-computer protocols should be seen as ceremonies, as the act of typing a password or shoving a smart-card into a reader are interpreted as such by users [4]. This seems sound; we need to recapture the anthropological aspect. Another useful idea was the comment here in 2004 by Frank Stajano that users wear different hats when operating a PDA in different modes [5].

Our mission is not to tell the user which VM in the laptop she's talking to, though. It's to tell the laptop which user VM it's talking to. We have to turn things round.

The simplest proposal is that the user should wear a physical hat signifying her mode of operation. In order to access `alice.mil`, Alice should put on her service cap, which will be recognised by the laptop's camera; to log on to his bank, Bob will put on a banker's bowler hat. For a `.play` machine, a party hat is fine.

There are other ways in which this could be implemented. For example, to access your work machine, you might just put your work ID badge round your neck. And of course, there will be a temptation to shift everything to software — so that the hat you're wearing is simply reflected back to you in an icon on the screen. But what I'm arguing for here is a change in perception. The objective is to be sure that the user is in the right frame of mind, not that the user "can" find out what VM she's talking to. (And as for the worry about whether you have the wrong user, I'm not interested in that here.) So rather than thinking about the problem as a system engineering one, I'd rather think of it as a somewhere between applied psychology, biometrics, and anthropology.

Interesting possibilities arise from the work of Peter Robinson and others in affect-based computing [6]. Now that computers are routinely equipped with video cameras and microphones, a machine can study its operator's facial expressions, gestures, speech and posture to observe emotions such as impatience, perplexity, and anger. This new field also has some useful warnings for the engineer; for example, people's emotional reactions to robots are very different from their reactions to people, so it cannot simply be assumed that having a hat icon on-screen will have the same effect on Alice as wearing a hat on her head. The social aspects matter; so do the physical aspects. The old world of rituals and manners, which condition our behaviour and our expectations of others, is different from online. If homo interneticus spends twelve hours a day sitting on a sofa with a laptop, much that used to go into human interaction will be lost. In fact, we don't even have a proper word for this loss!

In conclusion, I argue that to build robust protocols that are good enough to authenticate virtual machines to each other, we must first understand that the VMs in question include those in the brain as well as in the software, and that the authentication must be mutual. Protocol design thus comes down to usability testing, and something a bit more. Maths and formal methods give way to experimental psychology. But ultimately, at the deepest level, this is about anthropology. It's how systems get embedded in culture, in the interplay of verbal and non-verbal communications, and how our evolutionary past conditions the way we behave. The physical, and the ritual, have value that we need to rediscover. Or perhaps the next generation will reinvent it anyway, in the same way that pidgins become creoles, and all we have to do is figure out how to provide the avatars — or even just a basic lexicon of gestures to reopen the nonverbal channel.

References

[1] Ariely, D., Loewenstein, G.: The Heat of the Moment: The Effect of Sexual Arousal on Sexual Decision Making. Journal of Behavioral Decision Making 19, 87–98 (2006)

[2] Bonneau, J., Preibusch, S.: The Privacy Jungle: On the Market for Data Protection in Social Networks. In: Workshop on the Economics of Information Security (2009)

[3] Blaze, M.: Toward a broader view of security protocols. In: Christianson, B., Crispo, B., Malcolm, J.A., Roe, M. (eds.) Security Protocols 2004. LNCS, vol. 3957, pp. 106–120. Springer, Heidelberg (2006)

[4] Ellison, C.: Ceremony Design and Analysis. IACR eprint 399

[5] Stajano, F.: One user, many hats; and, sometimes, no hat: Towards a secure yet usable PDA. In: Christianson, B., Crispo, B., Malcolm, J.A., Roe, M. (eds.) Security Protocols 2004. LNCS, vol. 3957, pp. 51–64. Springer, Heidelberg (2006)

[6] Robinson, P., el Kaliouby, R.: Computation of emotions in man and machines. Phil. Trans. Roy. Soc. B 364 (April 2009)

It's the Anthropology, Stupid!
(Transcript of Discussion)

Ross Anderson

University of Cambridge

We have talked about the interactions between security and economics, security and psychology, and Bruce has been talking about the interaction with jurisprudence[1]. So in this talk I thought we would try and colonise yet one more of the University's disparate departments, and see if we can steal anything interesting from the anthropologists. I'm going to be agnostic about whether we're talking about the biological anthropologists or the social anthropologists, as you may know, these are two warring tribes.

The thinking started with virtualisation. We may be heading towards a world in which, by the time we retire, you end up with virtual machines everywhere. We've already got virtualised applications, storage servers in the cloud. It's a small step of the imagination that to think that we'll have virtual clients in our laptops or in your VR headsets as well. And this means that you may have a number of different entites or sub-users, say `bob.bank`, `bob.work`, `bob.play` – if you're doing classified work `bob.gov` – and you can imagine how this might work from a technical point of view. You might be running Xen or VMware on your laptop, you have got your government partition, or your work partition or your play partition, sitting under a particular instance of the operating system. Then this virtual machine on your laptop talks to various virtual machines in the cloud. It could be fairly complex; your work laptop could be talking to all sorts of services in the cloud, in `salesforce.com`, your own employer's cloud, and so on and so forth. So how is it all going to hang together?

Well we see the beginnings of some work on this, robust protocols, trustworthy key storage. As Jonathan was talking about earlier[2], many of the protocols we already use – TLS, SSH, and so on – will work fine provided we can tie them down reasonably at the ends. Tying them down at the ends might be slightly difficult because we might want to ground some machines geographically: we may want to see to it that the machine with the classified stuff on it stays in Britain, and the machine with the Dalai Lama's stuff on it doesn't go to China, and so on. There are various procedural and technical things you can try to do here. Better inter-VM separation is of course an area of research, with blue pills and red pills, and a client is particularly bad. With servers it's easy, because servers are very simple machines. But in a laptop, for example, suppose you were running your government VM, how can you be sure that it controls at the moment your sound-card, your video camera, and your microphone? How many covert channels are there in a video-card? Do you even know what's inside a

---

[1] Christianson, these proceedings.

[2] Anderson, these proceedings.

B. Christianson and J. Malcolm (Eds.): Security Protocols 2010, LNCS 7061, pp. 131–141, 2014.
© Springer-Verlag Berlin Heidelberg 2014

video-card? The PC vendor probably doesn't! There may be one or two guys at the video-card manufacturer who know this, but hey, they're not speaking.

What do you need from the user's point of view? Well you need some means of logging on; you need a dependable way for Bob to distinguish Bob's `PC.play` from Bob's `PC.bank`. The PC with which you do your banking shouldn't have all the crud on it that you get from playing computer games, and certainly Facebook and so on and so forth. And indeed if somebody can place a virtual bank or a simulacrum of a bank onto Bob's `PC.play`, and trick Bob into thinking that it's actually Bob's `PC.bank`, well that's your standard phishing attack, and that's got to be a bad thing.

So the traditional approach of fixing this at the client end is that you put a lot of effort into trying to understand the machine, and as I mentioned, the client side as a tunnel in to the server side. You think about the covert channels. You then, if you're a military systems designer, have a trusted boot sequence, or a trusted attention sequence. If you pick control-alt-delete, it infallibly takes you to a screen which says, which machine do you want to log on to, `bob.pc.bank`, `bob.pc.work`, or `bob.pc.play`? If you can get the engineering of that right so that it cannot be nobbled by malware, then lucky you – you can maybe sell millions of machines to the government. And of course the people who are working for the government, you can train them and discipline them; you can cause people to hit control-alt-delete as a robotic motion before they move between secret and top secret, or between secrets of a bank, or whatever. That's how these things are done.

The big problem though is, what about the mass market? Not the million people who work for the government and do classified stuff, but the hundreds of millions of people who account for almost all of your sales. Will this sort of thing work with random civilians? Well, of course not. So maybe it's time to try a bit of fresh thinking here, as Bruce remarked. To a first approximation all attacks are by insiders, and also to a first approximation they all start as errors. So what benefit would you get from the mandatory access control in your military or intelligence system? Basically it's mostly stopping well-trained people from entering high data into low by accident. If someone is deliberately wicked then you catch him by other means. Aldrich Ames was caught, for example, when the Director of the CIA noticed a Jaguar in the staff car park, and he called in his counter intelligence chief and said, "Oi, who belongs to that Jaguar?" This is nothing to do with computers.

How can you go about reducing the error rate? This is something that systems engineers, other than just security engineers, are interested in. How do you go about stopping people entering high data into low by accident, or flying the plane into the ground by accident, or doing other dumb things by accident? Well safety systems literature teaches us that this is largely about context and cues. There was a big survey by the motor industry folks – if you go and look at my software engineering notes there's a reference to it – the error rates that you get in car factories are found to depend almost entirely on the number of cues people have towards correct action. Practice, rather than actually have to think.

Things that people are trained to do they can do by reflex, do by context, are very much more dependable.

The next thing that I want to throw into the mix is the fact that in our community we've often found that protocols fail because you identify the wrong way. You can do secure banking by getting the bank to identify the user, get the user to put in a password, problem solved. We now know of course that it's at least as important to get the user to identify the bank, to know whether you are entering your password into `HSBC.com` or `HSBC.mafia.com`.

So going back to our problem of how the user is to understand whether she is talking to `alice.pc.bank`, or `alice.pc.work`, or `alice.pc.play`, it's not enough for the laptop to just display, "You are now talking to `alice.pc.work`", or to provide a secure attention sequence which says, "Please choose which of these `alice.pc.*` you actually want to log on to". We should actually be thinking about the other direction as well. And the key insight is this: that you have virtual machines not just in the laptop but also in the brain. People operate in different contexts. They behave differently when they are assuming different roles. And you can indeed think of people to some extent as having multiple personalities! The sort of person that you are at work, the sort of person you are when doing a solemn banking transaction, or conducting a religious ritual, is different again from the sort of person you are having a pint down the pub with your mates. These are different people defined by context.

So the issue here is not just which VM you are talking to in the cloud, but which VM in the user's brain is the system talking to, what mood is the user in, what does the user believe about context, about the likely consequences of their actions.

Jonathan Anderson: How universally applicable is this VM stuff? I've heard that people who have very high systematising quotients tend very much towards this compartmentalised VM view of the brain, but those with more of an empathising quotient are a little bit more connected, and all in one big mess sort of thing. Sorry, that sounded very derogatory.

Reply: Well I suspect that there are fairly universal aspects of this, and if you believe in the evolutionary psychology agenda, there are large numbers of modules in the brain which perform different functions, and if consciousness is an emergent phenomenon of this then you would expect the type of consciousness that you're enjoying at some particular time to vary as a function of those modules that are active and doing work, and you see this in the literature in various ways. But we can talk about that later.

My point is, if all attacks are insiders you need to know which insider, and there is some behavioural literature on this. George Loewenstein and others, for example, have written on the hot-cold empathy gap: most people when they're in a cold emotional state are not very good at predicting how they will react to certain circumstances when they are angry, or when they are sexually aroused, or whatever, and they described this as being the hot-cold empathy gap.

Now even though we are not that good at predicting how we will react in a brawl situation, we are generically aware of the risks, and we construct all sorts of mechanisms to see to it that we don't get into trouble. You know, people adopt various mechanisms all the time, with the experience to see to it that we don't drink too much in circumstances when we might get into a fight or whatever, and these strategies that we have adopted to cope with risks in meat-space don't necessarily move across to cyber-space, because we haven't had the experience. Facebook's only been around for a few years. And Joe and Soren made as point last year that Facebook users may be more open to scams because they're operating in a noisy, distracting environment where people flip from this task to that task in a state of continuous partial arousal, and this isn't the sort of condition in which you want to be making banking decisions, it's like a pub atmosphere or a party atmosphere – deliberately so, in order to attract and lock in the users.

So what happens if `alice.play` talks to a `machine.bank`? That could be a bad thing. So how would we deal with this in meat-space? Well there's a whole bunch of stuff. A very important thing is that we've got all these non-verbal channels that we use for communication: expression, gesture, tone of voice, and so on. These are very much older than speech; other primates have got the same mechanisms, so they have been around for tens of millions of years. Another thing is that these are interactive, and that may I think be one of the keys to making progress on this. We don't get into a synchronised emotional state with somebody just by looking at a photograph of them looking happy or sad; this is something that comes about as you interact.

Now this is obviously of some survival value because so many human cultures have overlaid all this with all sorts of rituals, like the wine ordering protocol that Matt Blaze was talking about[3]. There are manners formalised with ways of doing interactions that with a bit of luck bring people's emotional state close enough together that even if they start off in very different states of happiness, or anger, or arousal, or whatever, they come close enough that we can do something resembling business. Then there's jargon, jargon like ours, which conveys a sense of group membership. Chants: the people who study the evolution of music have got a big fight on at the moment about whether music is oratory cheesecake, you know, something that we enjoy because evolution fitted us to like sugar, and salt, and milk, or is it something much more primal? The people here at Cambridge take the view that music in the form of chant probably arose before speech did, based upon how monkeys and other primates roar, "eerr, eerr!" to wind themselves up for a fight or a hunting expedition or whatever. It could be that chant might actually have pre-dated speech, and might have evolved into speech.

And then there are dress codes. Now this is interesting, because when you dress people up as soldiers, or as dental students, you're not merely identifying them as your own side and the enemy, so each side knows which way to shoot, you're also inculcating behaviour. So you are interactively inducing a certain state of mind, and you've even got your equivalent follow-the-lead: "Company

---

[3] See LNCS 3957 "Toward a Broader View of Security Protocols", esp. pp 126–7.

Atten – tion!" The silence in the conversation gets everybody looking, paying attention to the sergeant-major; it's control-alt-shutup.

Dental students, again, the fact that you're wearing your scrubs socialises you, right? Down the pub these young ladies and gentlemen may be as rascally as anybody else, but when they're in the operating theatre, then of course all the medical ethics kick in and you have to pay attention to the patient – remember this, remember that, watch out for your hygiene, remember your CPR course, don't give them too much anaesthetic, duty, discipline, care, inculcated by means of dress.

Dress for all sorts of purposes, dress for power, dress for religious ritual, it's all there, a huge history of it; this is something that we as humans do. So what could we do in terms of claiming this interaction for the purposes of authentication? After all, we've been using this sort of thing for authentication in human societies for thousands of years.

Well a couple of years ago Matt pointed out that many of the real-world evolved social protocols, such as those for ordering wines[4], actually have the attributes of security protocols, in that we give the right kind of assurances to both sides in formal terms. Of course, they do something a little bit more in that they, being a ritual, inculcate in you in the fact that you're doing a certain thing, you're having a glass of nice wine in a restaurant, and there are certain cultural expectations of how people behave. Carl Ellison came up with the idea of human-computer interactions as ceremonies: where one of the participants to a protocol as a human, he says call it a ceremony, I think that was also a useful step but Carl didn't take it any further than that. A third idea was Frank's idea from four or five years ago[5], where he was talking about how you would tell what application was running on a mobile phone, and his idea was that you might put up a little icon of a hat depending on what you were doing, a play hat, a banker's hat, or whatever.

So our suggestion is this paper is that perhaps what you need to do is to actually wear a hat in order to operate your laptop. So the laptop's got a video camera in it, the laptop can see what hat you're wearing, so if you want to bank, the only way you can logon to your bank is to take the top hat, put it on, and you sit there in front of the laptop. Then the laptop says, "Aha, you are a banker!" Boom, logon screen to HSBC. We're geeks, we work in places like Google or Microsoft, that's the kind of hat that people wear there, so alright, logon to bloggs@google.com. If you want to be a pirate, you put on your felt tricorn, and your laptop says, "Aha, we're up to no good today!" and it pulls up Tor. And then of course the party hat takes you to Facebook or whatever.

Virgil Gligor: What if you put on the wrong hat for the purpose?

Reply: There are things you can do with hats physically, for example, you can do composability with hats, right, by the physical design of the hat you can see to it that the pirate hat won't go on top of the banker's top hat, so you can't

---

[4] LNCS 3957, p 110.
[5] LNCS 3957, p 51.

be a pirate and a banker at the same time, at least you can't be a pirate on top of a banker, but maybe you've heard of a banker on top of a pirate.

Sandy Clark: I can see one problem here with people in offices who would like to be surfing baseball when they should be working.

Reply: Now, the point here is that up until now, when we discuss such things in the protocols context we said, well hey, "Everything becomes software", that's Wilkes law, so fine, just put up a little icon in the corner saying, this is a pirate hat, so you're now using Tor. But the point of this paper today, what Frank and I are saying, is that we actually want to keep the behavioural channel open.

Now how might you do this in real life? Well if you're working for somewhere like the civil service they'll probably say you must keep your access badge around your neck so that the computer can see it and read the barcode. There are other ways you might do it better, for example you might have an active audio feedback channel, and there's a chap at LSC who has done some interesting work in getting speech that people utter, and putting it through some kind of signal processing, which changes the emotional tone on it, so it can make your voice sound happier or sadder in near real time by processing it, and they then feed that back to you and it actually affects your mood.

So there are mechanisms that other researchers are starting to work on that begin to give you the tools to provide the emotional interaction from a machine to a human. Now this gets you out of the field of system engineering into applied psychology and anthropology, and hence the title of my talk. Now we have got some people at the computer lab who do this. Peter Robinson has got people on the second floor who analyse facial expressions, gestures, and tones of voice, as a means of helping computers and automated devices judge the mood of the users. So your SatNav for example in future will know whether you're happy or confused, or furious, or whatever, and will be able to modulate its responses appropriately.

Some people at LSC have looked at the responses that people have when doing behavioural experiments depending on whether they think they're talking to a person or to a robot. And one of the ways in which psychology experiments fail is that if you just put the instructions up on the screen, the person thinks that they're talking to a computer. Now one of the ways you can deal with this experimentally is that if you put the experimenter behind the computer, you get the experimenter to interact socially with the experimental subject for ten minutes before you run the experiment, and that gives you completely different results. Why? Because if you think you're talking to a computer, it's just a dumb machine, it doesn't engage the dopamine system in your brain, and your emotions remain flat.

So this is something that we should be looking at a fair bit more. The human call centre compared with a voice response system – this is an important business problem. And what about physical aspects of conversation? If we're moving towards a world in which lots of people spend their nights sitting on their sofa with a laptop (a complaint made frequently by wife against self and grandson), is this just an issue of overweight and cardiovascular health, or are there more subtle things going on? What's the difference between sofa banking, which is what people do at the moment, and Wii banking? Suppose in order to bank you've got to leap around with a controller in each hand – would it be better, would it be worse? So far you'll only do this Wii stuff with computer games. I'm not just talking gesture-based authentication, what else is there?

So my point is that it's not just about knowing the user's mood, it's about putting her in the right mood, and assuring that she doesn't get out of that mood without the machine noticing. And again, we've got all sorts of mechanisms that we see in meat-space that are used to do this such as singing the national anthem or reciting a prayer. Authentication should induce solemnity as well as just measuring it! "I hereby declare under the penalties for perjury that the password that I'm about to enter is my true password, my only password, and nothing but my password." This still has to be invented, but you get the flavour of what I'm driving at.

And so there's a sense in which 'the password that you enter everywhere' won't do for quite a lot of purposes, it may have other effects, as Joe [Bonneau] has mentioned, from time to time, but will it do for banking? You would hope that it wouldn't. But then if the password we use is protected by physical channel mechanisms and by emotional channel mechanisms, then how on earth do you authenticate the user? We know there is a shortage of personal information for use in authentication, and surely there's also a shortage of personal gesture, of allowable ritual, and how will these problems work out once you start doing authentication in more physical and emotional ways? We may see the whole history of password research replaying itself once you start doing things in a somewhat more human and ceremonial way.

So the argument in this paper is that authentication protocols to VMs are fine, but we have to acknowledge that some of them are in the brain, not just in software. And mutual authentication means more than just usability testing. And this leads us on to deeper questions. How do systems get embedded in culture? You know, "The street finds its own uses for things", and sometimes it uses them in ways that we as security engineers don't anticipate.

If you haven't read it I suggest you have a look at dana boyd's thesis, which is linked from my Security and Psychology resource page. She did a study of American teens and she found out, for example, that teenagers in California tend to share their passwords as a sign of intimacy at a certain stage in the dating process. Somewhere between first kiss and getting into bed, you give her your Facebook password so you can say, "Darling, you and I are now one, you can masquerade as me." And then of course, when you decide to dump her, you change the password. Now if this is the ritual that has grown up around the technology, then of course the technology needs a redesign because the assumptions that we used to have about passwords, namely that they're personal, no longer hold.

So a bit of this is about rediscovering ritual, and there's a bit of it which is about giving people the tools with which they could invent it. Perhaps geeks just aren't good enough at ritual; perhaps you need prophets or priests to invent ritual, whatever; so you just make the tools available, or the street available, and people find ways to use it. And then of course you've got the problem that once a ritual has arisen how do you redevelop the systems to cope with it? Perhaps you can no longer achieve your original objectives. So that's one argument, that when it comes to authenticating people, things are a lot more complex than we might think.

We have to think about emotional channels, we have to think about ritual, or as the title of the talk puts it, it's about the anthropology as well, it's not just the systems engineering.

Jeff Yan: If there are too many hats, people are not handling that, just like with passwords, we cannot handle too many passwords, right.

Reply: Exactly, this is what I'm saying, we probably can't handle too many rituals.

Jeff Yan: Do you have any thoughts to address this problem?

Reply: No.

Jeff Yan: I think actually the idea of using this detectable computing to adjust the issues you are introducing actually could have some issues of user acceptance, so sort of like big brother type systems.

Reply: Well sure, it depends how it's built and it's sold. Some organisations just go about selling their products completely wrong and it puts everybody off, so a new technology can be completely sterilised by inappropriate marketing. Think of genetically modified crops; if they had sold that first as a means of producing medicines rather than a means of selling more weedkiller, then perhaps they would now be widely used in the UK, but they aren't.

Vashek Matyas: There was one suggestion that we made in the late 90s for authentication that would probably help here, it was not taken up at that time. It was that we would use speech recognition together with speaker verification, and thus give protection against replay attacks. When I engage with my banking system and the banking system asks me to say, for example, my blue coffee today was very good, putting challenges of this kind and asking for my response, and checking both that it was this challenge I responded to and that it was indeed me.

Reply: The thing to do here would not be to think entirely about the type 1 and type 2 errors on the voice prints, but about what you're actually doing with this speech ritual. Are you going to be effective at seeing to it that it can't be spoofed to the user, that it makes the user take care, that it puts them in an appropriate frame of mind?

Saša Radomirović: There are a few simple things that one can do already, I mean, we know that the colour red makes us more alert to danger, so if say the entire screen turns red when you are logging in to banking, you are already putting the human into some sort of condition, you additionally terminate all MySpace actions, while the user is doing that you are maybe at least conditioning him to the situation, that this is now a different context, this is something that is different from playing games.

Reply: Yes, there are some things like that that could be done.

Malte Schwarzkopf: One existing means that is used, which is along the lines of what you were talking about especially in terms of this "saying your prayers" kind of thing, is that sometimes a web page will require you to actually spell out a statement, yes, I agree to the licence agreement: you actually have to type it rather than just tick a box. I was wondering if you're aware of any existing work that has evaluated whether this does any better than other systems.

Reply: I think that such things are a terrible annoyance and not fit for purpose, and if you simply require people to stand on one leg and recite the Lord's Prayer instead of typing "yes I agree", then you'll find that even fewer people will use your horrible product, and it would be an awful lot simpler just to supply the product with a standard click licence.

Malte Schwarzkopf: Yes, the question was not about usability but whether there are any measurable security effects of that.

Reply: Well I tend to see such things as being just an annoyance.

Joseph Bonneau: It seems like a problem here is that having everything on your computer allows you to switch context so quickly and that's one of the benefits of it, and particularly if people get into problems with gmail because they mix personal and work, and everybody dumps everything into one gmail account. And similarly with Facebook because now people have so many different social contexts on the one thing, they have their parents, and work colleagues, and all of their mates that they hang out with at the pub, on one place. So it seems like you're trying to find a way to slow down the rate at which people can switch between contexts, and making them do some physical thing, which is how is too in meat-space: you have to at least walk across the street to get from the pub to the bank, at which point you realise you're going somewhere else. So like you said, people may not stand for it if you insist on some mandatory 30 second delay between these two different tabs on your browser. I guess the question is, will people accept this notion that, 'We won't let you go as fast as you theoretically could between different tasks because we think that's unsafe.'

Reply: Well in that case perhaps you have to have an understanding of the law and policy level, that if you are so keen to get people's banking business that you let people do banking when they're in a condition of uncertain mind – you know, 150 milliseconds away from Facebook – then there's going to be a certain error rate, and if your business model causes you to get your customers to operate the fast error rate, then some part of the costs of that are for your account. At the other end of the scale, we've already got the FBI giving advice to American businesses that if you're doing business banking, and therefore a potential target of this new wave of social malware, then they say (and that's policy here at Cambridge as well) you should have one or more PCs that are used only for banking – that do not have a general browser or mail clients on them, that are kept in a locked room to which only five people have access. It may simply become a technical necessity for transactions of large value, like authenticating the University's payroll of eight thousand people, to be conducted essentially in a SCIF[6]. And there's an interesting question, is there anything between a SCIF and Facebook that works?

Joseph Bonneau: I like the suggestion that you have a mandatory timeout. It's like airline pilots have 24 hours from bottle to throttle, we want ten minutes from Facebook to bank.

Reply: Maybe that's of some value, yes.

Paulo Verissimo: You were talking about the extreme of what I might call the complete promiscuity of social relations. I have two kids, 23, 20, and I have these weird conversations with them about that, I mean, I get there and they have ten screens running, and so sometimes there's a screw-up, right, because they think they are talking to the girlfriend, and they're talking to mum, or something like that. So what Ross is proposing is very valid, and we have been thinking about stuff in this direction, as you will see tomorrow[7], and we have to think in ways of breaking this promiscuity, in computer science lingo of course. It's probably difficult, but I think that's definitely the way. You're quite right, it's in the minds of new people that this is possible, we can't do everything at the same place.

Jonathan Anderson: I think it's not so much about imposing these kinds of things, but if you provide these effective tools I think people might see value in it. Google Labs I think had a drunk filter on gmail for a while where you could enable this thing that said, ah you seem a little out of it, are you sure you really want to send this email? And apparently people found value in that. So if that was pushed down into essentially your hypervisor, and it could sense which brain VM you are in at that level, instead of at the gmail level, then maybe it will say, "Ah are you sure you want to be in gmail at all because you don't seem like you're in a state for that? Why don't we just send you to your YouTube VM (or something where you're not allowed to upload) instead, because you seem to be only really fit for that?"

Bruce Christianson: Well one of the reasons people multi-task is because of server lag, so you think, while I'm waiting for the bank to get back to me on that transaction I'll just go and do whatever it is. Apart from getting banks to have faster servers, one thing might be to think about what things require the same emotional state, so that you only switch to things that require you to be in the same state of mind.

Paul Wernick: Or perhaps a hierarchy so that you can go from more to less serious easily.

Bruce Christianson: But then you've got that transaction that's half-way through, and now it's asking you some question. By the time you've been through the ten minutes to go back up to serious hat work, it will have aborted. Your trolley is empty.

Jonathan Anderson: But while you're waiting for this transaction why don't you read this bit in the New York Times about financial policies.

Bruce Christianson: Yes, that is the idea.

---

[6] Sensitive Compartmented Information Facility.

[7] Verissimo, these proceedings.

Reply: But people may do particular tasks online in order to modify their emotional state, and it's not just listening to a music station. People are dead tired and just want to relax, you might just sit there and do some routine task just to unwind, so it's complex and dynamic. Perhaps what we need to do is to provide the tools, provide the hooks, and then let the street provide the ritual. I just see this as an evolutionary process; you must supply the raw material, and then Mr Darwin in due course supplies the organs.

Paul Wernick: But does that require a relinquishing of control by the security engineers, that they must be comfortable with?

Jonathan Anderson: That's why we need to design sensible security APIs in the sort of way that we can say, "The following things we think are OK, and now you can compose them however you like."

Paul Wernick: It's much easier to do something that uses them in a fixed way.

Jonathan Anderson: In the short term.

Security Design in Human Computation Games

Su-Yang Yu and Jeff Yan

School of Computing Science
Newcastle University
United Kingdom, NE1 7RU
{s.y.yu,jeff.yan}@ncl.ac.uk

Abstract. We consider a binary labelling problem: for some machine learning applications, two types of distinct objects are required to be labeled respectively, before a classifier can be trained. We show that the famous ESP game and variants would not work well on this binary labelling problem. We discuss how to design a new human computation game to solve this problem. It turns out that interesting but subtle security issues emerge in the new game. We introduce novel gaming mechanisms, such as 'guess disagreement', which improve the game's security, usability and productivity simultaneously.

Keywords: Binary labeling, collusion, cheating, CAPTCHA, 'Cat or Dog' game.

1 Introduction

The emerging research area of human computation studies how to solicit voluntary human efforts to solve difficult problems that known computer algorithms cannot yet tackle efficiently. Typical human computation systems include computer games that people play just for fun, but their game play contributes to collectively solving large-scale computational problems.

It has been known for long that an essential security issue in online game design is tackling cheats [7]. Human computation games are typically web based, and they are not an exception.

In this paper, we first consider a binary labelling problem that the famous ESP game [4] would not work well: for some applications, two types of objects are required to be labeled respectively; each type will have a distinct label, but the total number of possible labels is two. Our aim is to design a new human computation game to address this problem. It turns out that that some interesting but subtle security issues have to be addressed in the new game.

We first give some details of the binary labeling problem, and discuss why the state of the art cannot offer a satisfactory solution. Then, we discuss the design of our new game, including main game mechanisms, design rationale behind, and some key implementation details – security, usability, and game productivity are key issues in our design. Next, we report a pilot study that was designed to evaluate the fun level and the utility of the game.

B. Christianson and J. Malcolm (Eds.): Security Protocols 2010, LNCS 7061, pp. 142–153, 2014.
© Springer-Verlag Berlin Heidelberg 2014

2   The Binary Labeling Problem

CAPTCHA (Completely Automated Public Turing test to tell Computers and Humans Apart) [5] is now almost a standard security technology, and has been widely deployed by commercial websites as a defence against undesirable or malicious Internet bots. It is widely accepted that a robustness evaluation is necessary before the deployment of any CAPTCHA, since if a deployed CAPTCHA is not strong enough, bots can easily bypass its defence, rendering it useless.

Asirra [1] is an image-recognition based CAPTCHA proposed by Microsoft. Instead of asking a user to recognize a distorted text, this CAPTCHA requires people to tell whether an image is a cat or dog. In 2008, Golle [2] proposed a machine learning method for evaluating the strength of Asirra. In his work, a large set of sample images was manually labeled as cat or dog according to the content of the images. Then image features such as color, texture and shape were extracted from each sample image to build and train a binary classifier, which was then used to recognize whether a new image is cat or dog. This process turns out to be an effective method for evaluating how robust an image based CAPTCHA such as Asirra is in resistance to adversarial attacks. Labeling a large sample set (13,000 images in the case of [2]) is a key step in this method. However, it cannot be automated since the state of the art of computer vision does not work well in recognizing images of cats and dogs – otherwise the CAPTCHA would have no reason to exist at all. It is tedious and expensive to label these images by hand.

On the other hand, a key component of Asirra is a huge database of labeled images of cats and dogs. Asirra relies on this database to generate CAPTCHA challenges, and determine whether an answer given by a user is correct or not. For security reasons, this database is kept confidential. That is why Golle [2] had to manually label a large number of images for his independent security evaluation.

The Asirra database has over three millions of labeled images, and it grows by nearly 10,000 images everyday [1]. All the images are provided by Petfinder.com, the largest web site in the world devoted to finding homes for homeless animals, and their volunteer workers have manually created the image labels. Given the amount of images involved, this labeling process is even more tedious and more expensive than what is required for evaluating image CAPTCHA's robustness. That is, to keep Asirra running, a large amount of human labor has been, and will be, involved with maintaining its database.

The specific problem that we consider is therefore to label images of cats and dogs both for enabling the Asirra service and for carrying out its robustness evaluation. To generalize it, the problem we want to solve is binary labeling, where two types of objects are required to be labeled respectively; each type will have a distinct label, but the total number of possible labels is two. Other practical scenarios also require binary labeling. For example, in order to evaluate their recent quantum computer, Google researchers had to manually label car images and those that do not contain any cars [9].

3   Why Would the State of the Art Not Work?

The famous ESP game [4] was designed to create labels for images on the Internet and thus improving the quality of image search. It is a two-player collaborative game. An image randomly picked from the Internet is displayed to both players who cannot communicate with each other. Each is asked to guess what the partner is typing. When both players type the same word, it turns out that that word can be an accurate label for describing the image. This simple game has achieved a huge success – it not only has collected a large number of useful labels for images on the Internet (Google licensed this game to create their own image labeler), but also kicked off the new research field of human computation.

However, the ESP game would not work well to address the binary labelling problem that we discuss in the current paper, for the following reasons.

First, it would be easy to cheat in the game. To agree on an image in the ESP game, two players are not required to type the same word at the same time, but each must type the same word at some point while the image is displayed on the screen [4]. That is, if we denote by A a set of guesses that player a has entered, and by B a set of guesses that her partner has entered, once $A \cap B \neq \emptyset$, an agreement is reached by two players, and the intersection of A and B is accepted as a valid label for the image. Therefore, cheaters can exploit this agreement algorithm to cheat with binary labeling as follows: a player types in both possible labels for an image, and the other types in either. In the worst case, the cheaters can easily win the game without producing a single valid label – for example, the second player always gives a tag different from the content of an image. This cheat would not work with content-rich images, since possible labels for such images are typically neither fixed nor predictable.

Second, it would be boring to play the ESP game if there are only two possible tags for describing each image. A major fun element of the ESP game stems from that you have to guess how other people think. Typically, agreeing on an appropriate name for an image in the game creates an enjoyable feeling of 'extra-sensory perception' about each other within a partnership: 'hey, I read your mind!' This fun element is highly dependent on the choice of images used. If an image implies only a small number of possible labels, it will be trivial for two players to reach an agreement. Thus, the enjoyment from the ESP effect of 'reading each other's mind' will quickly diminish. To make a game fun to play, it is essential to make sure that its difficulty level is right. However, playing with images with only two possible labels would simply make the ESP game too easy, and thus not much fun to play. A plausible solution is to mix these images of cats or dogs with content-rich images in the game so that people do not have to do trivial labelling too often. However, this will slow down productivity for binary labeling. Moreover, the cheating issue discussed above is still applicable.

Third, some of the mechanisms in the ESP game would not work for binary labelling. For example, the ESP game proposed to detect cheaters involving with a global agreement strategy (e.g. both players type 'a' for every image) by monitoring the average time two players agree on images: a sharp drop in this average time indicates the existence of a cheating agreement [4]. For binary labeling, this method would fail to differentiate between cheaters using a global strategy and those honest but really good players who can both respond and type fast – the latter do not have to ponder for long, since there are only two fixed options for each image.

Taboo words – another key feature in ESP – cannot be applied in a binary labelling setting, either. In ESP, taboo words serves two purposes: i) to harvest additional labels from the images by blacklisting common labels from the images' past incarnations thus forcing players to enter new labels, and ii) to prevent the use of a global agreement strategy by making a label agreed by a pair of players a taboo word across an entire session of their game play – the idea is that two players cannot agree on different images with the same word in the same session. Unfortunately, in a binary labelling setting, the introduction of taboo words would make the game unplayable. Due to the first purpose that taboo words serve, since there are only two possible labels, the most common input will be the correct label, and thus making it the first taboo word. This will consequently force the players to provide only the wrong label, until the wrong label is also tabooed, by which all the valid inputs are effectively blacklisted. On the other hand, due to the second purpose of taboo words, each valid label will be allowed only once in a single game session. That is, only two images – for one image of cat and the other of dog – will be properly labeled.

Magic Bullet [8] is a game that we designed to label images that are not content-rich, such as those containing only a single character or a short text string. In a typical setting, MB is a four-player game in which two teams compete against each other, with two players in each team. All of the players will share the view of the same gaming area, a screen with two targets – one is for their team and the other for their opponents' team. During each round, a randomly chosen image is shown to all four players. The team who first agrees on the image wins the current round of the game, and the image will turn into a bullet and shoot to their target. The movement of the bullet can drastically change as if by magic. For example, the bullet starts to move towards the target of the team that hit a key first. But if the other team reaches an agreement first, the bullet will change its direction to hit the winning team's target. As such, the game was named 'Magic Bullet'. A lab study suggested that this game maintains a high level of fun for players, and that people's game play creates accurate labels for images that contain only individual characters [8]. However, this game is not suitable for binary labeling because its matching algorithm is the same as the one used in the ESP game and thus vulnerable to the simple cheating discussed earlier.

4   A 'Cat Or Dog' Game

'Cat or Dog' is an online game that turns a task of labelling images of cats and dogs into a fun experience. People play the game just for fun, but their game play labels each image used in the game with a very high accuracy. This game also provides a generic solution to the binary labeling problem.

4.1 General Description of the Game

The theme of our 'Cat or Dog' game is on a treasure island, where pet animals walk past an area carrying gold coins, and players are teamed up to compete against others in order to attain the gold by winning the animal's affections.

In a typical setting, four players are randomly selected and allocated into two teams, with two people in each team. There are two treasure chests on the screen one for each team, and are located on the left/right side of the game area (See Figure 1). In each game session, the players must try to out-score their opponents by getting golden coins from pet animals within the allocated time limit of 2 minutes.

Fig. 1. The 'Cat or Dog' game. Players try to obtain golden coins by winning the pet animals' affections through agreeing on their identifications. The dog is running back to her previous route after dropping some coins in the winning team's treasure chest.

Each game session consists of an arbitrary number of rounds. At the beginning of a round, a pet – a cat or a dog – will run between the treasure chests of two teams. The pet will appear on either the top or bottom end of the game screen and move towards the opposite end.

When the pet appears the players must identify the kind of animal she most looks like, and try to get her attention by pressing the corresponding key ('c' for 'cat' and 'd' for 'dog'). Each player will only get a single chance to call the pet during each round. That is, once a player has entered a key, their keyboard will be 'locked' until the next round. The pet will drop golden coins to the team that first agrees on their identification of her. However, the pet will become annoyed with the team who first disagrees on her identification, and will give the coins to their opponents instead. The pet will move towards the winning team, drop some golden coins in their treasure chest, and then run back to its previous route. When she is out of the game screen, it indicates the end of a round.

A round is over either when the allocated time for that round has past, or when a team has reached an agreement or a disagreement before their opponents do so.

The time of how long each round will be, i.e. the speed at which a pet moves, differs and is decided by the game server. It is significantly longer towards the beginning of a game session, and gradually speeds up towards the end of the session. The faster a pet moves, the higher number of points the winning team will get.

The round time is chosen to be between 2 and 5 seconds for the following reasons. First, we wanted the round to be fast enough since one major element of fun we expect is the speed of competition. Second, the animation must also be slow enough so that the images are still easily recognisable. This is due to the concerns for players getting eye strain from trying to recognise fast moving images for a relatively long period of time.

There are also two reasons for making the rounds gradually speed up in a session. First, this allows players time to slowly ease into the game. Second, this encourages the loosing team not to give up, as a higher speed also issues higher rewards so there is plenty of opportunity for them to catch up.

4.2 Main Design Rationale

The 'Cat or Dog' game is a variant of our own Magic Bullet game [8], with some innovative extensions that will be discussed below.

An initial design of the 'Cat or Dog' game we conceived was a direct variant of the MB game as follows. The character image is replaced by an image of a cat or a dog. Players are expected to type 'c' for cat and 'd' for dog, and the team that first reaches an agreement wins. But a new matching mechanism, which we call *turn-based matching*, will be used to determine whether two players have agreed on an image, and it works as follows. After a player has given a guess on the image, they will no longer be able to send out any additional guesses until their partner has also sent out something for that turn. Then instead of comparing all the keys both players have sent, only the keys during the same turn are compared against each other. If it is a match then they score the points;

if it is not a match then their keyboard is unlocked again to mark the start of the next turn.

However, this initial design would introduce some subtle usability and security issues. For example, in this design, an indicator such as a red/green light will be needed so that players know whether their keyboards are currently locked or unlocked respectively. For example, the light starts off as green at the beginning of a round. As soon as the player has entered a guess it turns red. The light will be reset to green again either when their partner has also given a guess or at the beginning of the next round. Without such an indicator, there would be a major usability issue: since there could be multiple turns in a round, a player would easily become confused about when to enter their guess, or whether their guess has been taken into count by the game.

However, cheaters could exploit this initial design of the game. Specifically, this design would allow the cheaters to collude through an in-game covert channel, which uses entities not normally viewed as a communication channel to transfer information. Some more apparent cheating threats in this game, together with their defence, will be discussed later in this paper. Some older cheating cases in online games involving covert channels were discussed in [7].

Typically, cheaters can be divided into two categories each with a unique motive as follows.

- Type 1: those who just want to pollute our data.
- Type 2: those who just want to score higher points than others.

Both types of cheaters will want to establish a protocol with their partner in the game to achieve their desired aims. Type 1 cheater will want to provide the label that is opposite to that of the image, and Type 2 cheaters will want to agree with their partner on a specific key so that they could react faster than their opponents.

In the course of game play, the indicator could leak critical information to the cheaters, enabling them to form a collusion protocol that would not have been probable in Magic Bullet. Since there are only two options ('c' or 'd') in 'Cat or Dog' as opposed to 36 (a-z & 0-9) in MB, after a player has given a guess, she can easily deduce what her partner has entered by looking at the indicator and the outcome of that turn.

A player can deduce what their partner has entered in a turn, because in this scenario there can only be 1 of 3 possible outcomes: i) their team has won that turn, ii) they have lost that turn, or iii) the turn is still ongoing and the indicator resets back to green. If they have lost that turn, then the player cannot deduce useful information, as her partner might have entered the same guess as she did, a guess different from the one she did, or simply have not entered anything yet. Otherwise, the key that the partner has entered can be derived as shown in Table 1.

The critical observation is that a cheater can easily convey via the indicator their intention of either always creating a wrong label (Type 1 cheating) or only agreeing on one kind of animal but not the other (Type 2 cheating), and such intention can be equally easily detected by a willing collaborator to establish a

Table 1. How cheaters can determine their partner's input using the indicators

Player Guess	Partner Guess	
	Turn won	Indicator resets
C	C	D
D	D	D

colluding protocol in the game. They do not have to know each other, and do not have to have agreed upon a cheating protocol before the game. Once the in-game protocol is established, the cheaters no longer need to recognise the content of any image. Therefore they can react faster than their honest opponents, and thus achieve their desired aims.

The current design of the 'Cat or Dog' game, as implemented (and described in the previous section), addresses the above issue by making the following three design choices:

i) The number of turns allowed for each round is limited to only one;
ii) The indicator is removed;
iii) 'Guess disagreement' is introduced as a game mechanism. That is, the team that first reaches a disagreement loses the current round.

By limiting the number of turns per round to one, we not only encourage players to be accurate, but also remove the necessity of an indicator. Limiting the number of turns to one per round and removing the indicator together not only makes it harder for a cheater to convey or deduce the critical information about the intentions, but also make both the game and its interface simpler and easier to follow – it is our goal to make the game and its interface as simple as possible, which we believe can be critical to make a human computation game successful. The turn limitation also slows down the pace at which two cheaters could establish a collusion protocol.

Unlike in ESP and MB, where only guess agreement is used as a game mechanism, 'guess disagreement' is introduced in our new game to serve the following purposes. First, this makes it even harder for a cheater to deduce what is entered by her partner, since there are now more possible ways than before for a team to win a round. Second, the penalty introduced by the 'first disagreement' rule also encourages players to be accurate. Common game mechanisms utilized in human computation games are summarized in [6], but no prior art has utilized 'guess disagreement'.

Overall, these three design choices will not only lower the chances of data pollution by Type 1 cheaters because it becomes much harder for them to establish a protocol with their partner, but also put off Type 2 cheaters, since they are more likely to be penalised more than they would gain whilst trying to establish a protocol. In other words, the current design of the game limits in-game (covert) communication to mitigate cheating, and encourages players to be accurate to improve the quality of labels produced by the game.

4.3 Implementation and Other Details

'Cat or Dog' is designed as a web-based game. It follows the client-server architecture, and is implemented with the Google Web Toolkit (GWT). GWT allows applications to be written in Java, and it will compile the code into optimized JavaScript for deployment. Since all major browsers support JavaScript by default, end-users do not have to install anything on their computers before they can play the game. Our game can run with all the major browsers on any operating system.

4.4 Further Cheating Mitigation

Our 'Cat or Dog' game also supports some further cheating mitigation methods, including the following.

- Player queuing and random pairing: players who log on at the same or similar time will not necessarily be paired together.
- IP address checks: to make sure that players are not paired with themselves or with people who have a similar address.
- Trap. Some images are manually labeled and will be used as trap at a random interval. If players keep getting the trap images wrong then they will get flagged as cheaters and blacklisted, all label data from them will be discarded.

Trap could be the ultimate cheating prevention method, but decreases the throughput of data produced by the game. So it makes sense to make a cheater's life harder by other means, such as those discussed earlier. In addition, it is likely that not all images used in a game session will be labelled. The unlabelled images can also include traps. This problem can be addressed by inserting more traps; however doing so could drastically lower the throughput rate of the game. Instead, it is better if any unlabelled images themselves were to be reused after a random number of rounds.

4.5 Bots

When there are not enough human players, our system will automatically enable bots to play with waiting people. Like in the MB game, we support two types of bots. One type acts as a single player by simply replaying data from old games, and the other (which we call a Tailored Response Bot or TRB for short) plays as a single team by performing actions at response times tailored to an opponent team's performance.

A TRB never has to decide which key to press. Whether or not the team represented by a TRB reaches an agreement on an image is entirely the result of flipping a coin. Typically, a TRB monitors response times of its opponent team in previous rounds of the current game session, and generates some response times for its own team around those of the opponent team (or uses predefined values at the beginning of a session). At these intervals, TRB will flip a biased coin, with the result being either an agreement being reached or not. The bias of the coin depends on the scores of the current game session; it will be more in favor of the TRB if the opponent team is winning and less otherwise. The purpose is to keep the TRB's score around that of its opponent team, this way the stronger player(s) in the opponent team can be pushed to test their abilities and the weaker player(s) would not feel too overwhelmed.

With the support of these bots, even a single human player can play our game. That is, the human player partners with a replay bot, competing against a TRB bot. This game type can be used to either verify the correctness of the labels, or detect cheaters. Further discussions of both types of bots are in [8].

5   Evaluations

Our evaluation includes two parts. First, we show that the game is indeed enjoyable. Second, we estimate the accuracy and throughput of the data produced by the game.

Since our game has not been formally released to the public, we carried out an evaluation with a pilot study. We have advertised for volunteers to people (including visiting students) in our computer science department and a local software company. All the feedbacks were collected in an anonymous way, but an informed consent was obtained from the participants.

The images used in our game were collected from the Asirra website [3]. We wrote a Java program to automatically request images used in this CAPTCHA, and to download them into a designated folder. Traps were not used in the pilot study.

5.1   The Level of Fun

We used a questionnaire to survey the level of fun that the players experienced when playing the game. Table 2 shows the average rating (on a five point scale) to questions related to the enjoyability of the game.

A limitation of this survey is that it had a limited scale. We will be soon making our game available online, and it is our future work to gauge the fun level of our game using a much larger number of participants. We are particularly interested to see how many people will come back to play the game again, and how often they will play.

5.2   Data Quality and Throughput

Label Accuracy. In our study, 68 game sessions (including incomplete ones) were played, in which in total of 1906 sample images were used, with 1613 labeled. A manual inspection shows that 1585 images were correctly labeled, giving an accuracy rate of 98.26%.

Throughput. On average, a single game session produced 13 (std dev=1.77) correct labels per minute, giving 780 labels per human hour. The average number

Table 2. How enjoyable is 'Cat or Dog'? Average rating on the scale of 1 to 5, provided by 23 players who filled in the survey after playing the game. Higher scores are better.
a 1=No fun at all, 2=not much fun, 3=average, 4=some good fun, and 5=extremely fun
b 1=strongly disagree, 2= somewhat disagree, 3= neither agree or disagree, 4= somewhat agree, and 5= strongly agree
c 1= highly unlikely, 2= unlikely, 3=maybe, 4= very likely, and 5=definitely
* Bots were disabled in order to measure this fun element.
** This relatively large value was largely caused by two participants who ticked Option 1 as their answers.

Question	Rating		
	mean	std dev	% at 4 or above
Did you find the game fun to play? a	3.74	0.75	68.19
Did you like playing with your partner? b*	3.83	0.94	59.10
Are you likely to play this game again? c	3.22	1.17**	36.36

of labels collected per minute in the ESP game by two players was 3.89, giving 233.4 labels per hour. It is reasonable that it takes more time on average to harvest a label in the ESP game than in the Cat or Dog game.

It is worthwhile to note that when a TRB bot is enabled in our game, the same labeling rate of 780 labels per hour will be achieved while only two human players are required. That is, two humans play in the same team, competing against a TRB. This effectively doubles the throughput per player.

On the other hand, the game supports a large number (denoted by n) of parallel sessions. The throughput of the game can be quickly scaled by a factor of n, which is constrained only by the network bandwidth and the game server's CPU and memory.

6   Conclusion

We have showed that our 'Cat or Dog' game is not only fun to play, but also produces highly accurate labels for images of cats and dogs. By labeling such images, the game can serve two security purposes. One is to enable the service of Microsoft's Asirra CAPTCHA, and the other to streamline the evaluation of Assira's robustness. In the mean while, the charity organization Petfinder.com can also deploy our game to make it both easy and fun for volunteers to create their pet catalogue.

Our game can be extended to tackle any other binary labelling problems, but a new story line might be needed for the extended game – what a story line is most suitable depends on the types of objects to be classified. To the best of our knowledge, this work is the first to discuss the weakness of the famous ESP game in terms of binary labeling, and offers the first effective alternative solution. As a whole, our game is a novel interactive system, with multiple innovations. In particular, we introduce 'guess disagreement', a novel mechanism for human computation games. This mechanism not only makes it harder for cheaters to collude in our game, but also improves the accuracy of labels produced by the game. It is interesting future work to explore this mechanism's applicability to the design of future human computation games.

In designing our game, we have also learned an interesting lesson: By making an appropriate design choice (i.e. allowing only one turn per round in the game), we not only simplified the game, its interface and the way a player interacts with the game, but also mitigated a serious security threat. This illustrates that simplifying the design of a system can improve its usability and security simultaneously.

Acknowledgements. We thank all participants of our study, and thank Brian Randell, Anirban Bhattacharyya, Ahmad El Ahmad and Haryani Zakari for their help and support.

References

1. Elson, J., Douceur, J.R., Howell, J., Saul, J.: Asirra: a CAPTCHA that exploits interest-aligned manual image categorization. In: ACM CCS 2007, pp. 366–374 (2007)
2. Golle, P.: Machine learning attacks against the Asirra CAPTCHA. In: CCS 2008, pp. 535–542. ACM Press (2008)
3. MSR Asirra: A Human Interactive Proof,
   http://research.microsoft.com/asirra/ (as accessed on April 18, 2009)
4. von Ahn, L., Dabbish, L.: Labeling Images with a Computer Game. In: CHI, pp. 319–326. ACM Press (2004)
5. von Ahn, L., Blum, M., Langford, J.: Telling Humans and Computer Apart Automatically. CACM 47(2) (2004)
6. von Ahn, L., Dabbish, L.: Designing games with a purpose. CACM 51(8), 58–67 (2008)
7. Yan, J.: Security Design in Online Games. In: Proc. of the 19th Annual Computer Security Applications Conference (ACSAC), pp. 286–295. IEEE Computer Society (2003)
8. Yan, J., Yu, S.-Y.: Streamlining Attacks on CAPTCHAs with a Computer Game. In: Proc. of the Twenty-first International Joint Conference on Artificial Intelligence (IJCAI 2009), Pasadena, California, USA, July 11-17, pp. 2095–2100 (2009)
9. Neven, H., Denchev, V.S., Drew-Brook, M., Zhang, J., Macready, W.G., Rose, G.: Binary Classification using Hardware Implementation of Quantum Annealing. In: Neural Information Processing Systems Conference (NIPS 2009) (2009)

Security Design in Human Computation Games
(Transcript of Discussion)

Jeff Yan

School of Computing Science, University of Newcastle, Newcastle upon Tyne, UK

This is a joint work with my student Su-Yang, he is actually in the audience just over there, and his research is sponsored by Microsoft Research here in Cambridge.

So what is human computation about? Basically it is about getting voluntary human efforts to solve some difficult computational problems where no known algorithms exist to solve those kind of problems efficiently. And human computation systems are typically designed as computer games, because games offer independence, this can actually use, these can be used as incentives to attract volunteers. And in turn, the volunteers' game play collectively solves a computationally hard problem. That is the basic idea.

The work in this talk was inspired by the CAPTCHA called Asirra which was designed by a team at Microsoft Research. The idea is that because state of the art computation algorithms cannot do well in recognising cats and dogs, so this interface was presented to any user who wanted to access to an online service. In order to be authenticated as a human being, this user has to pick cat or dog images correctly.

So what exactly is the problem we want to address? Asirra security relies on the fact that the puzzle of recognising that dogs and cats is not solvable by computer algorithms. This means the following. In order to enable this Asirra service we have to give it a huge database of images, of course those images are for dogs and cats. At the same time we also need to actually store labels for cats, so that the system knows whether the answer input by a user is correct or not. I'll give you some figures: when the Microsoft researchers first put this Asirra online, there were three million images, all labelled, and the image database actually grows at the rate of about ten thousand images every day. And all these many images actually are manually labelled by a charity of volunteers, basically the images are from a charity which is called Petfinders, they actually look after pets people do not want, and they want to send the pets to other people.

On the other hand, if you want to evaluate the robustness of a CAPTCHA like Asirra, you also need a lot of manually labelled examples, for example, Philip Golle actually got his friends to manually label more than 13,000 images, so that he could actually chart whether this Asirra is secure enough. So the problem we are addressing is actually the labelling of these kinds of images, and specifically we are interested in binary labelling. That is to say the labels are just cat or dog, there is a binary choice. But of course if you get this process done manually it is pretty tedious.

Another case of this binary label was witnessed by Google's research. They recently demonstrated their quantum computing design, so in this demo they

B. Christianson and J. Malcolm (Eds.): Security Protocols 2010, LNCS 7061, pp. 154–160, 2014.

showed a binary classification algorithm implemented by their quantum computer. And in order to do so, they have to give a lot of examples, a lot of images examples of labels. But in this Google binary labelling case, they are interested in images of cars and images of non-cars. And they also got this labelling done manually again. So what we really want is a simple manual game, and people can play this game for fun, but at the same time the game play can label cats and dogs for us, and for the charity Petfinder.com. The people who run Petfinder.com still use a lot of the volunteers to manually label their images of cats and dogs, and they are interested in the game, so those charity workers can have some fun while offering their free time to the charity.

Most of you might be aware of the famous game, which is called the ESP game. This is a popular human computation game, and it works as follows. It is basically a two-player game. In this game an actual image will be displayed to two players, and then each of the players is asked to guess what his or her partner thinks about this image, and then they enter their guess into their system. And it turns out that if two players choose the same words to describe this image, and that word can be a nice label or a tag to describe the content of this image, because the computer does not do well in recognising images as of now. So of course the first question to ask is whether this ESP game is a solution for us to address this binary labelling problem.

Our arguments are the following. We think actually this ESP game is not good for this binary task for the following two reasons. The first reason is it would be boring to play this ESP game if we expect the labels are binary, for example, as a cat or dog, people will not play this game, it's too simple. And as far as we see the main fun bit in this ESP game is that they would actually be surprised, if indeed a partner read their mind, so we actually reach a consensus about a particular word. But this ESP effect only works well on these content-rich images. If, for example, there are only two choices, people would find it very boring to play, and if there are too many choices to describe a content-rich image, that will not work either. So in order to make this ESP fun, basically you have to carefully choose what kind of images are going to be used in the system, so that enough of those choices are provided, and not more and not less. So this is the fun element is not good enough to do binary labelling.

At the same time the ESP game would allow some cheating in the game, because of how the ESP game decides whether two players match, actually they use the following algorithm, for example, a very simple case, this image and this image are displayed to two players. So player 1 enter his first guess, for example, K, and then enters his second guess Y, but actually at the same time player 2 guesses V. Now of course there's no matching between the inputs from the two players, and then player 2 enters guess Y. And now because both players have the same guess Y, an agreement about this image is reached. This is the algorithm used in the ESP game. Apparently this will not work well with binary labelling, because there is a very simple cheating case. For example, a player simply enters both cat and dog, so they always reach agreement, and the result doesn't produce any meaningful labels at all. And in other cases one player enters cat and dog all the time, and his partner always cat, so again the system will not produce useful labels, so this is a cheating problem, it will make this ESP game not productive for labelling images of cat and dog at all.

And so how do we address these two issues? We have a number of ideas. The first idea is to make the game fun, so we introduced a competition, basically we wanted to design a game that's played by two teams. Each team has two players, so basically a two versus two competition. For example, the game could be like this, the cat/dog image is actually split to each of these four pairs. The team that first reaches an agreement about this image, for example, two players enter cat, wins this round. So the point is that in order to win this game you have to be fast and accurate, because no in-game communication is allowed, so the players would have found it difficult to collude, to cheat. So we introduced a competition, and in order to address the cheating, as I mentioned a while ago, we introduced something called a turn based on matching. So basically we are proposing to change the matching algorithm in the ESP game.

The idea is very simple, for two players in the same team, after player A enters a guess, for example G_A, this player cannot enter another guess until her partner enters a guess G_B. Basically, once player A enters a guess, his keyboard is locked and he cannot enter another guess. And then if we only compare G_A with G_B, this means the inputs in the same team are compared. So this can avoid the problem of abuse of their their agreement algorithm. But in order to make this cheating mitigation idea work, in our initial design we realised that in the game user interface an indicator is necessary, for example, a green or red light, which tells each player whether at the current moment your input is allowed, if it is red your keyboard is locked, and you couldn't actually enter anything. If you need not use this indicator, there could be a major usability issue because we call this a roundup game: there could be many more turns in a single run, so if we didn't have this indicator then a player would be easily confused when to enter a guess or whether their input has been taken into account, this would make the game less fun, and not workable. Our argument is that, because we want to support the two ideas, you actually have to introduce a unique user interface.

The initial design could cause an interesting security problem. Before we look at this security problem, we observe we can classify cheaters into two categories. Type 1 cheaters, are those who just want to pollute our data, their only aim is to provide the wrong data, the wrong label, and so pollute our collected data. Type 2 cheaters are different, they are not malicious enough, they actually just want to beat other players, they want to get more scores by being in more rounds. So the aim for the Type 2 cheaters is to agree on an image faster than their opponents. For example, they could reach a colluding protocol, for any image we all enter "C", means a cat, then they would have an edge to beat their opponents, because they could agree on an image faster.

The security problem we realised with the initial design is collusion while you are actually in-game: a covert channel could actually help both types of cheaters. And let's see how. The cheating scenario is the following. Basically a player can deduce a partner's input for the following reasons: for each turn of this game, it has only three possible outcomes. The first outcome is, this team have lost this turn, the second outcome is, this team won this turn, and the third outcome is that a round is not done yet, so the game is actually ongoing, and at the same time the lights for both players in this team will be reset to green, so that each player knows they are still playing the game, they're still allowed to enter their inputs.

Let's look at these three scenarios one by one, how this cheating could be done. The team of the first scenario, if this team has lost the current turn, is not of much interest because the players could not deduce much from this. There are three cases in this scenario. The partner might enter the same input as A, and their partner might enter a different input, or the partner might not input anything yet, because this turn was won by their opponents, and that means the opponents have reached an agreement earlier than this team. So if this team have lost this turn, basically they couldn't cheat at all. But the interesting thing is the other two scenarios. For if this team has won the current turn, or this round is still ongoing, not finished yet, we can see what information cheaters can get. Basically if player A's guess is "C" for cat, then this player can deduce what his partner entered according to their own account of the current algorithm, for example, if this current turn is won by this team, then player A is pretty sure his partner must have entered the "C". And if the indicator resets that means this run is ongoing, that means his partner must have entered a different guess, "D", because it is just a binary choice, so it's very clear for partner A to know what choice has been entered by their partner B. Similarly, if the player guesses "D", dog, and his team won this turn, then he is pretty sure that the partner actually entered "D". If this game is going on, then the partner must have entered a "C".

So the problem with this guessing game is the following: a cheater can easily convey information via the indicator and so convey their intention to their partner. Basically the inversion can be added, always creating the wrong label, thus to facilitate Type 1 cheating. Or their intention could be holding at green on one choice but not the other, so as to facilitate Type 2 cheating. And similarly important is that such intention can be equally easily detected by a willing colluder, so they could establish a colluding protocol in the game, and they do not have to know each other, they do not have to do anything else, they just play the game, and manipulate the outcome, and the indicator is on, and they can easily establish a colluding protocol, to do both types of cheating.

And so of course we had to redesign the game. The first change is that we made sure the number of turns allowed for each round is limited to only one, so in one round of the game only a single turn is allowed. This player enters, and then his partner enters a guess, and this finishes the turn. And if they can't reach agreement then they move on, and enter the second turn. Because we just need to the one turn, the indicator can be removed. The third rule we introduced was to enforce a new mechanism which is called guess disagreement. This means that the team that first reaches a disagreement, they have lost the current round. We can see how these three rules work. Basically this makes it harder for a colluder to convey or deduce information, because otherwise will not be there anymore. And the third change also makes it harder to collude, because now there are more possible ways for a team to win, because if you make a mistake earlier than your opponent, your opponent wins, similarly, if your opponent makes a mistake earlier than you did, then you win this turn. So this makes their deducing the information, the inference harder. And of course the first two changes make our user interface and user interaction a lot simpler, so that's good. And guess disagreement, actually encourages the guess accuracy, and puts off Type 2 cheaters, because if they do not reach agreement, they will be penalised.

So that's the change we have done to our original design. And in order to make the game a little bit more fun we also changed the story-line. So on the screen each user actually will see two chest boxes, this is actually for treasure, so for example, this is for team 1, this is for team 2. Each user will see the same thing, right, and the pet, just like cat or dog, will walk from up to down, or down to up, and then if the team reaches an agreement (that this is a cat) faster than their opponents, then the cat will drop some golden coins into the chest. We implemented this game and did a pilot study, and the results are pretty useful: we got an accuracy for labels more than 98%, and the throughput is about 13 correct labels per minute precision, and this means actually we can get 780 labels per hour precision. And this could be implemented by using a mobile. We also asked the people to tell us how enjoyable they found the game, and the figures are quite positive; we won't go into the details here. We also used this botnet that can replace a single team, this botnet can play against two humans, so basically this can input the throughput of the human. So this means actually we put in more than 50,000 labels per hour, but this is not interesting for this audience.

I think the discussion points are the following. We think the security design of our game is about the game rules, the design of game rules are innovative. And we claim that this essentially is a security protocol design. So my question is, would it be interesting to subject the design of game rules to formal method analysis? And if this is interesting, how could we do that, how could we actually apply formal methods to a detect security bugs in the game rules? I have no idea how to do that yet, because I'm not a formal methods person. And the second discussion point that's interesting to me is, are there any other real life binary labelling cases, because actually I want to make the motivation of this game design stronger, it would be good if you can offer some other examples of binary labelling that's relevant in real life. The third point I think is relevant is that apparently from my talk we can clearly see that security appeals to the design of human computation games, and so my question is, how could we make more use of the human condition for security? One answer we have figured out, we are interested to design actually a game as a CAPTCHA, basically this game is only playable by humans, computers cannot play this game. So we can actually deploy this game as a CAPTCHA. And of course, if we can think of other ways of making use of human condition for security, that would be really interesting. That's it.

Saša Radomirović: So do the game partners know each other in this game, or are they randomly assigned?

Reply: Randomly assigned, they never know each other.

Saša Radomirović: So even if there's one person who thinks that, well if I choose a strategy, right, choice 1 throughout the game, isn't there a danger that over time people realise that this might be his partner's way to win the games? If you randomly assigned, you all the time notice that your partner always seems to agree with you when it was choice number 1, or disagrees with you when it was choice number 2, so in time people will converge to just win the game by making choice 1 all the time.

Reply: Yes, actually we have to deal with this kind of cheating, for example, we can use traps, for example, if we label the image, to detect these kind of cheating.

Saša Radomirović: How?

Reply: Because for the usual game positions, their images do not have labels at all, so even we don't know what the labels should be addressed. But in order to detect cheaters we can insert some pre-labelled images, so when answers we collect from the players are not correct, we know they are cheaters. So that's another way of cheat detection.

Jonathan Anderson: Or give them the same image several times, and have option 1 for cat the first time, and dog the second. That's a way that you could check for people doing this without having to have any pre-labelling, just to check their consistency.

Reply: Yes.

Ross Anderson: But what's the threat model here, it strikes me that if you're running a CAPTCHA for, let's say, Yahoo, there might be 40,000 people per day, genuine humans trying to open mail accounts, and your botnet might be trying to open 100,000 accounts a day, so you could actually find that the attackers were most of the people playing the game, and so you would end up with attacker playing attacker, and then any passable deterministic algorithm will do.

Reply: Basically we could try to make the game a CAPTCHA so if an attacker really wants play this game, they have to actually produce labels for us.

Ross Anderson: You'd have to make it more complex, you'd have to do things like re-labelled images, you'd have to use the images again and again, you'd have to run various detection algorithms to see whether there was an agreement algorithm being used other than the human based one that you expected.

Reply: Yes, definitely.

James Malcolm: It seems quite slow; I think you said 14 or 15 matches per minute, that's four seconds to recognise the CAPTCHA result, I don't think it takes me that long. Is there a big overhead somewhere?

Reply: You're talking about the throughput of the labels, right?

James Malcolm: Yes. How long does it take to recognise a cat, a couple of seconds.

Joseph Bonneau: You just type in, and there's a little delay before the next image comes up.

James Malcolm: But four seconds seems quite slow.

Malte Schwarzkopf: It's not only just delay of recognition, also you have a synchronised round.

Reply: And if your partner has made a mistake, basically we cannot get around it, that will delay their performance.

James Malcolm: So it's not just the speed of the two people playing, or the four people playing, you have to make sure that they've all got to the certain point?

Reply: Yes, because we also need to make sure the players can have fun, otherwise they will not play this game, and then you will get nothing. So besides cheating mitigation, we also have to do some things to make the game fun.

Malte Schwarzkopf: Well attaching to that, you seem to be saying that mistakes are not the exception but they're fairly common, but with a simple task of telling cats from dogs, surely mistakes like this are extremely rare, because we know computers are not good at this, but humans, as James has said, can just tell a cat from a dog very easily, and there are no borderline cases where you're not quite sure?

Reply: Well one reason is indeed, actually there are quite some borderline cases, even to recognise it, that's either a cat or dog.

Malte Schwarzkopf: Well my perception is that this game is very much about speed, it's just, I can see something, can I type faster than the other team, it's not about the sort of recognition.

Reply: Both speed and accuracy matter. If you do not recognise a picture correctly your opponents could beat you to win the round.

Malte Schwarzkopf: I would argue that, you know, cat and dog are both three letters, but if you did have two words that are not the same length, then the winning strategy is to always type the shorter one.

Reply: Yes, but for this case actually we only allow people to enter a single character, "C" for cat, "D" for dog.

Vashek Matyas: I have a question, did you actually do some research into how complicated it would be for a computer mitigation to see whether they put cat or dog?

Reply: You mean how difficult for computer to recognise cat or dog, yes, there is data in the literature, their success rate is not much better than 50%, they're essentially guessing, right, not much good.

Virtually Perfect Democracy

Giampaolo Bella, Peter Y.A. Ryan, and Vanessa Teague

[1] Dipartimento di Matematica e Informatica
Università di Catania, Italy
giamp@dmi.unict.it
[2] Dept. Computer Science and Communications
University of Luxembourg
peter.ryan@uni.lu
[3] Dept. Computer Science and Software Engineering
University of Melbourne
vteague@csse.unimelb.edu.au

Abstract. In the 2009 Security Protocols Workshop, the Pretty Good Democracy scheme was presented. This scheme has the appeal of allowing voters to cast votes remotely, e.g. via the Internet, and confirm correct receipt in a single session. The scheme provides a degree of end-to-end verifiability: receipt of the correct acknowledgement code provides assurance that the vote will be accurately included in the final tally. The scheme does not require any trust in a voter client device. It does however have a number of vulnerabilities: privacy and accuracy depend on vote codes being kept secret. It also suffers the usual coercion style threats common to most remote voting schemes.

In this paper we investigate how to counter the above threats by introducing modest cryptographic capabilities, and modest trust assumptions, to the voting client. Of course, we are simply shifting trust, but we are transforming it and, arguably, making the trusted devices more accountable. Which design is deemed more secure will depend on the threat environment.

1 Introduction

Our scheme is based on *code voting*, which aims to avoid requiring the voter to trust any computational device or digital signature in order to vote. Instead, each voter receives a private code book which enables them to communicate securely with the voter server. Typically these schemes provide the voter with an *acknowledgement code*, which provides assurance that they communicated with the correct voting server and that their code was correctly received. However, they do not give any assurance that the vote will subsequently be correctly included in the overall count.

In [RT09], the Pretty Good Democracy scheme was introduced. As in code voting, each voter receives a code sheet with a unique *ID number* and a list of *vote codes*, one for each candidate. Unlike Code voting, there is a single *ack code* per code sheet. The important enhancement over code voting is that the

B. Christianson and J. Malcolm (Eds.): Security Protocols 2010, LNCS 7061, pp. 161–166, 2014.
© Springer-Verlag Berlin Heidelberg 2014

knowledge of the codes is now distributed so that the Vote Server must cooperate with a threshold set of Trustees in order to access the correct acknowledgement code. Thus, when the voter receives the correct code back from the Vote Server after having provided her credentials and vote code, she can be confident that the correct vote code will have been registered. She also receives unconditional proof that the votes were correctly tallied.

The arguments proving the correct registration of each vote depend on (at least) two significant assumptions:

– We do not have a colluding, malicious set of Trustees.
– Information about the vote codes does not leak out, in particular, to the Vote Server.

The first we will not discuss further. Taking a reasonably large threshold value and choosing the set of Trustees to be mutually distrustful etc. should make this assumption quite reasonable. In this paper we seek to strengthen the arguments supporting the second assumption by giving the voter's client modest cryptographic capabilities. We also explore how such techniques could help counter a number of other vulnerabilities identified in the original version of the scheme. The threats that we will focus on are the following three.

– Compromise of voting and/or acknowledgement codes.
– Coercion and vote-buying.
– Voters trying to undermine the credibility of the Vote Server by providing spurious vote codes.

We have not yet solved either of these problems completely. In the following three sections we investigate some attempts at solutions and explain why some issues still remain open.

2   Countering Code Leakage Threats

The scheme described in [RT09] presented a distributed construction to create the codes under encryption. This means that only a colluding threshold set of Trustees could determine the code values. However, to fit with the usual code voting approach, it is necessary at some point to extract these codes and print them to the code sheets. This means that much of the carefully constructed distributed trust is undermined by the existence of this pinch-point in the process.

Section 9.1 of [RT09] shows how to tally the results even when Vote IDs and Vote Codes are encrypted before being sent to the server. This solves the problem of a corrupt Vote Server who learns the codes, because the Vote Server cannot tell which of the known codes correspond to which encrypted IDs.

We investigate how to use a computational device with an independent communication channel to receive some of the code information, rather than printing all of it and sending it by post. The challenge is to allow the device to assist the voter in deriving her intended vote code, without allowing the device to send an alternative code.

Many countries use a smart-card for citizen identification. The assumption is that the smart-card can store a private key and perform some basic cryptographic operations such as encryption or signing, without revealing the key. This could be extremely useful for thwarting an attacker who intercepts communications between the voting client and the Vote Server. Standard cryptographic techniques would suffice for ensuring that the codes were sent from the holder of a particular card. We could attempt to achieve the same effect by sending a separate set of keys via an independent channel such as email, but it would be difficult to ensure that the two independent sets of code information were reliably joined.

An even more challenging problem is to prevent a voting client that knows the codes from casting an alternative one. This seems to require the voter doing some computation independent of the client, either in their head or using some alternative device such as a mobile phone.

3   Countering Coercion and Vote-Buying

Although PGD [RT09] is receipt-free, it is vulnerable to a coercer who intercepts the code sheet before the proper recipient votes. This seems unavoidable for this sort of scheme. However, we can address some of its vulnerabilities to a coercer who arrives after the code sheet. In PGD1:

1. the coercer can observe, via the bulletin board, whether the voter has cast a valid vote, and
2. the coercer can cast (or coerce the voter into casting) a (new) valid vote. Depending on the rules for resolving multiple votes, this may supersede or nullify the original vote, or prevent the voter from voting subsequently.

The first item is fairly easily resolved by the variant in which IDs are encrypted upon sending. (Section 9.1 of [RT09]). When the IDs are encrypted on the Bulletin Board, the coercer cannot tell whether a valid vote has already been cast. This also provides a simple solution to the second issue assuming that the voter has an opportunity to vote before the coercer arrives—we simply undertake to resolve ties by selecting the *first* valid vote cast for a particular ID. Then, even if the coercer casts another (otherwise valid) vote, it does not effect the tally.

3.1   Credentials

The more difficult coercer to defend against is one who arrives before the voter has voted. We have to assume that the voter receives the code sheet while the coercer is absent, and we also need to assume that the voter has some (later) access to the network without being observed by the coercer. Then we would like each voter to be able to cast a valid vote of their choice while making it impossible for the coercer to learn which vote they have cast. The same issue was successfully addressed in [JCJ05], but the implications of extending their technique to PGD are not immediately obvious. This is partly because the underlying cryptography is different, and partly because they assume a trusted voting client, which PGD otherwise avoids.

The idea in [JCJ05] is that each voter receives exactly one valid *credential*, which allows them to vote. Voters receive one true credential, but can generate plausible fake credentials with which to pretend to vote while they are being coerced. The voter must trust the computer to generate fake credentials based on the true one, which includes not only a correct cryptographic computation but also producing a printout or email that replicates the original way the credential was sent. Also, it must be difficult for the coercer to discover which was the true credential, even given access to the bulletin board and some access to the voter's computer (though obviously not access to the private data of the voting client, or it could simply query which code had been sent).

We are going to try to find a happy medium between the total trust of the voting device in [JCJ05] and the coercion vulnerability of PGD. The ideal would be to design the system so that

- a voter who is not being coerced has the same integrity guarantees as PGD, *including when the voting device is untrusted*, and
- a voter who is being coerced has a coercion-resistance strategy as effective as that in [JCJ05].

The conundrum is when or whether to return the ack codes.

- If we return the ack only for valid credentials, then the coercer can tell whether the vote was correctly cast or not.
- If we return the ack regardless of whether the credential was valid, then a cheating device can undetectably decline to cast a valid vote, even if the voter was not being coerced. (This is assuming that a cheating device can generate a fake credential.)

4   Countering Voter Threats

A number of significant threats towards the practical use of e-voting systems derive from the voter. Here, we focus on a particular one targeted at the general credibility and acceptance of the entire system. Voters who aim at undermining the public reputation of the system may try to insert spurious vote codes. Because these are fake codes, they should fail to obtain a corresponding ack code. Such failure may, depending on how the system is designed, become public and reach its malicious aim to some extent. Obviously, if the system required the voter to enter the vote code by keying it in rather than by clicking on it, spurious codes might also derive simply from mistakes rather than from deliberate maliciousness.

The introduction of an additional computational device in the system, which was advocated above in terms of smart-cards, might be useful also in this case.

Smart-cards may be seen as a form of protection not only for stored information, which typically is a long cryptographic key, but also for a specific computation. More simply, a modern smart-card is a minicomputer that protects both its memory and its executed program. If we assume that the smart-cards that many countries use for citizen identification are not programmable and store the citizen's private key, then the voter is endowed with a computational device that can do standard cryptography and is very difficult to tamper with. The functional interface of the smart-card will only react to well-formed inputs and, assuming that it is well programmed, will guard the stored secrets as the Crown jewels. A few years back, Anderson and Kuhn showed that tampering with modern smart-cards is possible though not straightforward [AK98].

Smart-cards appear to bear potential for addressing a variety of issues in e-voting. An important one is the notorious registration problem. For example, identification smart-cards carry the necessary information (birthdate) to establish whether an individual qualifies as a registered voter. We are working on a system that leverages on the physical tamper-evidence of smart-cards to thwart various forms of voter's misbehaviour.

One possibility is to deliver the ballots electronically to the smart-cards. If sent enciphered with the voter's private key, which the smart-card stores, the ballots may traverse the network confidentially. Vote codes could then be entirely kept from the voter, thus contributing to their confidentiality requirement stated earlier. The voter could choose his candidate name and then the smart-card could decrypt only the corresponding vote code and submit it protected in a standard fashion [RT09, §9.1]. For such a system to work effectively, we should assume at least the program interacting with the smart-card from the PC not to be compromised.

5   Discussion

Absolute security is unattainable. Some trust assumptions must remain. The question is: how to design the system to be as secure as possible in a given threat environment. The original PGD scheme avoided the need to place any trust in the voter's device but at the cost of assuming that vote codes are not leaked as a side-effect of the printing and distribution of the code sheets.

We have explored how introducing modest computational capabilities to the voter's device can reduce the reliance on the above assumption. We do this in a controlled way, minimising the the potential to do damage. Ultimately though, it would appear to be impossible to eliminate some degree of trust. We thus need well-founded techniques to evaluate the trade-offs between various schemes in the context of differing threat environments.

References

[AK98]   Anderson, R.J., Kuhn, M.J.: Low cost attacks on tamper resistant devices. In: Christianson, B., Crispo, B., Lomas, M., Roe, M. (eds.) Security Protocols 1997. LNCS, vol. 1361, pp. 125–136. Springer, Heidelberg (1998)

[JCJ05] Juels, A., Catalano, D., Jakobsson, M.: Coercion-resistant Electronic Elections. In: Proceedings of the 2005 ACM Workshop on Privacy in the Electronic Society, vol. 11 (2005)

[RT09]   Ryan, P.Y.A., Teague, V.: Pretty Good Democracy. In: Christianson, B., Malcolm, J.A., Matyáš, V., Roe, M. (eds.) Security Protocols 2009. LNCS, vol. 7028, pp. 111–130. Springer, Heidelberg (2013)

Virtually Perfect Democracy
(Transcript of Discussion)

Peter Y.A. Ryan

University of Luxembourg

This is joint work with Vanessa Teague from Melbourne, and Giampaolo Bella from Catania, neither of whom could unfortunately make it. Well first of all the title is a bit contrived, I should probably apologise for it, it kind of fits the theme. I'm not sure the content actually fits so well, we'll see about that. Sandy, yesterday you saying something about you managed to get out of voting; I must ask you more about why you were so keen to.

Sandy Clark: I escaped.

Reply: I think there's still a lot of fun to be had, and so I'm still wallowing in it. This will be a follow-on from the talk I gave last year[1], so I'll start with a very brief overview of the Pretty Good Democracy scheme, then I'll talk about the threats that we identified against that scheme, and then I'll talk rather speculatively about how we might counter some of those threats. Some of these potentially do lead us into virtualisation, but to be honest I'm not sure I understand virtualisation very well so maybe presenting it in front of this audience will generate some interesting ideas about how things like virtualisation, perhaps trusted devices and so on, might help.

With these kinds of voting system, the principle properties that we're aiming for are, first of all obviously, some sort of notion of integrity or accuracy, that the legitimately cast votes are accurately recorded in the final tally. Typically in the newer schemes we also have a stronger notion of verifiability, that the voters themselves and external observers have some way of confirming that in fact the count is accurate, so I'll be saying a little bit more about that. Alongside this we want the usual sort of ballot secrecy, or perhaps more subtle notions of receipt freeness and coercion resistance as well. We also want to do this in the context of trying to minimise the amount of trust that we have to place in either the technological components of the system, or indeed the people and the officials that are running it. So we want to move away from the trusted third party model of doing elections, which would obviously make the problem more tractable.

Pretty Good Democracy was itself based on an earlier scheme using Chaum Sure Code voting, so the idea here is very simple, that by snail-mail or some other supposedly secure channel you'd send out these code sheets to each of the voters, and each code sheet is effectively a private code book to communicate with the vote server. So you'd have some pairs of random codes against each candidate, you have a voting code and an acknowledgement code, and basically the protocol is, you login to a vote server, possibly with some additional authentication mechanism, and you present the vote server, perhaps with the ID

---

[1] See LNCS 8263 pp 123–133.

B. Christianson and J. Malcolm (Eds.): Security Protocols 2010, LNCS 7061, pp. 167–174, 2014.

of your sheet, and then the vote code for your voted candidate, and then ideally the vote server comes back with the correct acknowledgement code corresponding to that. And in fact the code sheet might look like this, a list of candidates, list of voting codes, and this list of acknowledgement codes; very simple. The point of it is that it sidesteps a lot of insecurities of the Internet, the crucial drawback of it (as I mentioned last year) is that there's no real verifiability; the correct ack code back just confirms the voting server received the correct voting paper, it doesn't guarantee that that's going to result in a vote being cast for the correct candidate in the final tally.

So what we were trying to do with Pretty Good democracy was to try and enhance that to give a higher degree of verifiability. And I think to some extent we achieved that, modulo a set of strong assumptions, which is what I'm going to be focussing on now. I won't go through the details because of time, and because some of you have seen some of it last year, but the key idea is that rather than have the vote server know all the database of the codes (as in code voting), in fact the vote server basically knows nothing, and the knowledge about these codes is cryptographically buried. And the whole set up is in such a way that the vote server essentially passes on vote codes sent to it by the voter, posts them to a web bulletin board, which actually decrypts the form, and then a threshold of Trustees have to collaborate to confirm that's a valid code, and to register it on a web bulletin board, and if that all works they then again collaborate in a threshold fashion to reveal the appropriate ack code. The whole point is that if the voter in a single session gets back a correct ack code, that's a strong indication that a threshold set of Trustees collaborated to correctly register their code on this web bulletin board. And then we can use some fairly conventional techniques in this field to do a verifiable tabulation of those registered votes, or more precisely where the codes are counted.

So that is the idea of Pretty Good Democracy; the details of how you set that up cryptographically are in last year's paper. But the key point is that getting the correct ack code back gives you a fairly strong guarantee that your code was correctly registered. But the crucial vulnerability, which was already mentioned last year, is that we are assuming here that the vote server doesn't somehow require knowledge of alternative codes on the code sheet, because clearly if it does manage to obtain that then it can undermine the accuracy property, it simply sends in the encryption of an alternative code, and that will be acknowledged by the Trustees of the valid code. And nothing will happen which will be detectable to point out there has been some corruption of the vote there. So the crucial point here is that we're very much assuming that the knowledge of these vote codes remains secret and doesn't leak to the web server. So that's really the issue we've been trying to address in this intervening year.

We already have a nice distributed construction for these cryptographic commitments to the bulletin board, we have a nice construction where a whole set of clerks, registrars, whatever you want to call them, had to collaborate in order to set all this up on the web bulletin board, and in such a way that no single entity would know any of the code information, because it's all encrypted on the web bulletin board. So that was very nice, but the problem is that at some point in the process we have to decrypt these and print them to a code sheet and distribute them. But this creates a sort of pinch point for all this nicely set up distributed trust, and that was kind of irritating, and of course that point is where a lot of the potential leakage of the code information could occur.

For Pretty Good Democracy the voting procedure is very simple. You logon to the server again as you did with code voting, you send in your ID of your ballot form, you send in the appropriate web code. Now what the server does then, that's a little bit more subtle than code voting, it creates an encryption of the vote code onto the public key of the Trustees, and in fact also for technical reasons there's zero knowledge proof of knowledge of that vote code, and it encrypts that to a web bulletin board. And then the Trustees collaborate to do a plaintext equivalence test on the appropriate row of the table with the web bulletin board to see whether that encrypted code matches one of the codes posted on the web bulletin board. And if that's OK then at that time it's flagged and they collectively reveal the acknowledgement code. We can probably skip on this technicality, the details of the proofs can be also posted, which is quite nice because it encounters some ballot stuffing potentially. So that's the basic scheme, does that make sense? I've gone through it extremely quickly, but I think the key ideas are quite simple.

There's a bunch of threats. I've already mentioned the key threat which I'm going to concentrate on today: that knowledge of these vote codes may be leaked and that would undermine both voter secrecy and the integrity of the scheme. I should just pause to remark that you could argue whether this is a fatal flaw. I am slightly ambivalent about this, I've discussed it: Ron[2], for example, responded saying it seemed quite an interesting scheme, on the other hand Josh[3] said, that's just fatal, I don't think it's a fatal flaw, so we have different views on this. But what we're trying to do is strengthen this assumption, make it much harder for things to leak, so at least the scheme perhaps is more viable for at least low level elections. I would like to think that maybe distributed versions can link to the IACR Internet voting system. OK, there's a lot of threats against it we identified, but I'm not going to talk about those today, so I'll merely touch on coercion for today.

Let me go through some of the ideas we've had for countermeasures to this vulnerability. The first idea we had actually seems to be remarkably effective. In particular we're exploring how, by introducing some trust in, for example, the voters device, we can (at the cost of introducing this degree of trust), mitigate the code leakage problem. One very simple possibility is to introduce a simple encryption capability into the voter's device, basically it has the public key of the Trustees so is able to encrypt the ID and the vote code before it gets sent to the vote server. So now the web server doesn't have to do that, and crucially the vote server doesn't see the plaintext of either the vote ID or the code. The point of that is of that even if the vote server does somehow acquire knowledge of the

---

[2] Ronald L. Rivest.

[3] Josh Benaloh.

table of vote codes, it's hard now for it to exploit because it doesn't know which row of the table on the web bulletin board to look at. So this actually seems quite nice, it's really introducing a very minimal trust assumption, basically from a security point of view that the device doesn't allow leaks to the vote server, let's say the plaintext of the ID or of the codes. Beyond that you don't really need to assume anything. So that's a mild trust assumption I think, but it actually seems to achieve quite a lot in terms of strengthening the underlying scheme. Of course we have to assume some additional stuff, that there isn't somehow a way of linking the message that you get, the request, back to say the voter's ID via IP addresses, and then if there's some sort of mixnet in the system between code sheets and voter, then of course you could still circumvent this. But there are probably ways of trying to avoid that kind of problem.

Some other simple ideas that we thought about to try and strengthen this. One is to have some sort of long-term knowledge between the voting system and the individual voter, which might be a social security number, or something like that. And the voter in some sense adds a bit of salt into their vote codes, and then there can be some homomorphic crypto process going on in the background, which means that the system does essentially the same mathematics. So that means potentially that an attacker would have to know not only the code, but also some information about the salt. Now that's sort of an interesting idea, of course it introduces immediately usability problems, already the voter is going to have to do some simple, easy simple mathematical operation, but that's going to be error prone to the voters themselves. And we are trying to make this system as simple and usable as possible. Another possibility that we've toyed with, which is actually borrowing an idea from the Scantegrity people, who have come up with a way you can actually print information, again in a sort of distributed way. If some of you have seen the Scantegrity scheme, it actually uses invisible ink, so you can have one process which acquires one set of the pixels and prints those in invisible ink onto the ballot sheets, and then another process takes over and is able cryptographically to acquire a complimentary set of pixels and print those, and then in final stage you reveal all the invisible ink, which reveals the information, but neither of these two processes actually knows anything about the information. So that's one way we could slightly reduce this pinch point and spread the collusion threshold slightly. How good that is, it's one of these trade-offs I guess, you weigh up.

Another very simple idea is to distribute the voter codes and the ack codes independently. Actually that doesn't of itself particularly help with the threat I'm talking about, but in conjunction with other things it's useful, as you will see in a moment.

So to go on to some slightly more sophisticated ideas, as I remarked earlier, the the distributed construction for all this cryptographic information looks very nice, and it's sort of irritating that we end up having to decrypt it all and print it. So what would be very nice is if we could come up with a way that we don't have to do this decryption and printing, we set up some kind of protocol in such a way that we only reveal the code of choice of the voter, and all the other codes remain encrypted, and in fact even the voter doesn't need to know the alternative code, they just need to know their code of choice. So we set the thing up in such a way that the alternative codes are never revealed, and if we can do that, that's crucial, because only if the vote server could learn of alternative codes, could they substitute them undetected into the scheme.

So that's one of our goals. But alongside this of course, whatever protocol we have, ideally we'd like to set it up in such a way that the voter can be confident that this code that's revealed to them is the correct one for their candidate. OK, it's more subtle than previously because previously the voter got a code sheet and it was very clear what the vote code and ack code corresponding to their candidate were, and we had some random auditing processes in the background which would detect any corruption with these printed committed values. If we're losing some of the protocol through this revealing of the single code, we don't have that mechanism now, we have to find some other way of assuring the voter that the code that they put into here is the correct code for their code sheet. I'll come back to that point a little bit later.

Another thing we toyed with, though I don't think any of the three authors knows too much about these things, was smart tokens ID, and it was actually Giampaolo's suggestion, so again, there are probably people in the audience who know a lot more about these. But I believe that you can actually set these things up in such a way that they enforce some kind of policy, and in particular we can envisage a policy here where the device only allows a single encryption during the period of the election with a particular key. So that in itself would, this would guarantee, if you set things up right, that only a single code could be revealed per voter during the period of an election. So I would welcome comments on how strong these smart tokens are in terms of enforcing such policies.

Virtualisation is something else, we ran some ideas, but again, I don't think any of us really understand virtualisation well enough to be sure how well this can enforce the kind of assumptions that we need. So again, I would very much welcome comments in the discussion period afterwards about to what extent virtualisation could help us with this particular problem.

Also some cryptographic mechanisms we thought about; again I won't go into the technical details, but one simple idea is to add an extra layer to the construction that I alluded to earlier, so that these encryption terms have a super-encryption layer with say a symmetric key, with a different key for each term. These are locking keys, if you like, distributed again by snail-mail, printed with the appropriate one against each candidate. So this now means that the voter can present to their device the appropriate unlocking key, which will allow the device access to reveal that particular term, and then perhaps use the private key of the voter to reveal the actual code. So that's again, a mechanism which we can use to prevent the device ever learning the alternate codes, apart from the one designated by the voter.

Another primitive which sounds promising here, but I haven't checked the details of precisely how it would work out, is to use oblivious transfer type protocols. That seems to be the right kind of primitive here, because the idea in oblivious transfer is to send several encrypted messages in such a way that only one of these can be decrypted by the recipient, and the sender won't know which one has been sent. Because that is very useful if you want to make sure that the sender in this context doesn't know which candidate the voter is choosing and to hide the code. So that looks like a primitive that could be very useful in this context. And also very speculatively it seems like quantum mechanics should help us do this, and using collapsible wave functions to reveal some dimension of information while destroying information in conjugate dimensions, feels like it should be useful, but again we haven't thought out the details of that.

Another line of thought which emerged in the last few days is that up to now we've been tending to think of both these schemes as basically conventional voting, where you have some kind of separate authority, or audit distributable authority, managing the election, and then the disjoined set of voters. Of course we could think in terms of more boardroom style voting systems, where the voters actually manage their own election, rather than having separate authorities, and again, I haven't really had time to think this through, it seems to work as a scheme. Superficially it sounds like it would be rather heavyweight compared to other boardroom voting schemes, although I should sit down and actually look at the complexity of computations, but that would actually help with these trust assumptions, as the voters themselves are controlling the creation and the distribution of this cryptographic material, that perhaps would make the trust assumptions a bit more easy. And that might work perhaps for small-scale elections, it doesn't seem like it would scale very well for large-scale elections, but maybe we should take a subset of the voters themselves control the election, maybe in the IACR context that might work. I don't quite how you'd choose that subset for an election.

So far I've been quite narrowly concentrating on this issue of how do we try and ensure that only a single code is revealed. A dual point of that is, how do we try and ensure that it's the correct code that gets revealed, and that's quite tricky as well. And the naïve answer is to say, well, that will become clear when the voter's gone through the protocol, and if they get the correct ack code back that should be a guarantee that the vote code that they got via this protocol was correct. But this is supposing again that they have some of the code sheet which has the ack code is written against the candidates. And of course that now immediately means that the ack codes become critical from a secrecy and integrity point of view. So we're potentially getting ourselves into some kind of regress here if we're not careful. So I'm not entirely clear how best to solve that.

And the other observation is, I think I skipped over this, but the original Pretty Good Democracy rather than having a distinctive set of ack codes, different for each candidate, actually proposed a single ack code sheet. That was for receipt freeness, particularly if you moved that post onto a bulletin board, and if we're going to post the fact that a vote has been cast, and also an ack code, we clearly mustn't have distinct ack codes for each candidate because that would immediately violate the receipt freeness. But if we're going to use this kind of mechanism to try and validate the code, then clearly we're going to have to fall back on distinct layer codes rather than single ones, if that makes sense. But of course, this immediately starts to cause problems from a receipt freeness point of view. Now arguably, rather than posting the ack codes in this context, we would just send them back in the session to the voter, so unless the voter is being monitored during the session, or somebody is monitoring communications, then perhaps we still have receipt freeness. But again, we're into rather tricky ground about assumptions, about communications and so forth.

I don't have time to go into coercion resistance, but if you worry about that, you also have to worry about when you send back ack codes. If a voter is, for example, trying to re-vote to avoid coercion, then you really have to worry about what happens, should an ack code be sent back at that point, or should it be refused on the grounds that the vote has already been cast, if you do that of course it indicates to the coercer that the vote has already been cast by the voter, and so forth. So you get some very tricky interactions between these various properties that we're trying to achieve. So the key question to which I don't yet know the answer is, is there some other more direct way of validating the code when using this kind of protocol, other than just basing it on getting the correct ack code back.

Coercion-resistance is still an issue with this scheme, and particularly how to try and solve it. We have to be quite careful how this interacts with what happens on the web bulletin board.

So let me conclude. This is a hard problem, we had a little bit of a crack at it, in particular we tried to think about how we could strengthen the scheme using perhaps some trusted devices, virtualisation, whatever, and I don't think we're expert enough really to make much progress on that front. There are I think some quite nice ideas about how cryptography can be used. And yes, there are plenty of open questions, so I'm going to be wallowing in the voting systems for a bit longer. Thank you.

Ross Anderson: The important thing about an election is that the real customers are the party observers. You have to somehow sell the idea that the election was fair to whoever lost it. And that's not the case with all elections, if you're electing people to a club, for example, then the people who don't get elected have no say, and perhaps it's the people who proposed the people who don't get elected that do, but in general, it's a social process that involves marketing to the losers, and in such a circumstance, having bundles of paper ballots sitting on a table in a town hall, is not a bad thing.

Reply: This is true, yes, an optically based audit.

Ross Anderson: So there's perhaps at least as much of a visualisation theme here as there is a cryptography theme. Where more than three black balls cause a person not to be elected, then the procedure is easy, you empty out the basin and you count the white balls and the black balls. I have yet to see an electronic voting system that provides as compelling an HCI as a table covered with bundles, each bundle containing a hundred ballot papers, or a basin into which you turn out all the white balls and black balls.

Reply: Yes, this is true, it's tricky, and of course what some schemes are doing is combining electronic and conventional paper systems. There's a project in fact going on in Israel doing exactly that; whether that's a smart way to go, I'm not sure, but it does help you in terms of persuasion. Of course potentially you will have problems between the two counts, but the fundamental point is that paper voting is not infallible either, as we know, and there's a history of slipping two black balls into the urn, particularly if you're in charge of the election.

Ross Anderson: Well one thing we've observed over the past few years with elections is that if you coerce an election you generally get away with it, whereas if you steal an election you generally don't. Example of coercing an election: Putin's re-election in Russia, all civil servants were told to vote for him or lose their jobs, etc, so when he won nobody was surprised, and nobody was ready to take to the streets. Example of a stolen election: the recent election in Kenya, people thought that they had managed to overthrow the government, but the government said, no you didn't, the result was that large numbers of people go on the streets, there was fighting, there was burning, there was bloodshed. So there's a curious thing here in that perhaps coercion is the least bad of the abuses that can happen. If the election is going to be rigged it's better it's coerced than it's stolen.

Sandy Clark: It's bad for who, it's bad for the people who retain power?

Paulo Verissimo: Yes, based on the analysis of those two cases, coercion could have generated riots also, I mean, imagine that the Kenyan president would tell the public servants that they should vote for him or would else lose their jobs, maybe they would come out on the streets, it all depends on the social condition.

Jonathan Anderson: But if you have coercion at least it's the sort of thing that has to be spread across an awful lot of people, and it would be the kind of thing that human observers would probably notice happening, whereas if you steal an election, it's something that could be done in one place at an opportune moment, when you have a moment that nobody's looking. So maybe even for transparency coercion is better than stealing.

Jeff Yan: It might be true in countries like the UK and the US, but in Russia, for people there not to vote as Putin wanted, they would die.

Saša Radomirović: In the west we have a lot of elections that are close calls, so on those it's not coercion that matters, because they could have gone either way.

Jeff Yan: But here you can actually have a case in court, if you have evidence for coercion in an election. But in Russia, nobody cares, right. Actually I'm interested in the human aspects in this kind of crypto-based protocol voting system — what is the research agenda for that?

Reply: That's probably quite a long answer actually.

Security Protocols for Secret Santa

Sjouke Mauw, Saša Radomirović, and Peter Y. A. Ryan

University of Luxembourg
SnT and FSTC
6, rue Richard Coudenhove-Kalergi
L-1359, Luxembourg
{sjouke.mauw,peter.ryan}@uni.lu, sasa.radomirovic@inf.ethz.ch

1 Introduction

The motivation for the current report lies in a number of questions concerning the current state of the art in security protocol design and analysis. Why is it so hard to develop a complete set of security requirements for a particular problem? For instance, even in the seemingly simple case of defining the secrecy property of an encryption algorithm it has taken decades to reach a degree of consensus, and even now new definitions are required in specific contexts. Similarly, even after more than twenty years of research on e-voting, there is still a lack of consensus as to which properties an e-voting protocol should satisfy. What did we learn from this research experience on e-voting? Can we apply the knowledge accumulated in this domain to similar domains and problems? Is there a methodology underlying the process of understanding a security protocol domain?

One could argue that such a methodology can not exist, because security requirements analysis is an instantiation of the general problem of requirements analysis and thus suffers from the same problems, such as ambiguity, incompleteness and implicit assumptions. Nevertheless, security protocol history shows that there are several patterns in the evolution of security requirements that can be identified and from which we can learn.

As a first example we look at the development of the notion of privacy in e-voting. While privacy initially amounted to vote secrecy, it was later on refined into receipt-freeness, stating that a voter cannot prove whom he voted for. Thus, privacy must be guaranteed, even if there is a reason for the voter to cooperate with the adversary. The notion of receipt-freeness, in turn, was refined into coercion resistance, capturing an even stronger form of cooperation with the adversary. As a consequence of the shift from honest participants to participants showing several forms of dishonest behaviour, we see a shift of the security requirements from basic privacy to *enforced privacy*. This drift towards insider attacks was also at the basis of the well-known developments concerning the Needham-Schroeder authentication protocol. This protocol was proven correct with respect to outside attackers. A problem that was overlooked by the authors was the possibility for a malicious insider to abuse an authentication session between him and a user to attack another user. Lowe's fix of

B. Christianson and J. Malcolm (Eds.): Security Protocols 2010, LNCS 7061, pp. 175–184, 2014.

the Needham-Schroeder protocol prevents such insider attacks. The resulting Needham-Schroeder-Lowe protocol guarantees the following form of agreement: If Alice believes to be communicating with Bob, then Bob believes to be communicating with Alice. We could even take this one step further and consider a stronger form of authentication, namely one where a user not only convinces himself of the authenticity of his communication partner, but can also use the communication to prove this fact to a third party. Protocols that achieve this property are called non-repudiation protocols.

A second class of examples comes from the discrepancy between a real-world problem and its idealized abstraction. In the real world, there are side-channels, a voter can be physically threatened and random-number generators are predictable. In the ideal world, the attacker adheres to the abstract model's strict code of conduct. If the attacker's abilities are defined by cryptographic games or Dolev-Yao inference rules, then dumpster diving and rubber-hoses are off-limits.

Looking at the history of security protocols, we can make a distinction between three approaches towards requirements analysis. The first approach consists of postulating a set of requirements, e.g., based on the similarity of the problem with well-studied existing problems. The second approach is driven by an analysis of possible threats. The set of all threats defines the unwanted behaviour and thus specifies the security requirements. Following Roscoe [10], these approaches can be considered as *extensional*, i.e., they refer to the externally observable effect. Achieving a complete specification in this way is rather hard. The third approach starts by designing an ideal solution that explains how to securely solve the problem under idealized assumptions. For instance, one may assume a Trusted Third Party, resilient, secure and anonymizing communication channels, trusted communication partners, and so on. Such an ideal solution may be considered as a specification of what the final solution should achieve. In Roscoe's terminology, this is the *intensional* approach. One of the problems with this approach is that it may suffer from over-specification.

The current state-of-the-art in the field of security protocol design is far from providing clear and explicit answers to the questions raised above. Therefore, we propose to study new, simple security protocol domains so as to identify common patterns in the domain analysis and apply them to new situations.

As a first exercise, we propose to study the Secret Santa problem. Secret Santa is known in many western countries under different names, such as Chris Kindle, sinterklaassurprises and julklapp. The informal description is as follows. Members of a group are randomly assigned other members to whom they anonymously give a gift. To provide a level of anonymity, simple protocols are used, such as drawing strips of paper (with a name) from a hat. This is a centralized, probabilistic solution, i.e. one that is not guaranteed to terminate successfully. A non-probabilistic service is offered through various web sites, but these require a TTP. An interesting question is whether there are distributed, non-probabilistic solutions without TTP.

2   Related Work

The Secret Santa protocol problem was first described in the scientific literature by Crépeau and Kilian [2] in 1994. They propose a solution using only a deck of playing cards. Later, in 2002, Gerard Tel uses the problem as an example in his text book [12]. He describes a probabilistic, decentralized solution. One of his students studied the problem in more detail and developed implementations of different solutions [13]. Liberti and Raimondi studied the problem from a different point of view. They are not proposing a protocol but an algorithm to determine if a solution exists under certain constraints, including an anonymity requirement [7]. Recently, Heather, Schneider, and Teague [5] proposed a solution with physical objects only.

3   The Secret Santa Problem

The Secret Santa problem boils down to anonymously establishing a random derangement of the participants. In addition, we require that cheating participants, i.e. those that don't follow this derangement when buying a present, can be identified. Formally,

Definition 1. *Let P be a set of size $N > 2$, containing participants. A Secret Santa protocol is a (distributed) protocol that establishes a function $f : P \to P$ such that*

1. *(bijective) f is a bijection;*
2. *(irreflexive) $\forall_{p \in P} f(p) \neq p$;*
3. *(random) f is random, i.e. none of the participants can influence the choice of f in such a way as to cause it to be distinguishable from random;*
4. *(anonymous) A group of conspiring participants $Q \subseteq P$ will not learn more about function f than can be deduced from $\{f(q) \mid q \in Q\}$.*
5. *(verifiable) If there is a participant $p' \in P$ who has not received a present after the exchange, we can identify the cheater, i.e. the participant $p \in P$ for which $f(p) = p'$.*

These requirements seem to easily follow from the (short and informal) problem description. But there were several choices made that led up to the formulation presented above. For instance, we have taken the stance that in a real-world Secret Santa protocol, there is nothing that can be done to prevent a group of conspirators from exchanging their assignments. Thus the anonymity and verifiability conditions express what we think is the best we can achieve.

Alternatively, we could have argued that unless there is a necessary trade-off present in the requirements, we should always strive for the strongest set of requirements. In this setting, we might state the verifiability requirement as follows.

5'. *(verifiable) After exchanging the presents it is verifiable that every cheating participant $p \in P$, i.e. one that has not given a present to $f(p)$, can be identified.*

Both of these formulations are based on catching cheaters. As a further alternative to the verifiability requirement, we could consider forcing participants to prove compliance.

5". (verifiable) After successfully executing the protocol, every participant $p \in P$ can prove that the image of p is indeed $f(p)$.

Aside from the problem of finding the "right" formulation for these requirements, it is not evident that the list is complete. Indeed, why are notions similar to receipt-freeness, coercion resistance, abuse-freeness and universal verifiability left out? Do we need to require a fairness property stating that whenever a participant gives a present, he will eventually receive a present?

Since correctness of a security protocol is relative to a particular adversary model, a specification of the adversary model must also be provided. We choose the Dolev-Yao adversary model with conspiring participants. Alternatively, we could have chosen honest but curious participants. This would mean that they strictly follow the protocol, but nevertheless try to learn other participant's secrets, e.g., by performing some extra local calculations. The discrepancy between the real world and the idealized world shows because we ignore covert channels that may appear when people bring or open presents.

4   Solutions

In this section we sketch several solutions for the Secret Santa problem. The traditional solution is to draw strips of paper from a hat. This solution is probabilistic, since a participant may draw his own name from the hat, which violates the second requirement of Definition 1. In fact, for a party of three, this solution will fail more frequently than it will work. This is furthermore a centralized solution, since the participants need to gather around a hat, but it does not require a trusted third party.

The solution proposed by Crépeau and Kilian [2] assumes an honest but curious party who is responsible for picking the permutation using a deck of cards only. Participants are represented by specific sequences of cards in the deck. The protocol consists of N rounds. The ith round consists of a random cyclic shift of the cards, after which the participant represented by the topmost sequence of cards is assigned to participant i. The encoding of participants through card sequences and the card sequences separating these encodings are designed in such a way that the boundaries of such a sequence can be blindly determined and that it can be verified blindly whether a participant's sequence is assigned to himself. If such a self-assignment is detected, the algorithm is repeated from scratch, making this a probabilistic solution. The verifiability requirement is not considered by Crépeau and Kilian.

Heather, Schneider, and Teague [5] describe a simple, centralized solution, requiring nothing further than envelopes, cards, and pens. Their solution is guaranteed to produce a cyclic permutation. Thus no donor will need to buy a gift for himself. However, their solution cannot produce derangements which are not cyclic permutations. Thus, every donor also knows that he will not receive a gift from his recipient.

If the participants also have a second set of larger envelopes, colored sheets of paper, and a paper puncher available, then Heather et al.'s solution can be generalized to a protocol which produces arbitrary derangements and tests the participants' patience. The details are left as an exercise for the reader.

4.1   Trusted Third Party

The simplest and most obvious solution is to use a trusted third party which will generate a random derangement f and securely communicate $f(p)$ to participant p. The trusted third party will then receive from p the present for $f(p)$ and distribute the presents to the participants. The following algorithm will (deterministically) generate a random derangement.

$D := P$;
$R := P$;
while $D \neq \emptyset$
do $p := \mathbf{any}(D)$;
    if $|D| = 2 \wedge |R \cap D| = 1 \wedge p \notin R \cap D$
      then $f(p) := \mathbf{random}(D - \{p\})$;
      else $f(p) := \mathbf{random}(R - \{p\})$;
    fi;
    $D := D - \{p\}$;
    $R := R - \{f(p)\}$;
od;

This solution satisfies requirements (1) through (5), but neither (5′) nor (5″). For (5′) the trusted third party must keep the participants in isolation for the duration of the protocol. For (5″) each participant p would need to be given a receipt signed by the trusted third party.

4.2   Decentralized Solutions

We give brief descriptions of a couple of decentralized solutions heuristically satisfying the requirements of Definition 1.

Homomorphic Encryption. We denote by $\{m, r\}_k$ an ElGamal encryption of a plaintext m with random number r and key k. Thus $k = (G, q, g, y)$, where $G = \langle g \rangle$ is a cyclic group of order q in which the Decision Diffie-Hellman problem is intractable, and $y = g^s$, s secret. The notation $\{m, r\}_k$ then corresponds to the pair $(g^r, y^r m)$. If we want to be less explicit with respect to the random factor introduced or the public key, we will simply leave them out, writing $\{m\}$ instead of $\{m, r\}_k$.

ElGamal encryption has the following homomorphic properties:

$$\{m_1, r_1\} \cdot \{m_2, r_2\} = \{m_1 m_2, r_1 + r_2\}$$

and

$$\{m_1, r_1\}^n = \{m_1^n, r_1 \cdot n\}.$$

The decentralized Secret Santa protocol now runs as follows.

1. Setup.
   The participants generate a public key $pk = (G, q, g, y)$ for the ElGamal cryptosystem such that only large enough coalitions of participants may recover the corresponding private key. All encryptions are performed using pk. The participants are labeled 1 through N and assigned the elements g^1 through $g^N \in G$, respectively. The participants publicly form encryptions of each of the elements in the set $\{g^1, \ldots, g^N\}$. Thus the vector $\langle \{g^1\}, \{g^2\}, \ldots, \{g^N\} \rangle$ is obtained.

2. Shuffle.
   Each participant gets to do a re-encryption shuffle of the vector. Thus they end up with
   $$\langle \{g^{\pi(1)}\}, \{g^{\pi(2)}\}, \ldots, \{g^{\pi(N)}\} \rangle$$
   for some permutation π of the set $\{1, \ldots, N\}$.
   The participants can be kept honest during this step using, for example, Furukawa and Sako's scheme for proving correctness of a shuffle [3].

3. Derangement test.
   The participants perform a distributed plaintext equality test [6] in which $\{g^{\pi(i)}\}$ is compared to $\{g^i\}$ for $1 \leq i \leq N$. They form the vector
   $$\langle (\{g^{\pi(1)}\}/\{g^1\})^{r_1}, \ldots, (\{g^{\pi(N)}\}/\{g^N\})^{r_N} \rangle,$$
   where $r_1, \ldots, r_N$ are random values all participants privately contribute to. At least one component of this vector is equal to $\{1\}$ if and only if π is not a derangement. If π is not a derangement, go to step 2. Since the number of derangements of an n-element set is equal to the nearest integer to $n!/e$ [11], only a few repetitions of steps 2 and 3 are expected.

4. Revealing $\pi(i)$ to participant i only.
   Let v be the vector $\langle \{g^{\pi(1)}\}, \ldots, \{g^{\pi(N)}\} \rangle$. The i-th component of this vector contains the encrypted assignment for donor i. The vector is noted by all participants. Each participant i generates a random secret number r_i which will serve as a blinding term and publicly announces the encryption $\{g^{r_i}\}$ over an authenticated channel. The participants compute the product $\{g^{\pi(i)}\} \cdot \{g^{r_i}\} = \{g^{\pi(i)} \cdot g^{r_i}\}$ for all i. Then all terms $\{g^{\pi(i)} \cdot g^{r_i}\}$ are decrypted and each participant i recovers $\pi(i)$.
   Note that recovering $\pi(i)$ from $g^{\pi(i)}$ will not be a problem, because all $\pi(i)$ will be numbers from 1 to N, where N is the number of participants in the scheme.

Note further that participants might submit blinding terms which are functions of the encrypted terms $\{g^{\pi(j)}\}$ for $1 \leq j \leq N$ in order to obtain information about other participant's assignments. To prevent this, each participant could be required to encrypt his blinding term using a submission secure augmented cryptosystem [14]. In the present case, the Cramer-Shoup cryptosystem [1] is a suitable choice. This allows the participants to verify that the submitted encrypted blinding terms are correctly formed without decrypting the blinding terms and then continue to use the embedded ElGamal encryption $\{g^{\pi(j)}\}$ as above. To prevent simple replays, the participants also need to verify that all ciphertexts are unique.

5. Presents.

Presents labeled with the recipient's name are put in one of N identical boxes. The boxes are sealed. Before their contents are revealed, the boxes are shuffled by each of the participants while the other participants are waiting outside.

6. Verification.

Verification is necessary if one or more participants have not received a present. If participant j has not received a present, the cheating donor is discovered by a plaintext equality test as in step 3: The participants encrypt g^j, obtaining $\{g^j\}$ and compare it with every entry in the vector v, which was noted in step 4. Thus the vector

$$\langle (\{g^{\pi(1)}\}/\{g^j\})^{r_1}, \ldots, (\{g^{\pi(N)}\}/\{g^j\})^{r_N} \rangle$$

is formed, where $r_1, \ldots, r_N$ are random values all participants have privately contributed to. Since v is a permutation of $\{g^1\}, \ldots, \{g^N\}$, exactly one component will be $\{1\}$. If the i-th component is $\{1\}$, then participant i is declared to be a cheater.

Fully Homomorphic Encryption. If we permit ourselves the use of a *fully homomorphic* encryption algorithm, such as that presented in [4], then we can describe a conceptually simpler derangement test step. We write $\{\!|m|\!\}$ for the fully homomorphic encryption of m and briefly sketch the derangement test step of the protocol. All other steps are performed analogously to the solution based on homomorphic encryption.

For the derangement test, the participants compute $\{\!|\pi(i) - i|\!\}$ using the additive homomorphism. The participants then exploit the multiplicative homomorphism to compute the encryption of the product of the $\{\!|\pi(i) - i|\!\}$ terms:

$$\lambda := \prod_1^N \{\!|\pi(i) - i|\!\}$$

If a plaintext equality test shows that λ is equivalent to $\{\!|0|\!\}$, then we know that there is at least one fixed point and so the permutation is not a derangement. If λ is not an encryption of 0, then we know that the permutation is a derangement but nothing further.

Verifiable Parallel Permutations. If we want to avoid the N plaintext equality tests in the derangement test step of the protocol based on homomorphic encryption, but prefer not to use a fully homomorphic encryption scheme, we can use an approach that exploits verifiable parallel permutations [8,9]. We suppose again that our cryptosystem is ElGamal, where g is the generator of the ElGamal group G. G is an order q subgroup of $\mathbb{Z}_p^*$, for suitable prime numbers p and q, both of which are much larger than the number of participants N.

The solution requires the parallel shuffling of $N + 1$ vectors. The following replaces the steps 1 through 3 of the homomorphic encryption solution described above. We start by constructing publicly the N vectors $w_1, \ldots, w_n$. These vectors contain encryptions of $g^0 = 1$ in all but one component. Each vector w_i contains the encryption of g in its i-th component:

$$w_1 = \langle \{g\}, \{1\}, \{1\}, \ldots, \{1\} \rangle$$
$$w_2 = \langle \{1\}, \{g\}, \{1\}, \ldots, \{1\} \rangle$$
$$\vdots$$
$$w_i = \langle \{1\}, \{1\}, \ldots, \{g\}, \ldots, \{1\} \rangle \qquad (\{g\} \text{ is in } i\text{-th component})$$
$$\vdots$$
$$w_N = \langle \{1\}, \{1\}, \ldots, \{1\}, \{g\} \rangle$$

Now a vector z is created that is the encryption of the values g^1 through g^N:

$$z := \langle \{g^1\}, \{g^2\}, \ldots, \{g^N\} \rangle$$

Consider w_1 through w_N and z as row vectors of an N times $N + 1$ matrix. We now parallel shuffle the columns of this matrix to get the $N + 1$ shuffled row vectors $w_1', \ldots, w_N'$ and z'. We now form the term

$$\lambda := \prod_1^N \{w_{ii}'\},$$

where w_{ii}' denotes the i-th component of the vector w_i'. If, when we decrypt λ we find that it is equal to 1 then z' represents a derangement. This is because an identical shuffle was applied to these $N + 1$ vectors. Suppose that z' does not represent a derangement. Then there exists a component j which is equal to an encryption $\{g^j\}$. By the parallel shuffle, w_{jj}', i.e. the j-th component of w_j', is equal to an encryption $\{g\}$. Since N is much smaller than q, λ cannot be an encryption $\{1\}$.

Thus we have $z' = \langle \{g^{\pi(1)}\}, \ldots, \{g^{\pi(N)}\} \rangle$ for some derangement π and we can continue with step 4 of the homomorphic encryption solution described above.

5   Conclusions

The purpose of this paper was to stress the problem of requirements analysis for security protocols. In order to make a step towards a methodology for the understanding of security protocol problems, we propose to conduct a series of case studies on new problems. We used the Secret Santa problem as an exercise and discussed requirements and some possible solutions. Although we think that we have identified the most interesting requirements they are not demonstrably complete. As indicated, there are several ways in which the set of requirements can be extended and there are different variations of the given requirements. It is also interesting to formalize the requirements and the proposed solutions as a first step towards formal verification. An interesting question is also to design efficient non-probabilistic decentralized solutions. By studying the relation between the TTP-based ideal solution and the decentralised solutions one could achieve a better understanding of the different requirements analysis approaches that we identified.

An interesting approach for identifying new case studies could be found in the distributed algorithms literature, which is rich of problems that in addition to the functional requirements often have a security dimension as well.

References

1. Cramer, R., Shoup, V.: Design and analysis of practical public-key encryption schemes secure against adaptive chosen ciphertext attack. SIAM J. Comput. 33(1), 167–226 (2004)
2. Crépeau, C., Kilian, J.: Discreet solitary games. In: Stinson, D.R. (ed.) CRYPTO 1993. LNCS, vol. 773, pp. 319–330. Springer, Heidelberg (1994)
3. Furukawa, J., Sako, K.: An efficient scheme for proving a shuffle. In: Kilian, J. (ed.) CRYPTO 2001. LNCS, vol. 2139, pp. 368–387. Springer, Heidelberg (2001)
4. Gentry, C.: Fully homomorphic encryption using ideal lattices. In: Proc. 41st Annual ACM Symposium on Theory of Computing (STOC 2009), pp. 169–178. ACM (2009)
5. Heather, J., Schneider, S., Teague, V.: Cryptographic protocols with everyday objects. Formal Aspects of Computing 26(1), 37–62 (2014)
6. Jakobsson, M., Juels, A.: Mix and match: Secure function evaluation via ciphertexts. In: Okamoto, T. (ed.) ASIACRYPT 2000. LNCS, vol. 1976, pp. 162–177. Springer, Heidelberg (2000)
7. Liberti, L., Raimondi, F.: The Secret Santa problem. In: Fleischer, R., Xu, J. (eds.) AAIM 2008. LNCS, vol. 5034, pp. 271–279. Springer, Heidelberg (2008)
8. Andrew Neff, C.: Verifiable mixing (shuffling) of ElGamal pairs (2004)
9. Ramchen, K., Teague, V.: Parallel shuffling and its application to Prêt à Voter. In: Proc. Int. Conf. on Electronic Voting Technology/Workshop on Trustworthy Elections (EVT/WOTE 2010) (2010)
10. Roscoe, A.W.: Intensional specifications of security protocols. In: Proc. 9th IEEE Computer Security Foundations Workshop (CSFW 1996), pp. 28–38. IEEE (1996)
11. Stanley, R.P.: Enumerative combinatorics, vol. 1. Wadsworth Publ. Co., Belmont (1986)

12. Tel, G.: Cryptografie – Beveiliging van de digitale maatschappij. Addison-Wesley (2002)
13. Verelst, J.: Secure computing and distributed solutions to the Secret Santa problem. Master's thesis, Computer Science Dept., University of Utrecht (2003)
14. Wikström, D.: Simplified submission of inputs to protocols. In: Ostrovsky, R., De Prisco, R., Visconti, I. (eds.) SCN 2008. LNCS, vol. 5229, pp. 293–308. Springer, Heidelberg (2008)

Security Protocols for Secret Santa
(Transcript of Discussion)

Sjouke Mauw

University of Luxembourg
SnT and FSTC
6, rue Richard Coudenhove-Kalergi
L-1359, Luxembourg

Designing security protocols is not complicated, unless you insist on making the same mistakes over and over. It depends on what you call designing; once you have the requirements it might be not too hard to make security protocols. But the complications are in finding the right requirements, and that's maybe the biggest question that I want to approach today: what to do with requirements in security protocols. My presentation is divided in two parts. First some general question asking; it's not answers that I will give today. Second I will look at a simple example, the example of Secret Santa. This is joint work with Saša Radomirović and Peter Ryan.

The original motivation of this subject was some feeling about what's happening in the e-voting world. I've been studying this field for two or three years now, and in the beginning I thought, OK, if I read a lot I will understand it, I'll really understand it. And I read a lot, studied it, the more I tried to understand it, the less I understood what requirements e-voting really needs. Maybe it's only my problem, but for example, while trying to verify, to formalise first the properties, if you look at it you see a lot of different interpretations of the same notions, meaning that it's too informal to really understand what's going on. And if you read the recent literature on verifiability, you see that where you started with individual verifiability in that I can verify that my vote has been counted correctly, and doing the personal verifiability means that everybody can look at the outcome themselves and verify that it really was a computation on the input that was provided. Well then came end-to-end verifiability, and recently I saw notions like classical individual verifiability, and constructive individual verifiability. And I somehow lost track of why we need all these developments. What's the process behind this? Is there a process, is this a random walk, or is there something deeper that I don't understand?

Looking at all these experiences it seems there's no methodology starting from sound engineering techniques to come to a set of requirements for a new application. So how come we don't have a methodology for this process?

If you look at some historical developments you see that in many fields there is this evolution of requirements going on. We start with a simple basic essential requirement, and we find it, we formulate it, we add new requirements, and somehow we see the evolution. We see this with e-voting: the evolution from privacy, which is a property that a voter can have, to enforced privacy, which is a property that's enforced upon a voter (he cannot give away his privacy).

B. Christianson and J. Malcolm (Eds.): Security Protocols 2010, LNCS 7061, pp. 185–190, 2014.
© Springer-Verlag Berlin Heidelberg 2014

And you see the intermediate step, so first we develop the receipt freeness, which means that he doesn't have a receipt after elections that he can show to a coercer, then there's some coercion notion introduced, which to my surprise is not a generalisation of receipt freeness, it's just partially overlapping with receipt freeness, but it should have been a generalisation. And then what we could call now enforced privacy, it means no way a voter can give up his privacy. So that's what you could call increasing cooperation of the agents for the adversary. And maybe as a general pattern here that we can have enforced end security property as a pattern put on the enforced authentication, what would that mean, that's unclear.

The second class of drivers for this evolution of requirements is the discrepancy between the real world and the idealised world. So in the idealised world you have this function, and this function should have different properties, and you must ensure that this is satisfied and then this requirement at the security level is satisfied. But in linking it back to the real world you see that there are side channels. For example, you have RFID tags: they are cheap, they can be opened, you can recover a session key, or whatever, and what will be the implications for the security, forward security, backward security, forward traceability, backward traceability, and all new machinery and implications of it, of this physical phenomenon that's coming in. You forget in your idealised world that there are agents living in the real world, that agents may have interactions that are not distinguished in your system, for example, the possibility of coercion. Or in contract signing we've seen ten years ago that apart from timeliness and fairness, suddenly there was the notion of abuse-freeness, meaning that somebody signing a contract can never prove to an outsider that he is in the position of either finishing the contract successfully, or stopping it, since he may have used that in another negotiation with another party, and say, hey look, if you give me better terms, I will do your contract problem, and that kind of thing. And that somehow we need an action between instances of the same protocol that's not foreseen. So this is a second class of drivers in this evolution, and probably you will know a lot more examples than I do, and maybe you can find more classes. And of course the question is, is this work completed, is this a random walk, and if it's a random walk, will it ever end, and will it end in a situation that everybody is happy, and will it always end in the same situation, I don't know. For contract signing for example, we have been quite stable for the last ten years now, I don't know of any additional requirements, do you know one?

Joseph Bonneau: Yes, we don't have balanced protocols.

Reply: Balanced, I missed that. So it seems that even my knowledge of contract signing is too weak to know what's happening. So what would we need to find a complete set of requirements, and of course if you look at the software engineering experience, support software engineering experience, all the main requirements, specification requirements formulation, and of course it's never complete, it's always relative to some users that want to use your system. And maybe what I would hope for is that these small domain security protocols have some specifics that enable us to formulate some guidelines, or patterns, how to proceed with a new requirement.

So you can basically see new ways how you can develop real life requirements. First of all you know that the new problem is similar to something you have solved already, or somebody else has solved, or maybe it's a reformulation of a physical problem like voting; in voting, you have your paper ballots, you have your protocols, and everybody knows what good voting means. And from there you devise your security requirements. Another approach is that rather than looking at what your system should do, you would look at what your system should not do. So you solicit people to fight with your system, to try to abuse it, and by identifying these threats, you specify your requirements, for example, what would be the threat in contract signing, when the signer withholds his signature. And a third approach is not to focus on requirements but to focus on the ideal behaviour of the system, for example, assume we have a trusted third party, assume we have secure, resilient, whatever, channels, what would be the simplest solution that would solve our problem, and that solution we take as the definition of our security requirements. And of course it's not a choice between one of these three, it's always a mix of the lot of them.

And as I said, we are far from formulating methodology, well, that's my opinion at the moment, and rather than trying to formulate a methodology I'd like to conduct a number of case studies trying to find out if there's some kind of pattern recurring in conducting these case studies, and maybe the patterns would help in making steps towards a methodology, but that's maybe wishful thinking. But I see that several other groups in Europe have somehow found this as a target, trying to take new problems, and trying to formulate security requirements, maybe you can reinforce the field through that. So what I want to do in the rest of the presentation is to take just one random case study, which is probably new to most of you, it was new to me when I started, and try to see what steps you can make. But I want to go into full details and see really what's the problem that we need to solve to have happier or better lives.

So what's the problem with Secret Santa? You celebrate by exchanging presents, but you don't want to buy presents for everybody, you want each person to buy only one present in such a way that everybody gets a present. So what you do, you put names on paper in a hat, and everybody picks a random name, hopefully not his own name, and then people buy presents, secretly bring it to the place where the presents are collected, and then, hey, after half an hour or so, somehow there is a box of presents for a lot of people. And of course, if you pick your own name you have to redo the whole process, it's a probabilistic process, large families have big problems with that. And it's a centralised solution, you have to come together to do what you do there.

OK, the first step is to make explicit the security requirements, so let's do it formally, well informally but precise enough to discuss it. So P is the set of participants, we have at least two participants, otherwise you can only give yourself a present, that's not a nice party then. So the point is to find the function f, a permutation of the participants, so that if I am p then I will give the present to the $f(p)$. So f must be a bijection, and it must be irreflexive in order not to give yourself a present. And this is the functional requirement, and now we can discuss the security requirements. So when we find this f is random, meaning that no participants can influence the outcome of this process in a way that isn't random, so I cannot force the process so that, for example, I want to buy a present for q because I have an excellent idea what present to buy, so I want to buy it. It has to be anonymous, so if you get a bad present you dont know who bought your present. But of course you can have conspiring participants, so if you have a group of people, and that's normal, people group together, the children, the family, to find out who gave whom a present, so if a group of people do not learn the outcome of this function f outside this group of people. And finally, if there's the exchange of the presents, and somebody doesn't get a present, he wants to identify the person who did not give the present, and hit him, or something else. So that's what we could call verifiability, or accountability, so if there is a participant, $p' \in P$ who has not received a present, we can identify the cheater p who had function result $f(p) = p'$. And so this is the kind of approach we can discuss. It didn't take long to find variations, so this is a slightly stronger verifiability result.

In the previous example you see that if two people swap the names of the people that they have to buy a present for, it will not be caught by this verifiability property, because it's still the case that everybody gets a present, but you don't get the present from whom you were expecting, from whom the f expected to be given. So this is a bit stronger. If the exchange of presents is verifiable, every cheating participant can be identified, thereby disallowing situations when people swap their strips of paper. You could formulate it in yet another way. So rather than say verifying that something went wrong, you can say, well every participant p can positively prove that he indeed bought a present for $f(p)$, which is the same result but from a different approach. And if you are creative you start asking yourself a question, OK, why not receipt-freeness? Of course in a family with presents it's maybe not a useful concept to do receipt-freeness, but if you want to use this protocol outside the simple domain you will have a lot of different properties, enforced anonymity, or plain fairness. If you give a present there must be a way to receive a present back. Or abuse-freeness, if you are taking part in two of these protocols can you abuse one to force the other one in a certain situation, maybe rather than having these individual properties, maybe have some universal requirements.

So already the discussion on the requirements is rather vague, you don't know when to be absolute, when to balance, and it depends on the situation what you want to use. So of course you should take into account the attacker model where you can have conspiring agents, or you can have honest but curious agents for example. Then you look at possible solutions, solution dimensions, for example, we have the solution with the hat, this is a typical physical solution, you have computer-like solutions, for example, you can get a web service that distributes this function for you in an honest way, trusted third parties, centralised, probabilistic, or not. So I list just a few where this decentralised solution would be the most interesting. This is the standard solution, it's physical, the problem is that it's probabilistic. I've tried to play with ways to make it not probabilistic, it's not easy, so if you want to see what the result of ElGamal, a physical device that helps you to solve the problem of distributing names along the same group, in a non-probabilistic way such that it satisfies the challenge, you have the ideal solution, you have a trusted third party who we can trust to make this function f, which is the derangement[1], and securely distributes the function.

Jonathan Anderson: Can we go back, how does it know to trust the third party with the hat, there has to be somebody who puts the strips of paper in the hat, shuffles it, and sees it?

Reply: My experience is that everybody writes his name on a piece of paper and then puts it in the hat so that everybody sees them do it.

Jonathan Anderson: So what if I write your name on my bit of paper?

Reply: Yes, so it's not verifiable.

Saša Radomirović: You won't get a present.

Joseph Bonneau: That doesn't matter, I still violate your assumptions.

Reply: So this hat solution is theoretical, it's not a real solution.

Joseph Bonneau: Well I guess with no trusted third party then it seems like there is no solution.

Reply: There are solutions where people have a paper, and one person writes all the names, it's verified by everybody, and it's cut into pieces under the eyes of everybody, and then somebody picks them up and puts them in the hat. So that's how you can solve it.

Jonathan Anderson: Well for everybody writing their own name, it's sort of a self enforcing protocol because the penalty for violating the protocol is that you get no present.

Reply: Yes, so if you talk about mechanism designs, even if there are some ways to cheat on this aggregate, everybody wants to increase their value of this aggregate, the mechanism is correct. So we played around with a crypto toolbox, just take random ingredients, homomorphic encryption and see if we can build a solution to that. There is a quite straightforward solution, but it involves a lot of non-trivial cryptography. You start with some kind of homomorphic encryption, then you make a list of all the participants, where participant 1 is the generator to the power of 1, and participant 2 is the generator to the power of 2. etc. You encrypt it with a public key in such way that if you have enough participants working together to decrypt, it will be decrypted, so it's a kind of threshold scheme.

Now every participant in turn will take this list and randomly shuffle it, and does a re-encryption of the list, and gives it to the next participant, and after one round of reshuffling and re-encryption every participant has put some randomness in this permutation, and then we can assume that it's a random permutation. One of the problems is that we have irreflexive lists, so it's not a derangement, if for example participant 1 has to buy a present for himself, so we

---

[1] "a derangement is a permutation of the elements of a set such that none of the elements appear in their original position" — Wikipedia.

have to do our test if it's a good derangement, but that's not too complicated, and if it's not a good derangement, you repeat this stuff until you are, so it's probabilistic. The next step is that you want verifiability, and for verifiability you want people to commit to the name that they will buy a present for, so you do some commitment by adding some personal randomness. Further you want that it's blind, and while decrypting this list in the group, everybody gets his element, and he wants his element to be blinded so that you're the only one can be blinded, well that's two factors that you have to add. So then the elements of the list are decrypted, everybody takes this element from the list. And when you buy your present you take your commitment with you and stick it to the present so that if there is a complaint everybody can use this commitment and check whether you really bought one. So that's the decentralised solution.

Of course this is just a very abstract scheme which you would want to formalise and analyse in a nice way. It's still complex, you may want to find simpler solutions. We have a probabilistic solution. Of course you would prefer a deterministic solution to work here without any problems. And the challenge we already said, can we find a physical solution which is deterministic, like the hat, without the drawing from the hat. The challenge is that this simple Secret Santa problem already explores a lot of the factors that we have in security requirements and specification. And just to get an understanding of what actually are these steps that you need to take to get a reasonable specification, I think we do need to make more studies, for example, we can take the well-known class of distributed algorithms that have standard, conventional properties, like self stabilisation, and try to find out what the security requirements are. Of course, many of these have already been studied in security contexts, but we have more protocols still to explore.

Ross Anderson: I am not entirely sure that one has to do this kind of Diffe-Hellman protocol, can't one do a kind of cut and choose? After all, given realistic assumptions and the realistic size of the participant groups, we might have 20 people in a family, among how many parties do they have to divide the trust? Two parties are enough, then you could have one party generate a million shuffles, and another party selects one, for example, and you can then make that a little bit more complex by, for example, decomposing the permutation such that you have permutations of type A and permutations of type B, such that you can compose any A and any B such that you can get a permutation such that $\phi(x)$ is never equal to x, and that would enable you to split the trust into three. So rather than go the full hog of using public key cryptography, there might be simpler ways to do it.

Reply: Yes, I agree.

Censorship of eBooks
(Extended Abstract)

Michael Roe

Microsoft Research

"In a century when the most dangerous books come into the hands of children as easily as into those of their fathers and their guardians, when reckless systematizing can pass itself off as philosophy, unbelief as strength of mind, and libertinage as imagination ..."
– Donatien Alphonse François de Sade, in *Eugenie de Franval*

Google Book Search has made available online scans of a very large number of out of copyright library books. The move from paper books to online access has the potential to make more books available to more readers than was possible before. But there is a potential downside: a centralized system where Google keeps the only digital copy of the book is potentially much more vulnerable to censorship. If Google decides, for whatever reason, not to make a book available, then readers have few alternative sources. Previously, if one library didn't stock a book then there were plenty of others that a reader could try.

Outline of this paper:

- To show that this is not a purely hypothetical problem, I will describe some recent examples of attempted censorship of eBooks.
- Are the emerging digital libraries highly centralized? What are the likely alternatives if one library doesn't hold the book?
- I will present the results of an experiment where I compare I list of books that have been banned in the past against Google, Project Gutenberg, The Internet Archive and the Bibliothèque nationale. The conclusion is that very few of these formerly controversial books are being censored today.

1   Recent Attempts at Censorship

1.1   Apple and *The Kama Sutra*

Apple controls which software is available for the iPhone. Third party software developers needs to get approval from Apple for their application before it can be made available through the App Store. Apple's tangle with book censorship began when a third party developer wrote an eBook reading program, called *Eucalyptus*, for the iPhone. The program could be used to read any of the eBooks available from Project Gutenberg; at present, there are over 20,000 to choose from. Initially, Apple refused to grant permission for this program on the grounds that people might use it to read one particular book — Richard

B. Christianson and J. Malcolm (Eds.): Security Protocols 2010, LNCS 7061, pp. 191–199, 2014.

Burton's translation of *The Kama Sutra*[1]. (On 24 January 2010 — some time after this incident — *The Kama Sutra* was the 4th most popular download from Project Gutenberg. It is therefore the most popular of the PG titles that are likely to be subject to censorship).

This incident has several interesting features:

– Is is an instance of censorship by a private company, not the government.
– It demonstrates that it is not just book scanning projects such as Google who have the power to censor books. The manufacturers of the devices used to read eBooks have the power of censorship, too.
– The attempt at censorship failed. The customers wouldn't stand for it.
– It illustrates the differing standards applied to books versus other media, such as computer software. Apple's attempted censorship of *The Kama Sutra* caused public protest, leading them to back down. However, they have continued to exercise control over which software can run on the iPhone.

1.2   Amazon and 1984

1.3   Amazon and Gay Literature

1.4   The Internet Watch Foundation and *Girls Scream Aloud*

The Internet Watch Foundation (IWF) operates a hotline to which members of the public can report instances of child sexual abuse images online. After checking that the reported image is in violation of UK law, the IWF's analysts add it to a black list. The black list is then used by many UK Internet Service Providers to prevent their customers gaining access to the blacklisted images. The IWF only provides the blacklist; each ISP has their own blocking technology.

The blocking technology is not specific to images. From a technical point of view, it could just as easily be used to block any Web content, including books. The only thing that stops it being used to ban books is that text-only books are not illegal under UK law, and the IWF has no mandate to add them to the blacklist.

In one incident, a member of the public reported an online story (text-only) to the IWF, who then referred it to the police for possible prosecution. The prosecution was not successful.

1.5   The Internet Archive and FBI Requests for Data

On 26 November 2007, the FBI served a "National Security Letter" on the Internet Archive, asking for details of one of its users. The Internet Archive were required to keep secret the fact that the request had been made; the only reason we know about it is that The Internet Archive, assisted by lawyers provided by the Electronic Frontier Foundation, were able to successfully challenge the request.

This is not an instance of censorship directly. But it shows that there is a real risk of the government monitoring which books people read online (and hence, that people may be intimidated into not downloading controversial works).

2   How Centralized is the Digital Library System?

The proposed settlement of a lawsuit against Google (The Authors Guild Inc., Association of American Publishers, Inc. et al. v. Google Inc.) would place Google in the unique position of being able to put online "orphan works" — books which are still in copyright but for which the copyright holder has not informed Google that they wish to opt out. None of Google's competitors (e.g. The Internet Archive or Project Gutenberg) have the advantage of this legal protection, and so they will not be able to act as alternative source for these orphaned works. The system is therefore extremely centralised and vulnerable to censorship — if Google doesn't make the book available, readers won't be able to get it elsewhere. (Of course, the copyright holder can still reprint the book. But "orphaned works" are expected to be those for which the original author or publisher has died, gone out of business etc., and so they mostly won't be available from the rights holder either).

For books for which the copyright has expired (rather than just being "orphaned") there are several competitors to Google, including Project Gutenberg and The Internet Archive. Furthermore, Project Gutenberg's eTexts are copied, reformatted and republished by a number of other organizations, including Feedbooks. Project Gutenberg's collection has also been issued on DVD ROM, and there are copies of this DVD available in many places. It would therefore be very hard for Project Gutenberg to suppress a book after they had put it on their web site — copies of the book would exist in too many other places. The last opportunity for them to suppress a book would be when they take the decision to upload the book. To the best of my knowledge, they have never done this, although of course they make sure that books are out of copyright before uploading them.

However, Google is the only one running a large-scale scanning operation. The Internet Archive was obtaining scans from Microsoft as well as Google, but Microsoft's scanning project is no longer in operation. Project Gutenberg gets most of its books from Distributed Proofreaders, who do some of their own scanning but mostly rely on scans from Google and The Internet Archive. The Boston Public Library's "Scan on Demand" service has also ceased operation. The result is that almost everything comes directly or indirectly from Google.

If Google were to suppress just a few well-known works, these would almost certainly be scanned by one of its competitors (e.g. Distributed Proofreaders). However, it is more doubtful that anyone has the scanning capability to to fill the gap if Google were to refuse to scan some large class of books.

Lastly, Google's ability to censor is enhanced because they also provide one of the most popular search engines. If a book isn't available through Google Book Search, a reader might well check to see if it's available from any of the other online sources by *performing a Google search.*

3   Experiment I

For this experiment, I took a list of books that had been the subject of censorship in the past, and compared it against the catalogues of three major sources of eBooks.

Method

The list was taken from Anne Haight's "Banned Books 387 B.C. to 1978 A.D." [3]. Other sources that could have been used instead include Charles Ripley Gillett's *Burned Books: Neglected chapters in British history and literature*[2].

I removed from the list any titles that were published after 1923, on the grounds that these will probably not be available online for copyright reasons. (In the U.S., books published before 1923 are out of copyright. Other countries have different copyright terms: for example, in EU countries copyright expires 70 years after the death of the author. This difference in copyright regimes can be seen in the choice of books the Bibliothèque nationale has put online). I also removed from the list titles that were newspapers, rather than books, and references that were more vague than a specific book (e.g. to an author's complete works).

It is worth noting that Anne Haight's list is strongly biased towards books in English (with some French titles). This may well matter — the current level of censorship might be very different for books in Chinese, for example.

This list was then compared against the holdings of several digital libraries:

- Project Gutenberg. Project Gutenberg's books are all contributed by volunteers, so it holds whatever books the volunteers feel like working on and PG's legal department confirms are out of copyright in the U.S. Project Gutenberg is heavily biased towards titles in English, with French being the second most popular language (26013 versus 1549 books, as of 24 January 2010).
- Google Book Search. Google's online collection was built by scanning the holdings of a number of libraries, most of which are in the U.S. (e.g. Harvard) with a few from Europe (e.g. the Bodleian library). As a result, Google's collection is strongly biased towards English-language titles published in the U.S. In the absence of censorship, we could expect it to contain the English-language titles from Anne Haight's list, but possibly not all the French ones.
- The Internet Archive. The Internet Archive holds copies of books that were scanned for Google Book Search; books that were scanned as part of a Microsoft project; and books that were OCR'd for Project Gutenberg.

For most of these sources, it was sufficient to check whether the book appeared in their catalogue. However, Google Book Search presented special problems:

- The books that are accessible through Google Book Search depend on which country you are in. Google takes your IP address, uses it to estimate which country you are in, and restricts your access to books accordingly. The main reason for this is the differences in copyright law between countries. While Project Gutenberg and others have taken the view that the applicable law is that of the country where their servers reside (i.e., the United States), Google tries to also comply with the copyright law of the reader's current location. Clearly, this could also be used for country-specific censorship: banning books in some countries and not others.

- Google Book Search can present a book in either "full view" or "snippet view". In snippet view, only part of the book is visible to the reader. Again, the justification for this is copyright law, under a theory that the law allows them to show a snippet view of books that are still in copyright. This could also be used for censorship: if they wished to suppress a book they had scanned, they could choose to restrict it to snippet view even when full view was legally permitted.
- These experiments were performed from the UK, which has a "life+70" copyright regime. Google doesn't actually find out when the author of the book died, but instead takes a very conservative view on what they make available in "life+70" countries. This means that several of the titles we wanted to check would not be visible from the UK.
- Google Book Search takes steps to discourage queries that are automatically generated by a computer, as opposed to being typed in by a human being. e.g. limiting the rate at which it will respond to queries; occasionally making users solve a CAPTCHA (a puzzle that is easy for humans, but hard for computers).

To overcome this problems, I used the Tor anonymizer to access Google Book Search. Tor is intended for anonymous web browsing (and, to some extent, for avoiding censorship). I used Tor to make Google think I was in a different country from my true location. By default, Tor will choose an "exit node" at random, meaning that the user will appear to be in a randomly-chosen country, but it is possible to use Tor in such a way that you appear to be in a country whose censorship status you wish to test.

The disadvantage of using Tor is that Google's defenses against automated queries were triggered more often. From Google's perspective, my queries and those of other Tor users appeared to originate from the same computer; this is how Tor provides anonymity. It however has the disadvantage that if any other Tor users sharing an exit node with me triggered Google's defenses, I was affected too.

Results

For works published in English after 1700, nearly everything was available online. The few exceptions were as follows:

- Sanger, Margaret. *Family Limitation.*
  This pamphlet provides information about contraception, and (in some editions) includes instructions for performing an abortion.

– Moore, George. *Flowers of Passion*. London: Provost, 1878.

In the nineteenth century, Mudie's circulating library refused to carry George Moore's *A Modern Lover*, because "two ladies from the country" had complained about a scene in the novel where the artist protagonist paints a picture of a nude model. At the time, most readers borrowed books from libraries rather than buying them, and so this had a major effect on distribution of the novel. George Moore complained about this censorship in a pamphlet entitled *Literature at nurse; or, Circulating morals*[4], arguing (among other things) that Mudie's should not censor books in this way because it had a monopoly. Moore attempted to bypass the library system by publishing his later works in cheap single-volume editions, rather than the more expensive three-volume editions preferred by the libraries.

In some ways, current concerns over censorship mirror those of the nineteenth century, with Amazon and Google in place of Mudie's and W H Smith's. It is therefore somewhat ironic that *Flowers of Passion*, a collection of George Moore's poems, should be one of the very few formerly controversial works that has not been scanned by Google.

– Warren, Mortimer A. *Almost Fourteen*.

This is a sex education book for teenagers. Google has scans of the second edition, which omits the material that was controversial in the first edition.

– Burton, Sir Richard Francis. *First Footsteps in East Africa*. London: Longman, Brown, Green and Longmans, 1856.

Appendix IV of this book was written in Latin, to reduce the risk of offending the reader. However, the publisher decided that this was not sufficient, and removed Appendix IV from most — but not all — copies of the book. The Project Gutenberg eText was OCR'd from scans provided by the Bibliothèque nationale, which were of a copy that was missing Appendix IV. The result is that the censored text is not available from any of three sources tested in this experiment (though at least some of it is available elsewhere on the Internet).

– *Venus in the Cloister*. London: Edmund Curll, 1724.

This is a work of fiction about a nun. It is mainly famous for being the subject of the first prosecution for obscenity under English law. As such, at one time it might have been considered the definitive example of an "illegal book". English law has changed since then, and this book is now available in paper form from a reputable academic publisher. However, it is still not available online from any of the sources we tested.

– Harbin, George. *The Hereditary Right of the Crown of England Asserted*. London: Richard Smith, 1713.

In this book, George Harbin argued that to be King of England, it is not sufficient to have *de facto* political power: the title must be legitimately inherited. In the "Glorious Revolution"[5] of 1688, James II had been overthrown by William of Orange. In 1701, parliament had passed the *Act of Settlement*, granting the throne to the protestant descendants of Sophia of Hanover. In 1714, her son ascended to the throne as George I. It is therefore easy to see why Harbin's book was controversial. Some of the issues (such the prohibition on the monarch being a Catholic) remain controversial to this day.

Coverage was less good for books before 1700, with 4 out of 11 seventeenth-century English works not available. Coverage was also poor for languages other than English. For example, the only Swedish work on the list (Peter Forsskal's *Tankar om borgerliga friheten* (Notes on Civil Liberty)) was not available.

4   Experiment II

Method

I took the titles from Anne Haight's book that were available via Project Gutenberg, and used Planet Lab to download them from a number of different countries. These downloads were performed automatically, by a computer program that computed an MD5 hash of the downloaded text and checked that it matched the expected value.

I encountered two problems with this experiment:

- Project Gutenberg's web server will sometimes close connection part-way through a download, leaving the user with an incomplete book. When this happens, the MD5 hash of the download will not match the expected value. I made this less likely to happen by reducing the rate at which my program downloaded books (which should be done anyway, to avoid overloading the PG web server), and had my program retry the download if the hash did not match the first time.
- Project Gutenberg occasionally updates their eBooks. During this experiment, *The Writings of Thomas Paine* and Henrik Ibsen's *Ghosts* were both updated. When this happens, the MD5 hash of the downloaded book doesn't match the expected value and retrying the download doesn't help. This can only be distinguished from genuine censorship by looking at the text of the book to see what has been changed.

Results

All of the Project Gutenberg eBooks were down-loadable from every location that was tested. We saw no evidence of Project Gutenberg selectively making books available, or of national firewalls restricting access to Project Gutenberg.

5   Experiment III

The French-language titles on Anne Haight's list were compared against the books that have been scanned by the Bibliothèque nationale for its online service, known as Gallica.

Results

The Bibliothèque nationale had scanned most of the French-language titles. The most notable omissions were some of the works of the Marquis de Sade.

- The story *Eugenie de Franval* is contained within some editions of *Les crimes de l'amour*, but not the edition that was scanned by the Bibliothèque nationale and then OCR'd for Project Gutenberg.

6   Experiment IV

The English-language titles from Anne Haight's list were downloaded from Google, using Tor to make the user appear to be in different countries.

Results

A dozen books on the list were accessible from the U.S., but not the U.K. This is consistent with Google not looking up the author's date of death, and instead blocking access from "life+70" countries to all books whose authors *could* have still been alive 70 years ago.

The one unexpected result was for a book that wasn't on Anne Haight's list, but shared a title with one that was (causing it to be accidentally included in an early version of this experiment): John Marston's *Histrio-Mastix*. This was published anonymously in 1610, and photographically reprinted (with a new introduction) in 1912. This ought to be out of copyright in the U.S., but (for unexplained reasons) Google only makes it available in snippet view.

7   Observations

7.1   Edition

It is important to check which edition of a book is available. In some cases, the edition that has been put online is one that omits the controversial material. An example is Mortimer Warren's *Almost Fourteen*; Google has the second edition, while omits much material that was contained in the first. The Project Gutenberg edition of de Sade's *Les crimes de l'amour* is based on the Bibliothèque nationale's scans, and both omit the story *Eugenie de Franval*. Releasing an edited edition may be a more effective form of censorship than suppressing the book entirely: readers might not seek a fuller edition elsewhere.

7.2   Language

It is also important to check which language the edition is in. A translation of a book reaches a new audience, and may attract the attention of censors who were not bothered by the original. The most obvious examples are the translations of the bible, but in Anne Haight's list we also see Vladimir Simkhovitch's *Marxism versus Socialism* (controversial when translated into Russian) and Gustave Flaubert's *Novembre* (controversial when translated into English).

7.3   Age of the Book

Out of copyright works may be less vulnerable to censorship because they are older. They are less likely to be subject to legal action for libel, because anyone mentioned in them is likely to be dead. Political issues that were controversial at the time of publication may be long settled by the time the copyright expires. (However, some political issues can be long lived. For example, the Indonesian War of Independence in 1945-49 took place many years after the publication of Multatuli's classic anti-imperialist novel, *Max Havelaar*). Newer books — such as the "orphaned works" in Google Book Search, or in-copyright books sold by Amazon for the Kindle reader — might be more subject to censorship than the pre-1923 titles examined in this paper.

8   Conclusions

There are several parties who have the technical means to censor online books. These include the manufacturers of equipment used to read eBooks (e.g. Apple's iPhone), Internet Service Providers (using a blacklist provided by the Internet Watch Foundation), book retailers such as Amazon and digital libraries such as Google Book Search.

However, nearly all of the historically controversial books I tested were readily available online. The current extent of censorship appears to be minimal, at least for pre-1923 books in English and French.

References

1. Burton, R.: The Kama Sutra of Vatsyayana. Kama Shastra Society (1883), Reprinted as Project Gutenberg eText 27827
2. Gillett, C.R.: Burned Books: Neglected chapters in British History and Literature. Columbia University Press (1932)
3. Haight, A., Haight, G.: Banned Books 387 B.C. To 1978 A.D. R. R. Bowker (1978)
4. Moore, G.: Literature at nurse, or Circulating morals. Vizetelly and Co. (1885)
5. House of Commons Information Office. The Glorious Revolution. Factsheet G4 (2009)

Censorship of eBooks
(Transcript of Discussion)

Michael Roe

University of Hertfordshire

The problem: paper books are being replaced by electronic versions, in quite a widespread way. Various companies have brought out eBook readers: there's the Amazon Kindle reader, the Sony reader, the Apple iPad can be used as an eBook reader as well. There are lots of hardware devices out there that people use for reading books. As for library books, Google is scanning a very large number of library books, and putting the scans online. Libraries have obviously become very tempted to get rid of all these nasty, expensive to store paper books, and just use Google. The question is: does this big move from paper to electronic form make censorship easier or will it make it harder?

The first thing to look at is the move to a very centralised system. Microsoft did have a rival scanning project, but sadly that project was discontinued. Boston Public Library also had their own scan on demand service, but they stopped. So basically the only one doing large-scale scanning is Google. Project Gutenberg are a potential rival to Google, but they get most of their eBooks from Distributed Proofreaders, who in turn get most of their scans from Google. The end result is that nearly everything comes via Google one way or another. And if that wasn't bad enough, one of the proposals for a legal settlement over the current copyright situation, would give Google a monopoly on orphan works, that is books for which the copyright has not actually expired, but for which there is no copyright holder still alive and able to say to Google, I don't want you to put my work on line. It could become very, very centralised to Google.

And what's the risk of centralisation? Well, the risk of centralisation is if the organisation doing the scanning doesn't like a book for one reason or another, then it doesn't get put online. This could be done in a deniable way. If you look at Google Book Search you will see that it's a common error for guy doing the scanning to turn over two pages at once. It would be very easy and almost undetectable if in a book where there was a page that said something controversial, they guy would just turn the page and not scan it. Nobody would be able to tell it wasn't an accident.

Bruce Christianson: How do people respond to the "you've missed a bit" assertions, do they go back and photocopy the missing page?

Reply: In the early days they did, but they seem to have stopped doing that. There are now too many books for them to do that, but certainly in the first stage of their book scanning project they would respond.

Bruce Christianson: But now it's gone forever.

Reply: So the good news is that past the scanning stage, distribution isn't centralised at all. Once Project Gutenberg has put stuff online it gets reformatted and redistributed by lots of different people: for example there's Feedbooks and Multi-

B. Christianson and J. Malcolm (Eds.): Security Protocols 2010, LNCS 7061, pp. 200–206, 2014.
© Springer-Verlag Berlin Heidelberg 2014

books. Lots of people take Project Gutenberg eBooks and convert them into some easy to read form. Project Gutenberg also burns its collection to DVDs, and the DVDs are in libraries, schools, etc. So once a book has been posted in digital form on the Internet, it becomes very hard to take it back. The vulnerable point where somebody has an opportunity to censor something is at the scanning stage.

Is this the kind of thing only security people worry about, or is it a real risk? The first indication that there might be a real risk was with Apple and *The Kama Sutra*. There was an application written for the iPhone called Eucalyptus that let people read Project Gutenberg eBooks, and initially Apple refused to let this program be run on the iPhone, on the grounds that of all the tens of thousands of books that were on Project Gutenberg, there was one particular book they didn't want people to be able read on the Apple iPhone, and that was Sir Richard Burton's translation of *The Kama Sutra*. One thing about this: it was censorship by a commercial entity, not government. It wasn't the US government demanding *The Kama Sutra* be banned, it was a private company that decided that some of their customers would not like this.

James Malcolm: Mike, how did they even think of this requirement?

Reply: If you look at the list of most popular downloads, *The Kama Sutra* is about number 4. So one could imagine the guys at Apple going, OK, what is this application, looking at the list of top books, and finding *The Kama Sutra*. If it had been number 11 on the most popular list, they might have missed it.

Malte Schwarzkopf: Did they give any justification or did they just say, we don't like this?

Reply: I think they referred the program's author to their policy for iPhone apps. An interesting thing here is the difference in our attitude towards printed books versus computer games. Although Apple backed down on censorship of books, there are still controls on sexually explicit computer games.

Bruce Christianson: Amazon just don't want you to read *1984*.

Reply: Yes, so the next thing that should worry you is *1984*. George Orwell died in 1950, which means in countries where copyright expires 50 years after the death of the author (like Canada), his works are out of copyright and anybody can reprint *1984*. But in countries like the UK or in the US, *1984* is still in copyright and you can't do this. A third party publisher made a mistake, and made *1984* available through Amazon on the Kindle in countries where it wasn't out of copyright. But when Amazon realised this mistake had been made, they just caused the book to disappear — even from the readers of people who had already bought it. And of all the books in all the world you could have had this happen to, this is just about the most ironic one. There you are, reading about a fictional dystopia in which paper books have been replaced by screens and the Ministry of Truth makes books vanish, and the next thing you know, the telescreen on which you have been reading *1984* tells you that there is no such book, that it doesn't exist.

That was about copyright, and the differences in different countries' copyright laws (which is a very interesting subject), but exactly the same thing could have happened if some government had come along to Amazon and said, withdraw this book from people who already have it.

And the fourth thing was also to do with Amazon. Lesbian and gay literature at one point vanished from their search facility. Although you could still buy the book, it wouldn't show up in a search. This was allegedly due to an error, which was corrected after a customer complaint, but it shows another way in which censorship can be applied. Rather than outrightly suppressing a book, you can suppress the catalogue information so that people who might be interested in reading it don't know it exists, or can't get to it.

Joseph Bonneau: Does Amazon do business in countries where gay literature would be illegal? I mean, they're forced to deal with some requirements like not selling *Mein Kampf* in Germany.

Reply: The concern here was that they went beyond that, and blocked the search for everyone.

Joseph Bonneau: Well the question was whether the mistake would be that the laws for access from Syria accidentally got propagated to the whole website.

Reply: Not being an Amazon insider I don't strictly know, but looking at it I think not. The error looks more like a difference of understanding between the people classifying books and the people implementing the censorship filter over what a particular classification label meant: gay pornography versus non-pornographic works about gay rights, or written by authors who were known to be gay, etc.

Joseph Bonneau: So is the policy for pornographic books in the west that they are for sale but they're not in search results?

Reply: I think so.

So we wanted to do some experiments and see what the current state of censorship is. The list I took for this was from a book by Anne Haight called *Banned Books*, which researched the history of censorship up until the 1970s. There are several other sources I could have chosen, and they would all have given a roughly similar set of books. I took this list and compared it against Google Book Search, The Internet Archive and Project Gutenberg. The conclusion is, if it was published in English after 1700, the chances are you can get it. Basically you can get everything, and there's almost nothing that's been censored. There's less coverage for languages other than English, but that's not because there's more censorship for other languages, it's because these sources have fewer books of any kind in other languages.

The limitation for this experiment is that I'm checking an English language list of banned books against libraries that have mostly English language titles, so this tells you nothing about censorship of eBooks in Chinese.

There's a very small set of books from that list (that were published in English, after about 1700) that Google hasn't scanned. Firstly: George Harbin's *The Hereditary Right of the Crown of England*. In only a half an hour talk I don't have time to explain the English Civil War and the Act of Settlement of 1701, but basically the reason why this book might be controversial is its implication that the king's accession to the throne wasn't legitimate, and the other guy is the rightful king. Which, you know, might cause some people to be upset.

The next one historically was *Venus in the Cloister*. It's a work of fiction about a nun, and it's chiefly famous because it is the first book to be prosecuted for obscenity under English law, and so clearly it's of historical importance.

In Sir Richard Burton's *First Footsteps in East Africa*, there's an appendix which he wrote in Latin, in order not to offend the reader. At the last minute his publisher decided that even putting it in Latin wasn't sufficient to protect the Victorian reading public, and tore out those pages from most copies of the book, but not all copies. It so happens that the copy that was scanned by the Bibliothèque Nationale, and OCR'd for Project Gutenberg, and hence the one everybody is using, is one of the copies of the books from which the pages were torn out. If they had done a bit more searching for a different copy of the book they could have got that missing appendix.

Then there is George Moore's *Flowers of Passion*. Now George Moore was also a big campaigner against censorship by the libraries in the 19th century. Again, this is not about government censorship, this is about commercial censorship. Most people borrowed books from libraries rather than buying them, and so WH Smith's and Mudie's had a monopoly on the library market and could decide what could be stocked by libraries. George Moore wrote pamphlets complaining against this, and saying they shouldn't do this because they are a monopoly. So it's really just like the Google situation, only in the 19th century. And the irony of this is that his book of poems is one of the few books that Google didn't scan.

I rather doubt that Google has any objection to any of those books. I don't think there's anything in them that would cause Google to suppress them, I think it's purely the after effect of previous censorship: because these books were censored in the past, the libraries don't have them, so when Google scans books from libraries it doesn't encounter them.

The second observation is, if you're creating a censorship scanner the book's language matters. It's not enough to check that the library has the book in its original language or in some language, you have to check that it's available in the language that is sensitive. For example, the Bible. Historically a lot of people have got themselves into trouble by publishing translations of the Bible into the vernacular.

The edition sometimes matters. You often see the cases where the first edition said something controversial that was dropped from later editions, so it's censorship if your library only has the second censored edition and doesn't have the original. And sometimes even the copy matters, of which the classic example is the Richard Burton book I described earlier. If most copies of the book have had pages torn out–the offensive bits–then it matters that your library has a copy that's got all the pages.

In the second experiment, we used Planet Lab to download all of these previously controversial books from many countries around the world, computed the MD5 hash on what we got and checked to see if the hash matched. When we tried to do this, we discovered that Project Gutenberg will sometimes close the connection halfway through a download, particularly if you're downloading lots of stuff quickly. And of course if this happens the MD5 hash won't match, because you're missing the end of the input. So you need to do some kind of exponential back-off, and regulate how fast you put in requests — which you need to do anyway because otherwise you're doing a denial of service attack on Project Gutenberg's servers.

The second problem was that Project Gutenberg occasionally changes the book. People report typos and other errata, and occasionally the errata get applied to the online text, and the online text is updated to a more recent standard.

So while I was doing this experiment they revised the works of Thomas Paine, and so the hash of the download didn't match — Thomas Paine was no longer saying the same thing this week as he was saying last week, even though he's been dead for a considerable length of time.

And it's only when you look at the changes that you realise that this is not due to censorship, but just to do with errata being corrected. This shows that if you're writing a program to automatically check censorship it's going to be harder than you might think, because even in the normal case where there's no censorship, books are changing quite often.

And as I expected, none of these formerly controversial books were blocked anywhere. Everywhere we checked, we could download everything.

The last experiment was to take the French works from Anne Haight's list and compare them to the Bibliothèque Nationale, which has their own scanning project. And they had nearly everything, apart from some things by the Marquis de Sade, who was a fairly well-known and important figure in French literature.

Bruce Christianson: He was a bit of a political hot potato as well.

Reply: Yes, but that's not why he's sensitive now. At one point when I was checking, they had online the political pamphlet *Frenchmen, another effort if you would be republicans* from the middle of *Philosophy in the Boudoir*, but not the preceding pornographic introduction. It's an example of what we care about changing over time.

Although we might be worried about online censorship, as far as I can tell, nobody is blocking access to Project Gutenberg, and Project Gutenberg will put anything online.

A limitation of this is that I'm only looking at English language books before 1923, because they're out of copyright. It could well be that censorship is happening more in other languages, in countries that haven't yet given up on censorship. Also, works after 1923 are more likely to be sensitive. For example, libel. Books before 1923 are unlikely to be libellous because anybody who is defamed in them is likely dead and no longer able to sue for libel. A book from the 19th century is less likely to still to be controversial for political reasons, although doing this I realised that some of the issues can run for an extraordinary long time. George Harbin was back in 17 something or other, but people are still writing letters to the newspapers about the legal rule that says a Catholic can't be king.

Ross Anderson: Perhaps ten years ago we had the first judgement — there's a note I believe on my website — that compelled The Guardian to change it's online archive in order to modify an article that was deemed to be libellous, and this is something Google was warned about. It's an interesting question as to whether, once the claimant dies, The Guardian will be prepared to restore it's archives to a complete condition. It might actually be worthwhile writing to them and posing the question.

Reply: There's at least one title in Anne Haight's list that is a newspaper article rather than a book. I didn't include it in this experiment because Google's book scanning project doesn't cover newspapers, but as a separate experiment I looked to see if it was actually online in the British Library's newspaper scanning project. It was, so newspaper articles from the 19th century that were the subjects of successful libel suits are available on line now, because the British Library has a print copy, and has scanned it and made it available now, now that the person's dead. But you're right, this may not happen from electronic works, because now the master copy is being censored as well.

Ross Anderson: And I've no idea what the legal position on this is.

Paul Wernick: I think there was a case just recently in front of the European Court, against The Times, and it was accepted that if you libel somebody in the paper, and it's been accepted, it's gone through the courts that you've defamed them, every time somebody reads the archive which still shows the defamation, without a note saying, by the way we had to retract this one. it's a new defamation.

Ross Anderson: But that shouldn't be an issue, because the right way of doing this, to my way of thinking, would be that the archive contains the defamatory article, plus a note at the end of it saying, this was found to be defamatory, and the link to the High Court judgement and to the later apology.

Paul Wernick: In the States it's only the first time it's published that you can sue. In Europe, now every time somebody reads that webpage it's a new instance of defamation, unless you put in the note you suggested.

Paul Wernick: But that will change the record.

Another experiment we could do — but haven't tried yet — is monitoring Google, because we know that Google is conservative about copyright law. In countries where the copyright expires seventy years after the death of an author, it is actually quite hard to know whether the book is out of copyright or not, because you don't have the actual date when the author died. So we know Google is conservative on what they make available, and the question is, how conservative are they being, and are there any anomalies? Are there any books that, given the rules they seem to be applying, ought to be available online, but mysteriously are not. We want to extend these scanning techniques to Google, as the next step.

One case that I haven't been able to test yet is where there are multiple translations of a book, so there are several editions with the same author and the same title, and some of them are in copyright and some aren't. If somebody was to do a new translation of Virgil, for example, they'll get a new copyright on that translation, and the database will say author Virgil and title *The Aeneid.* The question is, are Google and such like being over-restrictive with what they put online by withdrawing all the old out of copyright versions that match on author and title.

Joseph Bonneau: It would be interesting to look at where Google has a choice of which version of something to put on line, because you mentioned for a lot of books there's multiple editions, and it seems like their goal isn't to always have every single edition ever online. I mean, they essentially pick some representative edition.

Reply: Their approach seems to be that they just take everything off the library shelf and put it through the scanner.

Joseph Bonneau: It might be interesting to think about if you were Google how you would do censorship in a way that was harder to detect. They periodically make changes anyway to fix errors, so if you're scanning and trying to detect censorship, you have a lot of changes that you have to process. Maybe they can intentionally insert extra changes into the system just to frustrate that.

Sandy Clark: The scanning technology still has a lot of errors, so when you discover something was mis-scanned, you can't tell whether it was deliberately removed or if it was just an error.

Joseph Bonneau: Wikipedia has a pretty good system in place that if things get changed, they run it instantly by a human, and they delete the garbage pretty fast. I mean, if you were constantly scanning and finding all the changes you could feed them to a team of volunteer censorship detectors.

Paul Wernick: You're worrying about a conspiracy that isn't there yet, and not the conspiracy that is there, which is Google claiming rights over orphaned works.

Sandy Clark: What happens if the technology changes and we can't read these electronic documents anymore, and we get rid of all of the paper?

Reply: Project Gutenberg are very, very concerned about that, which is partly why their standard is still 80 column text, so that you can read it on the terminals that we had 30 years ago, because they're very reluctant to move to some new format that might go away again in a couple of years. There's a certain amount of sense in only using formats that have been around for long enough that we can be sure that they're going to be with us for a long time.

Paulo Verissimo: It strikes me that, the current situation where Google is retaining an enormous capacity of, let's call it, recopying stuff, and society is letting it do it, this principle that, why should I keep gigabytes of local copies that I can get there, is a little bit similar to the situation of the early middle ages where the copyist monks would be the only guys writing stuff. And, as you know, they rewrote classics, they mutilated at their own will, and we only later could find out about that by retrieving copies.

On the Value of Hybrid Security Testing

Saad Aloteibi and Frank Stajano

Computer Laboratory
University of Cambridge
{firstname.lastname}@cl.cam.ac.uk

Abstract. We propose a framework for designing a security tool that can take advantages from current approaches while increasing precision, scalability and debuggability. This could enable software developers to conduct comprehensive security testing automatically. The approaches we utilise are static, dynamic and taint analysis along with fuzzing. The rationale behind this is that the complexity of today's applications makes the discovery of their vulnerabilities difficult using a single approach. Therefore, a combination of them is what is needed to move towards efficient security checking.

1 Introduction

It is well known that ensuring the security of an application usually escapes software producers' task list during development [1]. Increasing complexity, agile approaches, marketing pressure [2] and other factors could all explain why security is not initially considered. After all, discovering a security vulnerability in an already shipped product can also be economically expensive for vendors either in terms of the cost of patching a single vulnerability, as in Microsoft cases [3], or it could negatively affect their market value when such vulnerabilities become public [2]. Hence, discovering application vulnerabilities is surely of interest to both security researchers and developers but the difference is on their priorities. Whilst, security researchers would like to put the code under their microscope and examine it precisely after having modelled the threats associated with their application, developers would not support this for obvious business reasons and appear willing to sacrifice soundness. Unfortunately, current security testing tools do not accommodate such conflicting priorities in an efficient manner. In this paper, we propose a framework for an automated testing tool that takes into consideration the business needs of software houses while preserving a conservative view. This is done by blending the strengths of current testing approaches and debugging techniques as well as carefully organising this combination to maximise the benefits.

2 Current Approaches

2.1 Static Analysis

Static analysis tools emulate the complier principles to scan the source code for possible anomalies. Techniques include simple search functionality [4], syntactical

B. Christianson and J. Malcolm (Eds.): Security Protocols 2010, LNCS 7061, pp. 207–213, 2014.

examination [5, 6] and abstract interpretation [7]. However, all of these suffer from the trade- off between relaxing the tool so that complex software can be analysed while accepting a huge number of false alarms or conducting deeper analysis, which may come at the price of scalability. For example, Flawfinder[1] [5] incorporates about 160 rule-sets of potential vulnerabilities that include buffer overflows, format string problems, race conditions and others. Code is then matched against these rules, and hits are reported to the user in a ranked order. Applying Flawfinder to complex software as Open Office resulted in 13,090 warnings. Scanning through these would require a considerable amount of man hours, not to mention the high volume of false positives. Nevertheless, the static analysis approach has the advantage of covering the whole code without the need for executing the program, which gives it an advantage over other methods [8].

2.2   Dynamic Analysis

The idea here is to monitor the program behaviour during executions so that precise judgments about the existence of a problem can be made. An example of this is program profiling, where the control flow paths of different test cases are analysed in order to identify codes that may need to be optimised to increase performance or may have latent problems [9]. Although this provides precise results compared with static analysis, it is thought to be inefficient in providing a high level of assurance for two reasons. Firstly, it depends on the test case that the program will run. So, generalisation about the analysis results cannot be made since the monitored behaviour would only apply for this specific test case and not for every possible run as in static analysis. Secondly, examining the behaviour of the program when executing typical input files is not enough on its own since vulnerabilities are usually triggered by coordinating changes that are difficult to produce using this approach.

2.3   Fuzzing

Conceptually, fuzzing can be regarded as a form of dynamic analysis. The main principle here is to provide unexpected inputs to the program and monitor its behaviour for the sake of catching bugs [10]. These inputs could be generated randomly[2] or based on grammatical rules that govern the inputs [11]. Interestingly, fuzzing has proved to be effective in revealing vulnerabilities and is being deployed as a component of the development process, as in Microsoft Security Development Life-cycle [12], and also by hacker communities [13]. However, it also inherits the problems of dynamic analysis since code coverage is not guaranteed and because it is highly dependent on the test case provided. Furthermore, fuzzing would be more effective if it were actually directed towards possible attack points which may have unhandled exceptions. Fuzzing alone cannot achieve this and would need to be made smarter by other means.

---

[1] We used version 1.27.

[2] This could be done by taking a valid input file and randomly change bytes on it.

3   Hybrid Security Testing Architecture

If we examine software vulnerability reports, we will find that the majority of them are triggered by maliciously crafted inputs. This root cause raises two questions:

- What is the input that triggers the problem?
- What is the instruction that executes the attack?

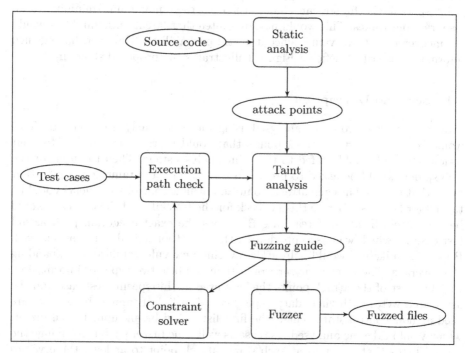

Fig. 1. Hybrid security testing architecture. The fuzzing guide includes flow information, vulnerable instructions and the tainted file.

Neither one of the aforementioned approaches can answer these questions if performed alone. Static analysis might be a good candidate for the second question but would be poor at the first. Dynamic analysis and fuzzing may provide an error-revealing input but it would be the developer's task to identify the cause of the flaw, which may not be trivial. In our framework, we aim to provide an answer to both questions. Initially, we concentrate on identifying codes that may cause a security breach, even with negligible probability. This is done statically by reasoning over the whole source code. We do not aim for precision here since each warning would automatically be checked at later stages to assess its severity, so we would accept a high rate of false positives and aim to keep the volume of false negatives low. Achieving the former goal would require three elements. Firstly, a test case that exercises the suspected code[3] would need to be provided. Secondly, it is important to pinpoint which bytes from the test case are used at this particular attack point. Thirdly, these bytes need to be changed to different values that may uncover the vulnerability. For the first element, a corpus of test cases could be provided by the user during testing or it could be crawled from the Internet. For the second, we utilise the concept of taint analysis[4] in order to map between input bytes and the attack point that uses them so they can be mutated. For the third, it is important to collect information about the data type of those bytes that are used at each attack point so that the fuzzer can change them to their maximum, minimum and, also, random values. This would not guarantee that latent vulnerabilities would be uncovered by these values since it is still probabilistic. However, having such information is still beneficial. Figure 1 illustrates the proposed structure.

3.1 Scenario Description

Firstly, a program would be analysed using the static analysis component. This would result in a list of attack points that could be ranked according to their seriousness and would be fed to the taint analysis stage. Then the user, or the web spider, would be asked to provide a test case for the taint analyser so that bytes that are used at each attack point and at flow control statements could be tagged for later use. Before this, a check for the feasibility of the test case would be conducted. That is, if test case B follows the exact execution path as did test case A, which was used previously, then the tool should not continue with B as it is unlikely it would help in discovering new vulnerabilities or expanding the coverage. The taint analyser would then produce two types of information. Firstly, a list of the attack points that are used at this specific test case and the associated bytes with their data type. Second, a list of tainted bytes that are used at flow control statements. The first list would be an input to the fuzzer, which would take the analysed test case as well. The fuzzer's job is to change the tagged bytes that are used at each single attack point to at least three values (maximum, minimum and random) and produce fuzzed files for each attack point. The reasons behind this are twofold. Firstly, we would like to identify the exact cause of the bug if it exists and, therefore, these points are considered individually. This is similar in concept to delta debugging. Secondly, changing only specific bits would ensure that the generated file would be syntactically valid and, hence, pass the initial parser check. The resulted fuzzed files would then be tested by debugging tools for bugs detection. The second list produced by the taint analyser would be used by a constraint solver along with the tainted file, so that we could automatically expand the coverage of a single test case without the need for using different ones. The expanded test cases would then be checked to decide whether or not such an execution path has been explored previously.

---

[3] Some might refer to this as a sensitive sink or an attack point.

[4] Taint analysis aims to identify user-driven data that affect values used at security critical instructions or flow control statements.

3.2   Essential Feature

It is quite difficult with the current fuzzing techniques to decide when enough testing has been performed, either because of the code coverage problem or due to the lack of attack points identification. In our approach, the logging of the following information is required:

– What should be fuzzed? which would be obtained from the static analysis component.
– What has been fuzzed? which is a result of the fuzzer component.

If all the attack points identified initially have already been fuzzed, then the user would be notified that testing has been completed and no further vulnerabilities can be detected. If there are some points that the provided test cases cannot reach, then users would at least know that the testing process did not cover the whole code and further procedures are needed to assure the security of the application.

3.3   Motivated Example

In the following, we present a security vulnerability that has been detected in the Open Office suite using this approach in manual settings. It is worth mentioning that it is remotely exploitable and has been proved by the developer.

```
1  switch(nOpcode) {
2  // has to pass 131 cases and go to default to reach the
       code
3  default:
4  // needs not to satisfy 11 if statements and go to the
       else branch
5  // nDataSize type is unsigned long
6  sal_uInt32 nTemp;
7  *pPict >> nTemp ;
8  nDataSize = nTemp;
9  nDataSize+=4;
10 }
```

This example illustrates a clear case of a programmer not following basic secure coding principles. That is, since nDataSize is used for allocating memory space and its value is calculated from untrusted input, then it is obvious that it must have been carefully bounded. To exploit this flaw, an attacker should modify the variable nOpcode to a particular value that would make the offending code reachable then change the nTemp to its maximum value (0xFFFFFFFF). This value will be assigned to nDataSize and then would result in integer overflow at nDataSize+=4 statement. The attacker would be able to direct the program to read from a specific location of his choice. Our proposed approach should be able to detect this problem. Firstly, the static analysis tool should produce a warning about the statement at line 9 for possible integer overflow since it is used in memory allocation. The taint analyser would show that nTemp is used at this attack point and pinpoint which bytes correspond to it in the input file. The fuzzer would change only these bytes to the maximum value and, hence, produce the conditions necessary to reveal this bug. The constraint solver would also receive the location of nOpcode in the input file and, therefore, the required constraints to reach this code could be negated.

4   Related Work

A relevant study done by Lanzi et al. proposed a similar idea [14]. However, their use of static analysis is only to acquire basic knowledge about the target application since they focused on executables. This was done via the construction of inter-procedural control flow graphs and loop identifications. Another study was conducted by Ganesh et al., who assumed that users have in mind a set of suspicious areas that they want to test [15]. By default, their method is configured to deal with system and function calls as such. This choice is logical since these libraries are mostly developed by different people and programmers may not understand some of the necessary preconditions that the library developers assume programmers should do. Nevertheless, this method completely depends on the provided test cases. That is, checks for attack points would be conducted for only the provided file but not for the whole program, which may in turn give a false sense of security. Furthermore, the identification of attack points is actually the heart of the problem and leaving it on the user is not desirable. Others in academia [8] and in the commercial field have also briefly and theoretically considered the benefits of merging only static and dynamic analysis.

5   Conclusion

If we want to build a robust security testing tool, we must understand that neither one of the current approaches can do this alone. Static analysis would provide code coverage but would also present results that would need to be filtered, requiring considerable effort. Dynamic solutions, including fuzzing, would bring specific results that would not be generalisable. Designers of security testing tools should also take the business needs of software developers into consideration without sacrificing completeness. We show that combining static, dynamic and taint analysis along with fuzzing can be more effective in covering the whole program conservatively while reducing the needs for post-processing. Equally important, we highlight the need for identifying the exact source of the bug so debugging can be efficient. Furthermore, we show that it is necessary to inform the user about whether or not sufficient fuzzing has been done.

References

[1] Pistoia, M., Erlingsson, U.: Programming languages and program analysis for security: a three-year retrospective. SIGPLAN Not. 43(12), 32–39 (2009)

[2] Telang, R., Wattal, S.: Impact of software vulnerability announcements on the market value of software vendors - an empirical investigation. In: Workshop on the Economics of Information Security, p. 677427. Harvard University, Cambridge (2005)

[3] Howard, M., Leblanc, D.: Writing Secure Code. Microsoft Press, Redmond (2001)

[4] Chess, B., McGraw, G.: Static analysis for security. IEEE Security Privacy 2, 76–79 (2004)

[5] Wheeler, D.A.: Flawfinder

[6] Viega, J., Bloch, J.T., Kohno, Y., McGraw, G.: ITS4: A static vulnerability scanner for C and C++ code. In: Proceedings of the 16th Annual Computer Security Applications Conference, ACSAC 2000, p. 257. IEEE Computer Society, Washington, DC (2000)

[7] Wagner, D., Foster, J.S., Brewer, E.A., Aiken, A.: A first step towards automated detection of buffer overrun vulnerabilities. In: Network and Distributed System Security Symposium, pp. 3–17 (2000)

[8] Ernst, M.D.: Static and Dynamic Analysis: Synergy and Duality. In: Workshop on Dynamic Analysis, Portland, OR, USA, pp. 24–27 (2003)

[9] Reps, T., Ball, T., Das, M., Larus, J.: The use of program profiling for software maintenance with applications to the year 2000 problem. In: Jazayeri, M. (ed.) ESEC 1997 and ESEC-FSE 1997. LNCS, vol. 1301, pp. 432–449. Springer, Heidelberg (1997)

[10] Sutton, M., Greene, A., Amini, P.: Fuzzing: Brute Force Vulnerability Discovery. Addison-Wesley Professional (2007)

[11] Godefroid, P., Kiezun, A., Levin, M.Y.: Grammar-based whitebox fuzzing. In: Proceedings of the 2008 ACM SIGPLAN Conference on Programming Language Design and Implementation, PLDI 2008, pp. 206–215. ACM, New York (2008)

[12] Microsoft Corporation: The Microsoft Security Development Lifecycle (SDL): Process Guidance

[13] Microsoft Corporation: Automated penetration testing with white-box fuzzing

[14] Lanzi, A., Martignoni, L., Monga, M., Paleari, R.: A smart fuzzer for x86 executables. In: Proceedings of the Third International Workshop on Software Engineering for Secure Systems, SESS 2007, p. 7. IEEE Computer Society, Washington, DC (2007)

[15] Ganesh, V., Leek, T., Rinard, M.: Taint-based directed whitebox fuzzing. In: Proceedings of the 31st International Conference on Software Engineering, ICSE 2009, pp. 474–484. IEEE Computer Society, Washington, DC (2009)

On the Value of Hybrid Security Testing
(Transcript of Discussion)

Saad Aloteibi

University of Cambridge

The first bug we found, we sent it to Open Office, they solved it, and they solved it in their own way, but if you have exactly 65K characters, then you will undoubtedly have the same problem, and that's basically Sandy's talk about the honeymoon effect[1]. Finally it was solved. The other interesting thing about this is, we tried it with Writer (which is the Microsoft Word of Open Office), and Writer handled it correctly, so I asked the Open Office people, well did you have a problem with the Writer, and they said, well yes, we did have this vulnerability with the Writer, but we have fixed it. So conceptually they should have done it for the other applications as well because they are the same, and this is again about the honeymoon effect, you just need one "+4", such as this, and check it with the pertinent applications.

Jonathan Anderson: How much manual work did you have to do to get your tool to find this, is this a bug that you knew was there, and you used your debug tool to find it?

Reply: No I didn't know about it, I did some static analysis, and when I did the static analysis with the bugfinder, and the bugfinder presented me with 13,000 warnings, one of them was this, when I saw it I realised that there was a problem here, so I told my fuzzer, go and produce this, and when it was produced then the problem was stopped. Also with the other vulnerability, we found it with the static analysis as well. The interesting thing is that you need to fuzz about 142 constants here for this, in which case there is about 131, you need to go to the default, and you need to also have a default, also devise about 100 `if` statements, you can go to the bug. So there the work of the constraint solver is important, because you will end up with 142 constants solved at the end. There is no honeymoon effect here.

The final conclusion is rather it's a matter of balance; I am not going to say that this approach will solve all security problems, but it will eliminate the low hanging fruit, and it will make it harder to find further vulnerabilities. It will not detect some logical problems; let's say you are fuzzing a web application that has some access control for say two kinds of users, an administrator and a normal user, if you fuzz it and gain the privilege of the administrator, you wouldn't know that, because there is no reasoning about the logic of the application itself.

The second point is that attackers are using fuzzing, so if you don't use it someone else will use it instead of you and find the problem with the application. We think that driving the fuzzing process will be more optimal than just

---

[1] Clark, these proceedings.

B. Christianson and J. Malcolm (Eds.): Security Protocols 2010, LNCS 7061, pp. 214–216, 2014.
© Springer-Verlag Berlin Heidelberg 2014

randomly fuzzing. And you need to use different approaches in a complimentary way, so that you can at least improve your software security.

Jonathan Anderson: What's the run time of these tools like? If you have a huge code base like Open Office and you want to run massive regressive testing or progression testing on all the kinds of vulnerabilities you found before, how long would it take to run? Would that take weeks?

Reply: We haven't actually implemented that, but there is a performance overhead here, it might take a longer time than it takes for a small application, because when you instrument a program you actually go about 20 or 30 times slower than the actual running, so there is a performance overhead. But it can be done in an automatic way, no-one needs to sit there and wait for the result of this static analysis.

Jonathan Anderson: And every time you test one of these fuzzed files, so each test case produces three of these fuzzed files, does that involve kind of starting Open Office, and saying, open this file, then close it?

Reply: Yes, well you authorise with the Open Office, you instrument it, you attach it to a debugger, you watch for synchronisation faults, that doesn't really assure you that, if there isn't, I mean, not all the vulnerability will result in a synchronisation fault, it might well execute without any crashes or warnings. So in this case you can do some logging of the results of the debugger, and then you process the output of that. And just to make it easier you need to attach it to the debugger or program test.

Bruce Christianson: I think regression testing is an interesting example though, because one of the things that we're always worrying about is whether you have good code coverage on your regression test suite. The only other approach I know for doing that involves fuzzing a program and seeing which mutations die, and writing new tests for mutations that don't die. This seems a more targeted way of doing that.

Reply: Yes, and as I mentioned, there is no valid proof here, you need actually to test out things in different ways, so formal proofs, there is a problem here with them, complexity matters because, for example this started as a student project, and it ended up with eight million lines of code so complexity makes it harder for the security tool to work, so they don't do any formal methods, except for the critical components, but they don't do it for the whole thing.

Ross Anderson: So what opportunity might there be for a security conscious company to deliberately evolve its directed fuzzing tools at the same time as it evolves its code? Is this perhaps where this work might lead?

Jonathan Anderson: Yes, I think it is. I guess if you're a really security conscious company you want to apply this technique, not at the integration test level where you're testing everything, but you really want to be able to break out just that bit that processes input. That gets a big performance win so that you can do a lot more testing.

Reply: The idea is actually that if you know that your enemy, the hacker, is using this against you, you should use it against yourself. It might not protect yourself from everything, but it will at least make it harder for the other side to find some way to break your code.

Security Made, Not Perfect, But Automatic

Paulo Verissimo

Universidade de Lisboa, Faculdade de Ciências, LaSIGE - Lisbon, Portugal
pjv@di.fc.ul.pt

1   Introduction

Threats to computer systems have been increasing over the past few years. Given
the dependence of society and businesses on computers, we have been spending
every day more to make computer systems and networks secure enough. Yet,
current practice and technology are based on intrusion prevention, and incorpo-
rate a lot of ad hoc procedures and man power, without being anywhere near
perfect, for reasonable scale systems. Maybe the next quantum leap in computer
systems security is to make it automatic, so that it can be cheap and effective.
The first possibility that comes to mind is to make systems out of tamper-proof
components, also said fully trustworthy: perfect components $\rightarrow$ perfect security,
all else being correct. Though this lied at the basis of the trusted computing
base work in the eighties, it is known today that it is impossible in practice
to implement reasonably complex systems whose components are vulnerability
free. This implies that systems in general cannot be made perfectly secure under the prevention paradigm. One interesting approach relies on providing some
isolation between virtual machines residing on a same hardware machine, which
can then act as if they were separate computers (see Figure 1).

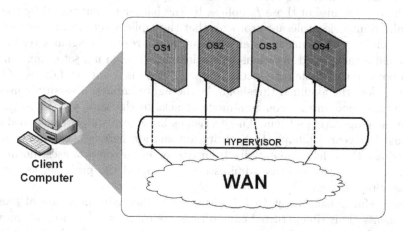

Fig. 1. Enjoying the isolation of Virtual Machines (VM)

Note however, that isolation is just mutual: all vulnerabilities residing in each
virtual machine's software are still exploitable. Not to mention the hypervisor

B. Christianson and J. Malcolm (Eds.): Security Protocols 2010, LNCS 7061, pp. 217–223, 2014.
© Springer-Verlag Berlin Heidelberg 2014

which, for now, we assume trustworthy, a plausible assumption for a wide range
of systems, given some recent results [6]. What about having just a few perfect
components? Computer systems have incorporated smart cards, security chips,
and the TCG/TPM initiative is perhaps the most relevant such attempt. The
idea is to make a chain of attestations that expands to the rest of the components
of the system, starting from a perfect (trusted) component that serves as the
root of trust. The objective is to certify the integrity at start-up or launch of
any application, or at designated moments in its execution. However, in between
nothing is guaranteed, e.g. concerning on-line attacks. And, the whole scheme is
based on the principle of global prevention.

Anyway, such a trusted component scheme based on intrusion prevention
works well on a single machine basis but it is obviously a single point of failure,
and the power of such a scheme is thus limited in distributed systems, which
include practically all current interesting applications.

2   Security with Hybrid Distributed System Models

An alternative paradigm to prevention would be tolerance: we could accept that
all components are to different extents imperfect and subject to intrusions, but
ensure, with the adequate mechanisms, that the whole is quasi-perfectly secure:
in fact, to a desired probability, given by the coverage of the basic assumptions.

Figure 2 exemplifies an intrusion-tolerant set of servers running state machines, and the compound ends up running a Byzantine fault-tolerant service
which, if individual components exhibit diversity from one another (to prevent
common-mode attacks), achieves quasi-perfect security if up to f individual replicas are compromised: the system automatically continues to function correctly
and the compromise of those f replicas by the hacker is neutralized by the decentralized intrusion-tolerant protocols that the replicas run among themselves.
This replicated set of machines ensures automatic resilience against very harsh
faults and attacks (said malicious Byzantine faults): even if a set of machines is
compromised, the whole runs secure protocols that mask out any failures, if they
remain below the assumed threshold. As the figure implies, diversity is used to
ensure that there are no common-mode attacks to the same vulnerability, e.g.
in the same operating system. These schemes have been widely researched over
the past few years [3],[5],[8],[1]. Security automation here is taken in the sense
that whilst there have potentially been one or more compromises, nothing is
required, e.g. of the security administrator, to mend the problem, as long as
sufficient replicas exist.

One useful enhancement to this situation is the re-introduction of trusted
components. This time, trusted components are used for tolerance, not prevention: the decentralized intrusion tolerance protocols leverage the inclusion of
trusted components to a new level, avoiding single points of failure, and amplifying the resilience of the remaining imperfect components. The power of
computing with trusted-trustworthy components like the TPM and others, can
be greatly enhanced if based on a modular/distributed computing model. Under

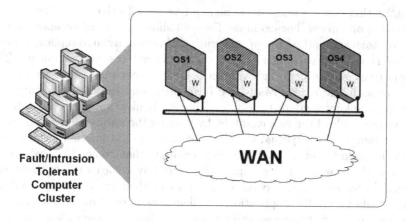

Fig. 2. Automatic resilience to malicious attacks by replicated and diverse execution

such a hybrid model (trusted and untrusted components or systems thereof) one can develop efficient intrusion tolerant algorithms that fulfill the vision of automatic security [11], by having those (COTS or application-specific) trusted components improve the managing of redundancy and diversity, and/or performing self-healing. For example, each replica in Figure 2 is enhanced by such a component (W), capable of assisting its security in crucial steps: authentication, intrusion detection, fail-safe shut-down in case of attack, rejuvenation, etc. For example, the use of very simple trusted components allowed reducing the usual quorum of necessary replicas for Byzantine State Machine Replication, from $3f+1$ to $2f+1$. Several researchers have been following that track lately [5],[4]. In the example of the figure, depicting a mid-scale setting (e.g. a server farm) the W components actually form a distributed subsystem connected through a secure private network, a "control network", whereby then can reach consensus on certain events and decisions [10].

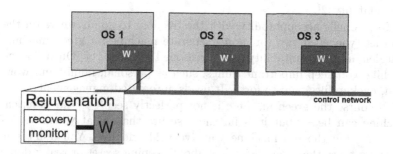

Fig. 3. Automatic self-healing of compromised components through software rejuvenation

Automation can be taken to a higher level of effectiveness, when reaching unattended operation. For example, Figure 3 shows a trusted-component based intrusion-tolerant method to automatically self-heal individual replicas that may have been compromised. The local proactive recovery trusted components (PRW) perform rejuvenation periodically, even as new attacks take place. Methods like proactive and reactive recovery have been used, and essentially restore a machine to some known good state [3],[9]. This mechanism enhances the automatic security protocols of the first example, by keeping the redundant replica quorum virtually intact in a perpetual way. So, the notion of automation is amplified to include unattended operation. The first example that comes to mind are critical servers. However, in this paper, we essentially wish to think about client machines, which currently spend a large part of their lives compromised. Self-healing could be a killer application for client machines, if done in a simple and cheap way, and in fact there is nothing in the mechanism exemplified that cannot be done in a client PC.

3   Fulfilling the Automatic Security Vision

After this introduction, it is now easier to extrapolate from here that hybrid distributed system models comprising components with different degrees of trustworthiness, from totally untrusted (may be compromised) to totally trusted (tamper-proof), may be the key to the solution we seek. They are realistic since they represent the setting of the distributed applications of today, with different loci of trust, and may also help materialize some visions of tomorrow, essentially addressing the current risks incurred by clients addressing applications and peers on large-scale and unknown settings like the Internet:

> ... In consequence, the current trend to use a single physical-logical PC for everything will reverse. I will be using my "office work" computer, my "web-browsing" computer, my "e-banking" computer and my "personal theatre" computer, and so forth. The fact that they may exist in a same box is irrelevant, because what matters is that they will be self-contained, non-interfering, and will have different levels of security and dependability [2].
>
> ... To reconcile accountability with the freedom to go anywhere on the Internet, you need two (or more) separate machines: a green machine that demands accountability, and a red one that does not. On the green machine you keep important things, such as personal, family and work data, backup files, and so forth. It needs automated management ...
>
> ... Of course the green machine is not perfectly secure — no practical machine can be — but it is far more secure than what you have today. [...] On the red machine you live wild and free. You don't put anything there that you really care about keeping secret or really don't want to lose. [...] Virtual machines can keep green isolated from red, though there are details to work out [...] give the user some control over

the flow of information between green and red without losing too much security [7].

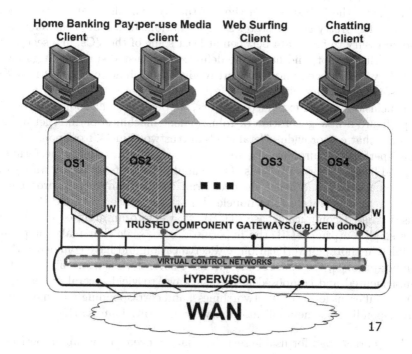

Fig. 4. Hybrid trustworthiness ("green"/"red") client machines

Let us imagine how the visions quoted above could be fulfilled under a hybrid distributed systems model. As said before, we draw from mechanisms previously used essentially for servers, and create new architectures intended for creating a robust client machine and, what's more, one addressing the visions just quoted. Figure 4 depicts the setting: a client machine composed of a hypervisor and the necessary number of virtual machines (VM) with the same or different operating systems. Each *virtual client* (VC) implements a function (e.g. the e-banking client, the web surfing client, etc.), and is composed of one or more VMs. Likewise, each VC is intended to have a given level of trustworthiness (e.g. from the vision statement in [7]: some will be "green", others "red", etc.). This may imply some of the redundancy and/or self-healing techniques illustrated above, adapted and enhanced to live on a hypervisor-based multi virtual-machine setting. That is, the bank wishes the home banking VC to exhibit virtually perfect security (green), and perhaps it is willing to pay for the development of a dedicated trustworthy cluster of Byzantine-resilient replicated VMs, with possibly diverse operating systems, implementing its VC. The relevant protocols run through one of the trusted component gateways. On the other hand, while we accept that the web browsing VC can be compromised for a while (red), no contamination should be possible amongst VCs. Some of these VCs can possess self-healing capability, and the web surfing or the chatting virtual clients are certainly good candidates for pretty simple stateless rejuvenation. In a real client machine, it is also necessary to pass data between at least some of the VCs, in a secure way. This is a critical spot, and hence the definition of trusted component gateways, enforced by a privileged and trustworthy virtual machine (e.g. *dom0* in a XEN hypervisor-based architecture).

In conclusion, in this extended abstract, we described the root ideas of what may prefigure a new generation of robust client machines for Internet applications: ones that can provide several levels of trustworthiness, from non-secure up to quasi-perfectly secure, because security has a cost, in usability, performance, price, and hence requires tradeoffs. They should be able to do it in a transparent and automatic way, and hence the decentralized intrusion tolerant protocols. In essence, from desperately (and hopelessly) trying to keep a whole PC operating as a trusted computing base (TCB), we went to an architecture that has a very small-footprint TCB, the hypervisor, on a scale that makes it possible to indulge in thorough verification and certification and have confidence that it is tamper-proof [6]. On top of that, we have several virtual machines that can be implemented and composed in diverse ways, to yield several virtual clients achieving different levels of trustworthiness, and correspondingly be more or less secure depending on the application in view. Quoting Lampson [7]:

> Things are so bad for usable security that we need to give up on perfection and focus on essentials.

Acknowledgments. This work was partially supported by the FCT, through the Multiannual and the CMU-Portugal Programmes.

References

1. Amir, Y., Danilov, C., Dolev, D., Kirsch, J., Lane, J., Nita-Rotaru, C., Olsen, J., Zage, D.: Scaling Byzantine fault-tolerant replication to wide area networks. In: Proceedings of the IEEE International Conference on Dependable Systems and Networks, pp. 105–114 (June 2006)
2. Bellovin, S.M., Benzel, T.V., Blakley, B., Denning, D.E., Diffie, W., Epstein, J., Verissimo, P.: Information assurance technology forecast 2008. IEEE Security & Privacy 6(1), 10–17 (2008)
3. Castro, M., Liskov, B.: Practical Byzantine fault-tolerance and proactive recovery. ACM Trans. on Computer Systems 20(4), 398–461 (2002)
4. Chun, B.-G., Maniatis, P., Shenker, S., Kubiatowicz, J.: Attested append-only memory: making adversaries stick to their word. In: Proceedings of the 21st ACM Symposium on Operating Systems Principles, pp. 189–204 (October 2007)

5. Correia, M., Neves, N.F., Verissimo, P.: How to tolerate half less one Byzantine nodes in practical distributed systems. In: Proceedings of the 23rd IEEE Symposium on Reliable Distributed Systems, pp. 174–183 (October 2004)
6. Klein, G., Elphinstone, K., Heiser, G., Andronick, J., Cock, D., Derrin, P., Elkaduwe, D., Engelhardt, K., Kolanski, R., Norrish, M., Sewell, T., Tuch, H., Winwood, S.: sel4: formal verification of an OS kernel. In: SOSP 2009: Proceedings of the ACM SIGOPS 22nd Symposium on Operating Systems Principles, pp. 207–220. ACM, New York (2009)
7. Lampson, B.: Privacy and security, usable security: how to get it. Commun. ACM 52(11), 25–27 (2009)
8. Martin, J.P., Alvisi, L.: Fast Byzantine consensus. In: Proceedings of the IEEE International Conference on Dependable Systems and Networks, pp. 402–411 (June 2005)
9. Sousa, P., Bessani, A.N., Correia, M., Neves, N.F., Verissimo, P.: Highly available intrusion-tolerant services with proactive-reactive recovery. IEEE Transactions on Parallel and Distributed Systems
10. Verissimo, P.: Travelling through wormholes: a new look at distributed systems models. SIGACT News (ACM Special Interest Group on Automata and Computability Theory) 37(1), 66–81 (2006)
11. Verissimo, P., Neves, N.F., Cachin, C., Poritz, J., Powell, D., Deswarte, Y., Stroud, R., Welch, I.: Intrusion-tolerant middleware: The road to automatic security. IEEE Security & Privacy 4(4), 54–62 (2006)

Security Made, Not Perfect, But Automatic
(Transcript of Discussion)

Paulo Verissimo

University of Lisbon

I decided to take the challenge of the organisers, the perfection of security, turn it around, and propose: if not perfect why not automatic? So we might ask if preventative security, meaning the canonical way of security, the only way to get it? Let me share a few thoughts about that. If we think that there is no trustworthiness, meaning a holistic perfection about what secure systems are, that behind our nice algorithms there's machinery, so there's no secure application without regard to the platform, or there is no effective policy in isolation of enforcing machinery, or that there is no information security in the absence of infrastructure security, then we might think, do we need at least some auxiliary paradigms to build secure systems. I'm going to talk about stuff that can be used in anything, servers, etc, but using it on the client side, maybe then there is no future in expensive security. Maybe we need, at least on the client side, to bring security to be sort of a commodity, something that is adaptive to the context where you're working on, and several people talked about that yesterday. And it should be automatic, getting out of our way.

Is that possible? Well let's see. If we look at security as prevention, that's the main word for us, the idea is trust that certain attacks will not occur, definitely taking vulnerabilities out of the system, and in essence preventing attacks from leading to intrusions.

Now systems in general — I'm not talking about perhaps certain components, but systems in general, and the more complex, the worse — they cannot be made perfectly secure under the prevention paradigm. So that's my statement. I've been working on alternative ways of solving the problem: what about thinking about some isolation, some modularisation to help us, or what about diversity and redundancy to make the hacker's life difficult, or really relying on just a few perfect components, components that are so small, and so well-controlled, that we again have great confidence? It's about realism of the assumption that the thing is perfect.

What about intrusion tolerance as a road to automatic security? So I'm going to talk about combining paradigms that have been around, interesting paradigms. We know that people have considered virtual machines as a very promising way of handling security problems. Some comments yesterday were made about that, and I will show you that it helps, but it doesn't solve it. Then other people have been thinking about Byzantine fault tolerance, BFT, so I don't how many of you are aware, it's state machine replication, so programs that respond to inputs and process things, and deterministically they can be replicated, and if they're replicated, if some of them die, the others continue doing the job. If they are diverse, the attacker power factor will increase linearly

B. Christianson and J. Malcolm (Eds.): Security Protocols 2010, LNCS 7061, pp. 224–232, 2014.
© Springer-Verlag Berlin Heidelberg 2014

with the number of replicas, and so maybe we get something out of it in the way of being resilient automatically. There's a lot of focus on that, but they have limitations also. I'm not going to be talking about those limitations here. have been working on.

And then thirdly, if this automatic thing is just working for you, right, and you forget about it, there's obviously a problem that the thing can get exhausted, you know, if the attacker starts methodically taking them out, one after the other. So I'm going to be talking then about self-healing with recovery of stuff. I think the most simple thing is that the software does more where you replace it with a new version, but there are other defensive approaches to do that.

So look at the isolation of virtual machines, people have talked about it yesterday, what happens is that I have this single machine, but actually it can be several machines, so it's neat because then I can isolate certain operations, and I can trust that WAN, I have this operating system taking care of this, operating system in the generic sense with applications. Well, it's nice, but it doesn't solve the whole problem. Why? First it's just mutual isolation, so each virtual machine is still exploitable. Secondly, the flavour of diversity that I'm showing here, which is you can have different configuration of systems, it's really not quite exploitable, because it's really separating just the functions of the homogeneous machine, and so if those things die you're in trouble, we need more. And thirdly the hypervisor is still the single point of failure. So at this point, you know, let's pretend it's not, let's pretend the hypervisor would not be the problem, but later on I'll have my bullet-proof jacket on, so in my last slide I'll let Virgil [Gligor] ask the question, and I'll answer the way we in our group are trying to handle it.

So let me get to intrusion-tolerance. The intrusion-tolerance paradigm assumes strange things, the idea is that systems are vulnerable, they have vulnerabilities, like we have diseases, we have bacteria in our bodies. And let's assume that systems can be attacked, and let's assume that they can be attacked with success, so there can be intrusions, so they can be intruded upon, so hackers can really screw up the component sources. But despite that the system will remain secure and operational in terms of what will be even a formal specification of safety properties. The idea is to use redundancy and diversity so that the hacker attacks individual components but doesn't get the whole system.

I'll give you an informal basic proposition of how the algorithm works. Given N processes, and f as a function of N, and H, a set of assumptions on the environment, which means also attackers and stuff, therefore at least N-f remain correct processes, algorithm A, your application, satisfies a predefined set of properties that is executed correctly. Now consider that H is your environment, where you have intruders, consider f, a number that is stipulated, which is the resilience of your system, and then this algorithm, despite attacks that break down up to f components of your system, replicas if you want, or servers, or whatever, will execute correctly.

Now, let's see how we can do it. We could have clusters of machines, this is what people have done with servers, there are already systems doing this. Machines run secure protocols; they're connected to the network, but they run secure protocols amongst them which are resilient to these attacks, they're the so-called Byzantine Resilient Protocols, or BFT protocols. And if you use diversity then you foil common-mode attacks, if the hacker knows how to attack one machine it doesn't mean that then he can do parallel attacks, people have to sequence them because they have to learn how to attack the second, and so on. And if you enhance this with perfect components, as people have done more recently, it's allowable, by the time principles we know of verification, etc, etc, to have small enough, and simple enough, meaning non-dynamic components that you prove correct, or verify correct, and say, this is perfect, and then you can construct algorithms. We have learned over this decade several ways we can construct algorithms that make these components amplify the security of the whole, or if you prefer, mitigate the insecurity of the remaining part of the machine. So we're still progressively fulfilling our dream, which is, this machine is not perfect, but we have a small perfect environment, and this could be stuff like smart-cards, TPM, or purpose made security chips, or appliances, or whatever.

In strong configurations that people have prototyped with, they can have a control network of their own, a secluded network, which is perfectly feasible inside a server, its the centre, and it's even more feasible for the client machine, as we can see. So they can have a non-attackable network because it's a second interface, where they can exchange information about attacks, or about the verification of hashes, or signatures, or whatever. I'm just exciting your imagination about the possibilities of algorithms that can be done that will enhance your algorithms suffering all the attacks, or, as Ross[1] was mentioning yesterday, your operations to the outside.

Now, this automatic thing is beautiful, but in a question of time the hacker will break them all down because intrusion-tolerance assumes that things are not perfect, and so the idea is that the attack factor may be calculated so that you can rejuvenate those replicas, and so the Ws can become W's, where you can have a rejuvenation engine. There have been prototypes for this, so this is doable, all that I'm saying until now is doable. I'll tell you what we intend, what are the challenges for the future.

Well the challenge for the future is really the perfect client machine security, so it's absolutely amazing that several people have addressed this problem. I think it's absolutely actual, and so our work with that is probably the next step, you know, servers have become reasonably stable, clients are really screwing up the whole scenario. A couple of years ago several of us were coming up with visions along those lines, very similar to what Ross was saying, saying, for example, I'll be using my office work, and my web browsing, my eBay computing, they will be the same machine, but it doesn't matter, because they will be self-contained, non-interfering, and may have different levels of security. So three years ago people had this vision and that's what started fermenting.

More recently Lampson was talking about similar things, in his metaphor, it's the green and the red machines. You must in your client, have green and red machines, virtually speaking, and the greens are good, the reds are not so good,

---

[1] Anderson, these proceedings.

and this is essentially what we were saying three years ago, we will have different levels of goodness and evil.

Right, how to get there, which is bringing virtual machines, and state machine replication together. Then you have a promisingly powerful technical algorithmic architectural paradigm. Technically what it means is that you have a machine that has a hypervisor. Then you have a pool of machines, and use this pool to construct clusters of virtual clients. So these are virtual machines in the sense of having a hypervisor, but what I'm going to talk about is virtual clients, it's the web browsing client, the banking client, and so forth. And so I'll get to my idea of green clients, and yellow clients, and red clients. The stuff that can be done is told in the paper. You really have to imagine these future systems, which can be done in current hardware, that's an interesting thing. Our experiments could have domain zero as a primordial if you want to trust the component gateway. Domain zero is complex enough to be attacked, and this hypervisor is also complex enough to be attacked, so when I'm finished ask me how I solved that problem. But let's pretend they're OK. This would act as a kind of low-level middleware to constrain the operations that can happen between those virtual clients. So what you have to imagine is that these virtual clients are working to the outside, they're connecting, they don't know each other, they're addressing, you know, size and places in the network, and what you have to do is to apply your policies that will constrain the passing of information between those virtual clients because that's a critical machine.

Now this passing of information, as was being said yesterday, is very complex because part of it will rely on the hats of the machine user, but we are very sceptical about the capacity of the person to make rational decisions. So we think that the first principle is to come up with a machine that uses very simple ideas. It could be pumps, you know the pump principle, directional passing of information whereby if you're doing a bank transaction, and you want to safeguard it, a connected virtual client of yours cannot send stuff into your banking transactions. So this is the research we want to do, obviously it is ongoing, and I think the purpose of this workshop is to discuss these ongoing ideas. We really think that we have to do something at this level as simple as I was saying, which will combine stuff that we want to study with the context awareness. So we've done stuff on context awareness in the past, in the context of complex embedded systems. So the idea would be to have these automated units, it could be robbers that go into nuclear areas, and they don't know the place, so they have to get there, and depending on what the place looks like, they will make decisions. And if you use some context awareness, then this context awareness is in some way connected to this trusted component gateway, it's this notion that knowing, not you the person, but the environment knowing where it is, that may constrain the sensitive passing of information. Because we really don't believe that a client will suddenly become very smart and stop doing nonsense.

This is a security installation of a facility, it could be anywhere, so the controls, and the security alarm, everything is there. And this thing here is how to disconnect the alarm, so it could be, Mr Thief, hears how to disconnect the alarm, thank you. And so the user will continue to do this kind of stuff, and we just have to help him.

Hypervisor, domain zero, whatever, these things have problems, yes, we know that, but you have to have secure enough systems depending on the applications. So the principle, that's what is important, is that you can recursively apply those intrusion-tolerance techniques to the hypervisor and we've been doing very nice work on virtual machines for several years now, and the idea is that, this is not perfect, but it's much better than what we have now, and for really sensitive applications, we know how to apply recursively the argument of introducing tolerance, to do an intrusion-tolerant hypervisor which will then overcome the vulnerabilities that Virgil certainly is going to talk about. And we all know that some people just trust these things too much.

Jonathan Anderson: Modern smartphone operating systems, which in a lot of ways are desktop operating systems with a couple of modifications, have all of the confinement properties that you're talking about for your different applications, of the non-interference and things, more rigorous structured security model than desktops have, and they don't hypervisors and virtual machines, and these extra levels of indirection, but there are reasons why desktop computers work the way they do, why we have the wide interfaces, and why applications can communicate with each other really easily. So can you comment on the model by which the uptake of this happens, this world where you have very strict controls on the different applications, and you can't install anything to this trusted dumb zero kind of thing because if you do then it can interfere with any of the applications.

Reply: Well if I understood your question, you were saying that that's a done deal, but I don't think that's correct.

Virgil Gligor: Why don't you pick up that question during my talk.

Jonathan Anderson: OK.

Virgil Gligor: But we'll let him answer anyway [laughter].

Reply: OK, so you see, phones, as far as I know, have a different issue. What they retain is the integrity of the original stuff, which is the communication, and they retain the hardware, so it's different. So if you accept that we can do new PC architectures, then that's different, because that's what they do, they retain the original part of the telecom, essential for real time, to guarantee the bandwidth, and because of crypto, you know, GSM, etc. And then they added years ago a little PC if you want, and that PC is as crappy as our PCs, and they run Windows mobile, and even the same VM, which is quite nice but you can see they have not solved the problems in the way we want to solve them. So this problem will happen in those phones. So it's happening, I mean, they're being attacked everyday.

Jonathan Anderson: A lot of the security wins that you get, the difference (for instance) between Mac OS and the iPhone OS, is that some of the security things which are optional here are turned on and mandatory in iPhone OS, for instance, and it does mitigate a lot of things, but they can only do that because there's no backwards compatibility requirement. So in order to move to this kind of model ...

Reply: In this kind of model, and my vision of several of these virtual clients, you can address that problem. So the problem is the following: you have this blue ray reader, or you have this commercial eBanking machine, those things are acceptable, they are black box systems controlled by a supplier, the supplier puts them there, it won't touch them, and this is how they protect them, right, you accept that this principle works for a set of several boxes. The problem is that the metaphor with the PCs is different, we think that PC is ours, we should do whatever we want with it. This is also why, when trusted computing appeared, there was so much controversy, because they appeared to be taking control of your PC away from you. Now imagine that you have this situation, so this is an OEM platform and your bank will say, oh you want to do eBanking with me, so here's this CD to install my virtual client, which is composed by the way of four virtual machines that do Byzantine agreement, and you cannot connect to anything else but the bank. You accept because what you just did was to buy a little black box, that's the metaphor of having several virtual PCs, you accepted because you know this is only for you to do home banking, and then you can switch to your other PC, which is yours where you can do anything. So an advantage of this is exactly to overcome that problem of allowing a normal user to have black boxes from suppliers of pay per view TV, for example, whilst controlling his PC, come on, you know, it's mine.

James Malcolm: But don't you think applications and users will say, but I really want to be able to automate the transfer of money from my other application. For example, I would really like to be able to tell my banking application to transfer some money for me on the basis of how much I won in this game; people will demand these things.

Reply: Yes, it's like this, but that's a personal feeling. People can be as stupid as they want, and so the people who want high performance cameras, so that they can be seen, this kind of thing, because they're stupid, that's the problem. So people must understand that they cannot have the whole thing connected. But this is the social problem we were discussing yesterday, it's a social problem, it's not for us, it's the newer guys, those guys who think that when they're sitting there at Facebook etc, everything is connected, and we must tell them, what I tell my kids, there are good streets and bad streets, this is how I was raised, I was raised that there are very secure streets where you can get, you know, with your nice diving watch, and other streets where you should take everything out of sight. And we should educate also those adults who want to be always connected.

Dieter Gollmann: I disagree, it has nothing to do with regeneration, it has to do with different applications interacting. I'm doing reviews for the European Commission. They want from my bank a signed statement that this is my correct account information, when I tried it here with Barclays in the past, Barclays looked at me and said, you are crazy, we don't do it. My German bank was more helpful. So I can imagine a situation where there is my banking client in this world, and I have a different client to interact with the European Commission, and the European Commission says, we want your banking client confirmation that this is your correct account information. And we get into this issue of who governs the interaction, and that's the difficult problem. Sorting out the virtual machines, the hypervisor, is the easy problem.

Bruce Christianson: It doesn't seem to be quite as hopeless as that because what you have the potential for here is a box, and inside it there's something that I trust, and there's something else inside of it the bank trusts, there's something else inside it that you trust, or the European Commission trusts, and they have a secure way of communicating with it, so at least there seems to be some hope that we could run transactions that everybody would agree on.

Ross Anderson: But the banks can't even sort out their own internal APIs and EMV for example, so what chance is there? It takes them 20 years to change anything; the world might be great if in theory you've got a David Chaum type mechanism, the separation of functional control between your bank at your tax collector, and so on, implementable it may be, in theory, but in practice, it won't happen.

Bruce Christianson: The wonderful thing about the PC revolution was that everybody threw away everything and started again with a blank sheet of paper. Now it's a shame (in retrospect) that they did so with no explicitness and no self-control, but perhaps that's what we need, some new computing revolution that allows everybody to start again.

Jonathan Anderson: Well in some ways that's happening, people do expect that by 2013 more people will be computing on the phone than they are on the computer and desktops. You have to run away some of the backwards compatibility, but some of the arguments going around concern me, because there's this assumption that people are too stupid to use computers, let's give them a box, put one button on it, we'll even push the button for them, before it ships from the factory so they don't have to worry about it. Whereas kind of the whole point of computing is that you can do new things that haven't been pre-imagined by the people who built it.

Bruce Christianson: But this approach is quite nice, because it lets you do the pre-imagined things, it comes with a package that will do them, but you're not confined to just those.

Jonathan Anderson: But James' point, it's not unrealistic that I might want to have some kind of application. So yes, it's good to have these secure ways to communicate with my bank, but you might be able to imagine new and interesting things that could be done if you could interact with them in a programmatic way, and if people could write software to do new and interesting things. I mean, I agree with Ross, eBanking is the wrong example, but there are lots of things where if you say, here are the set of things that are allowed to be done, and then you can go on YouTube separately, and that's different. But if of all the interesting things, you can only do A, B, C or D, multiple choice, pick one, and you can't invent new ways of doing things, I don't know about that.

Joseph Bonneau: There's a theory in general economics that let's you have both at the same time now, it's called libertarian paternalism, where you force people to do the right thing, if they don't make any choice, but people who want to make a choice can shoot themselves in the foot. An example in software design, if you look at the progression of Firefox, you have to click through three or four things, and basically assert, I know what I'm doing, I'll now override. So potentially we can design this in the same way, that you almost have to prove that you know something about computers in order to override the warning, but for 90% of users they just want a button.

Jonathan Anderson: But my point is that this VM architecture is basically operating systems, but a little bit more constricted in that the inter process communication is more limited. We've already had this kind of argument and debate in the market, and people decided, we want computers that provide wide interfaces so you can do new and interesting things, and if you build this kind of an architecture with these extremely narrow confined interfaces, then they're better be a mechanism to expand those interfaces, but of course as soon as they expand people say, oh why aren't we just using traditional architecture.

Reply: No, hold on, maybe you're missing the point. This is not, as I said, this is not VM, because VM doesn't solve the problem. VM gives you virtual machines, and I'm talking about virtual clients, which is a different abstraction, composed of several VMs. I don't think I said that clients are stupid, but I certainly said that they're not smart enough.

Jonathan Anderson: You said they were stupid earlier.

Reply: They're not smart enough, OK, it's a politically correct euphemism. When I mention context awareness, the idea is that there's got to be a means to put you on the right track, and you can decide not to go on the right track, but definitely in some applications, you will not be able to. Come on, we know banks do very stupid things, but one thing is for certain, when they have these terminals where you buy stuff in swipe cards, or put the cards, that's accepted. So the trust model, even though a lot psychological, is accepted, because it's something that is purpose made, you know, blah, blah, blah. So you see it's transporting the metaphor to here, it's not going to be perfect, but from the liability side probably it's going to improve. In Portugal, for example, the law is ambiguous, and so you sign a contract saying that, well, you know, our systems are perfect, and whatever happens with your login and password, it's you. I keep telling people this; it's this kind of thing that you want to solve in a better way, but it will not go away, it's creating trust, you will still have problems, but that's the same as on the street; but if you take precautions maybe the problem is solved.

Ross Anderson: Well there's a similar debate we had six or seven years ago[2], which is about trusted computing. Now one of the reasons we've had such rapid innovation in the world of computing is that there are lots of hundreds of millions of people out there with computers that can run the software that you write over the weekend after you've had your good idea. There are also

---

[2] Actually in 2000 AD, at the VIIIth Security Protocols Workshop, LNCS 2133.

hundreds of millions of computers with data on which this application can work, so if you write an application that does something cool with Word documents or Excel spreadsheets, or whatever, you have potentially got a billion dollar company within a year, and that never existed before because you could not scale that quickly. The implied threat with trusted computing was that the owners of legacy applications could lock down the data, they could encrypt using keys that would only be available to authorised applications, and they could then charge rental to innovators to get at all the stuff. Now I don't want to more than point people's attention at those debates here, but a number of those arguments may resurrect themselves in new formats, perhaps on different sides of the good or bad dividing line once people start thinking seriously about virtualisation. Because if you're going to a different virtual environment, who controls them? Does the bank control virtualisation, or Bob.bank, to use yesterday's terminology, and if so, can the bank forbid you from exploiting data other than to turn off your application?

Bruce Christianson: Jon made a very good point when he said people, application programs, want wide interfaces, whereas for security, we want the interfaces to be narrow. I think that says that the interface the application programmer sees should be through a non-trivial piece of code that someone else has written, that maps everything down onto the narrow interface underneath, and if you can't do that mapping then what you have is something that isn't secure. That may, or may not, be something you're willing to live with, but at least you'll know. In a lot of cases we use this wide interface because it's convenient, not because we actually have to for logical reasons.

Jonathan Anderson: And in some cases if the wide interface didn't exist, then the platform wouldn't be able to run the application.

Bruce Christianson: Yes, but we don't program in assembly code anymore, for the same reason[3].

---

[3] We decided that the narrower, high-level programming language interface was better, not just more restrictive, because it allowed us to automate a lot of the heavy lifting.

Security Limitations of Virtualization and How to Overcome Them

Virgil Gligor

Carnegie Mellon University
Pittsburgh, PA 15213
gligor@cmu.edu

Abstract. To be useful, security primitives must be available on commodity computers with demonstrable assurance and understandable by ordinary users with minimum effort. Trusted computing bases comprising a hypervisor, which implements the reference monitor, and virtual machines whose layered operating system services are formally verified, will continue to fail these criteria for client-side commodity computers. We argue that demonstrable high assurance will continue to elude commodity computers, and complex policies that require management of multiple subjects, object types, and permissions will continue to be misunderstood and misused by most users. We also argue that high-assurance, usable commodity computers require only two security primitives: *partitions for isolated code execution*, and *trustworthy communication* between partitions and between users and partitions. Usability requirements for isolated partitions are modest: users need to know when to use a small trusted system partition and when to switch to a larger untrusted one; developers need to isolate and assure only few security-sensitive code modules within an application; and security professionals needed to maintain only the trusted partition and a few isolated modules in the untrusted one. Trustworthy communication, which requires partitions and users to decide whether to accept input from or provide output to others, is more challenging because it requires trust, not merely secure (i.e., confidential and authentic) communication channels.

1 Introduction

The idea of using virtualization of computer system resources to provide isolated execution of user-level computations appeared nearly four decades ago. Specifically, use of virtual machine monitors (VMMs), or hypervisors, to implement reference monitor mechanisms for isolated virtual machine (VMs) was suggested in 1973 and implemented by at least two research projects in the 1970s (SDC KVM/370 [18]) and 1980s (DEC VAX/VMM [19]), respectively. There is enough evidence to suggest that virtual machine isolation is no longer a research topic in security. New hardware architectures enable modern VMMs to provide virtual-machine isolation efficiently. However, virtual-machine isolation has been achieved only with low degrees of assurance on commodity systems, and the reference monitor policies supported (e.g., multi-level access control [27]) have not

B. Christianson and J. Malcolm (Eds.): Security Protocols 2010, LNCS 7061, pp. 233–251, 2014.
© Springer-Verlag Berlin Heidelberg 2014

been easily understood by most users. Hence, security of virtualized client-side commodity computers remains an elusive goal. All available evidence suggests that this will not change in the near future.

In this paper, we examine some of the reasons for this state of affairs and suggest that high-assurance trusted computing bases (TCBs) using reference-monitor-based, layered commodity operating systems is unlikely to be practical in the future. Instead, high-assurance systems will survive only in special, or niche, systems and applications where security is critical; e.g., in defense, aerospace, and industrial control systems. Although this prediction is *not* specific to virtualized architectures and holds for most commodity systems (e.g., for security kernels of native operating systems [23,5,38] and separation/isolation kernels [9,10,12]), in this paper we focus on TCBs where the reference monitor are implemented in VMMs and layered operating systems in VMs, since recent mechanisms for virtualization have led to the belief that high-assurance commodity systems may in fact be just around the corner. To justify our prediction, we rely on two classes of observations, which explain both the persistent insecurity of commodity systems and the dearth of security primitives that are usable by ordinary users. We call these observations the "axioms" of insecurity and usable security, respectively, to emphasize their validity in the future. We also argue that two types of security primitives can help overcome these challenges of usable security for client-side commodity computers, namely *partitions for isolated code execution*, and *trustworthy communication* between partitions and between users and partitions.

Isolated Partitions. We envision two orthogonal forms of system partitions, neither of which explicitly aims at preventing information flow (and thus differ from a separation kernel's partitions [9,10]). Instead, they provide isolated execution environments, which protect code and data secrecy and integrity, and code execution from tampering. The first form of partitioning, which is inspired by Lampsons *red-green machine* separation [20,22], divides system resources into two partitions instead of virtualizing them, and switches between the partitions only under (human) user control exercised via a trusted path. Unlike most commodity VM systems, neither malware-infested operating systems nor applications can escape their partition behind the users back [8].

The second form of partitioning separates developer-selected, security-sensitive code blocks from untrusted operating system code and applications, and provides strong guarantees of data secrecy and integrity, as well as code execution integrity, to an external entity via attestation [7]. A necessary condition for the isolation of security sensitive code is the ability to modularize applications and insert secure channels between the separate modules. Since information flow control is not necessarily sought, these channels can be bidirectional. The design of security-sensitive code partitions relies on source-code analysis for modularity, where a module controls its input and output channels. Among the many applications of security-sensitive code block isolation, we envision the protection of secret and private keys used in hard drive encryption, SSH, SSL, and e-mail signing. We also envision that isolated code blocks will perform access-control policy enforcement for otherwise-untrusted applications.

Trustworthy Communication. Trustworthy communication requires secure channels between partitions and trusted paths between humans and their partitions. However, whether a partition accepts input from or provides sensitive output to another depends on the trust established between partitions or between humans and their partitions, not merely on the existence of secure channels. For example, a security-sensitive code block accepts only input whose validity it can verify in its own partition, or if it can recover from the failure to verify input validity. A code block outputs sensitive information to another partition only in areas that are legitimately accessible to the code of the receiving partition and only if it can determine that the receiver is at least accountable for the protection of sensitive information, if not fully trusted. Trustworthy communication between otherwise isolated partitions also requires secure (de)composition of systems into modules of different granularities, ranging from very coarse partitions, such as an entire operating system, to a single application module, each partition comprising different types of sensitive code and data.

Coarse-granularity partitions and trustworthy communication are intended to reflect a humans view of asset protection, whereas fine-granularity partitions reflect an application developer's concern of separating security-sensitive code modules from malware-infested code in untrusted operating systems and applications. We illustrate the two types of partitions for commodity operating systems and applications, and outline their implementation with non-virtualizing hypervisors [8,7].

High-Assurance Systems. For the purposes of this discussion, a high assurance system is one that implements a reference monitor as its foundation, and verifies operating system security layer-by-layer until a highly assured TCB is created for secure application development [37,28,36,23,5,19,18,38]. A reference monitor identifies all system subjects and objects, and is isolated from external attacks. It is always invoked for every subject reference to any object, and hence enforces a systems security policy. Finally, it is small enough for analysis and tests that assure its correctness [3]. The last requirement implies that the reference monitor is also simple and enough to enable correctness verification via formal proofs and hence provides high-assurance of correct implementation.

System layering is also essential for high assurance. Layering eliminates cyclic dependencies between modules of different layers and allows proofs for correctness of the type: if layer $n-1$ implements security property A correctly, then layer n implements security property B correctly, where the two properties may coincide. For high assurance, the entire TCB must have a stable configuration; i.e., the TCB cannot change (e.g., upgraded, patched) before the formal verification for the current system version is completed. In principle, layering also allows composable proofs of correctness for modular verification, which helps limit the verification time and effort to modified components. We use the qualifier of "low assurance" for systems where formally verified reference monitors and assured operating system layers are not implemented.

2   Axioms of Insecurity

The axioms of insecurity discussed below suggest that high-assurance TCBs are impractical given marketplace conditions and system usability requirements. Hence, it is futile to expect such systems for commodity computers in the foreseeable future; e.g., within the next fifteen years, which in computing technology is beyond our horizon.

Axiom 1. There will always be rapid innovation in computing and information technology and this will always lead to low-assurance commodity systems.

This statement has obviously been true for past commodity systems. The question is why will rapid innovation persist in the future and why will it continue to produce only low assurance systems? Computing and information technology markets are highly competitive, have a very low cost of entry, are largely unregulated, and explicitly exclude liability for buggy, unsafe and insecure systems. These market characteristics encourage rapid innovation. However, both the cost and delayed time to market of a highly assured TCB would be prohibitive for a commodity system to survive in a competitive marketplace that encourages rapid innovation. For example, it has been estimated that the cost per source line of code (SLoC) of a formally verified TCB implementation for high-assurance systems (i.e., at level EAL6 of the Common Criteria) to be $10K [29]. This suggests that the cost for a (very small) reference monitor of 20K SLoC would be about $200M, without accounting for the cost of the few millions of SLoC of higher operating systems layers. This also implies that the opportunity cost of a high-assurance TCB for client-side devices would be prohibitive.

Rapid innovation also creates a strong incentive to produce and use function-rich system components, perhaps of diverse provenance, that are inexpensive to produce, and hence of uncertain assurance. It also creates a strong incentive to perform frequent functional upgrades, which most often imply that a system may not be stable enough to preserve the validity of high-assurance evidence. This implies that the component supply chain of a commodity client machine reduces its assurance to the lowest common denominator.

We stress that Axiom 1 does *not* rule out high-assurance TCBs (e.g., EAL6 or 7 of the Common Criteria) for regulated market segments where such assurance is explicitly mandated and rewarded. Instead, Axiom 1 rules out high-assurance TCBs only for unregulated commodity markets that lack liability for insecure products.

Axiom 2. There will always be large software components in commodity systems whose security properties are not understood by most users.

The fact that commodity systems will always have large software components has already been recognized. For example, Lampson makes the stronger statement that, among software components, only giants survive [6]. The certainty of large software components in competitive markets is justified intuitively. Survival in such markets requires both high development productivity and retention of backward compatibility with already deployed systems. Together, these requirements naturally lead to large software components.

A common way to achieve high development productivity is to enhance existing software components with new functions, rather than to build new components from scratch, in response to diverse and evolving market demands. For example, adding multiple file formats and new protocol features are typical enhancements that increase software use in the marketplace. Adding new layers of abstraction to existing components to support new standard software tools, libraries, and development environments is a useful way of enhancing productivity. At the same time, backward compatibility with existing software requires retention of older and perhaps rarely used functions and interfaces. Naturally, addition of new functions while retaining old ones will always lead to software-component growth. Unfortunately, large software components have large attack surfaces [30,31]. This makes it difficult for most developers – not just for ordinary users – to figure out what security properties hold and which adversary attacks are countered.

Axiom 3. There will always be bugs, features, and operator/user errors that will lead to security vulnerabilities and there will always be adversaries to take advantage of them.

Axioms 1 and 2 already suggest that there will always be bugs in the software components of commodity systems, which will lead to security vulnerabilities. Similarly, in an earlier presentation we argued that new system technologies and features often introduce new vulnerabilities and new adversary behaviors [24]. However, this axiom is stronger, and not just because it predicts future user/operator errors that lead to security vulnerabilities. Instead, it is stronger because it postulates the existence of adversaries who will always exploit these vulnerabilities. The reason for this is fairly intuitive. Pervasive use of commodity systems creates tangible economic, political, and social incentives for an adversary to find and exploit such vulnerabilities. These include bug bounties paid to researchers who discover exploitable vulnerabilities by large software companies; payment for not exploiting zero-day vulnerabilities that disrupt business operations; e.g., extortion; for-hire theft of corporate intellectual property and trade secrets; bragging rights for attacks against public servers in support of various political causes; and real and perceived advantages derived from theft of government secrets. In short, adversaries' exploits of security vulnerabilities will continue to pay off and hence persist.

Note that Axiom 3 postulates the existence of adversary-exploitable, operator/user errors in the future, independent of Axioms 1 and 2. This implies that even if high-assurance client-side commodity systems hypothetically exist, there will still be adversary-exploitable, inevitable operator/user errors. Why will operator/user errors be inevitable? We find three reasons for this. First, many security features, including those for secure system configuration and access control management [32], are often user-unfriendly and inconvenient [22]. This is often the case because large-scale, design-time studies that can enhance usability are often forgone to decrease time-to-market delays in a competitive market. Second, even if all client-side security features would hypothetically become usable in time, social engineering experiments could always deceive, scam, and manipulate unsuspecting users into taking actions (e.g., import of malicious software via *pdf* files and *usb* memory sticks, or clicking on links for malicious websites) that would adversely affect user and application security, despite the security of the underlying system. Third, even security-savvy users who might not easily fall pray to social-engineering attacks cannot always predict new security vulnerabilities introduced by new features of the computing products they use. As Christopher Strachey used to reflect on innovative solutions to computing problems, "it is impossible to predict the consequences of being clever *cf.* [21]."

3   Axioms of Usable Security

The axioms of usable security attempt to capture what we believe most users want to protect, what they need when protection fails, and what security features they can learn easily. These suggest that design of simple and expressive user interfaces to security mechanisms, while necessary, are often insufficient for usable security.

Axiom 1. Most users want a high degree of security for a few types of sensitive transactions.

Most users are unwilling or unable to learn elaborate security mechanisms and prefer to rely on a few default (i.e., automated) procedures that protect their significant assets; e.g., high-value financial accounts, private health-care data, sensitive government information, and code critical processes. This is the case since most users mental models of real-life security enable them to distinguish between a few assets that are valuable and many that are not, and seek protection for the former while expecting unconstrained access to the latter [20]. Hence, most users expect to have at least of few transactions at their disposal that protect their assets with high a degree of confidence. At the same time, most users want to be unencumbered by security procedures when they do not access valuable assets and benefit from the freedom offered by unconstrained access to Internet services. In short, most users need a mechanism that enables them to switch between a secure world and a world of freedom in Internet interactions.

Axiom 2. Most users need feasible recourse from security breaches.

Most users seem to understand that there is no perfect security in the on-line world and hence require feasible recourse from security breaches. This usually implies the automated detection security breaches (e.g., by malicious software and insiders) and isolation of their effects, largely automated recovery mechanisms, and, if all else fails, accountability and attribution for the perpetrators of the detected breaches.

The need for feasible recourse arises from users mental models and expectations developed in the real world; e.g., guaranteed repairs from accidents, account insurance in case of stolen credit cards and other financial instruments, regaining ones identity and credentials after identity theft. Lack of detailed understanding of how the security mechanisms of commodity systems work often leads users to attribute real world properties to systems and networks and to expect similar recourse after security breaches. However, most users are able to learn new recourse procedures for the on-line world provided that these are feasible; e.g., accessible to them with little effort.

Axiom 3. Most users can benefit from security policy simplicity and uniformity.

Most commodity operating systems define security policies in terms of different types of user permissions to different system objects; e.g., permissions to files, directories, devices, interprocess communication objects, shared segments, and processes. Users are expected to understand how to configure application policies despite ample evidence that most are unable to express even relatively simple access restrictions for a single object type in practice [32]. As a consequence, users are often exposed to adversary attacks that could, in principle, be countered by sound policy configurations; e.g., by correct permission settings. Part of the problem is that, to counter an adversary attack against a specific application, a user must understand both the application specification and the definition of the attack. Lack of knowledge in either area inevitably leads to errors that leave users in an insecure state. Clearly, users could benefit from simple and uniform default policies for applications that make it obvious which adversary behaviors are countered by which policy. Hence, it is unlikely that most users can benefit from widely different and complex policies and use them effectively to counter threats.

Most users can also benefit from uniform interfaces to access control settings, and from having examples for how to use these settings when additional levels of control are required. Policy definition tools and aids (e.g., secure-state verification tools) are most often required to support user verification of correct permission settings.

4   Isolated Partitions

A possible role for the above "axioms" of insecurity and usable security is to help delimit the usefulness of different architectures for system security that could be employed effectively by ordinary users, system administrators, and application developers using commodity systems. We begin by arguing that, by itself, virtualization is not particularly useful for application security despite new hardware architectures that support it efficiently. Specifically, we examine whether virtualization, both early and modern, can support (1) isolated partitions, (2) secure channels and trusted paths, as a basis for trustworthy communication. and (3) high assurance TCBs. Then we focus on two types of isolated partitions and their salient features for high-assurance, usable commodity implementation.

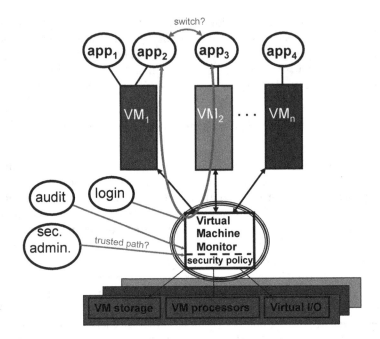

Fig. 1. Early Virtualization: Coarse-Grain VM Partitions and Unstructured VMMs

4.1   Virtualized Systems

Early Virtualization. The original notions of virtualization using Virtual Machine Monitors (VMMs), or hypervisors, originated with IBMs CP-67 and ended with VM/370 systems [2]. The original VMMs implemented only abstractions that enable a virtual machine (VM) to run an operating system and user applications efficiently. These included virtual storage (e.g., virtual memory, disk volumes, and possibly a rudimentary file system), virtual devices, and virtual processors. Using these abstractions, early virtual machines could support different operating systems, one per VM, and their applications; viz., Figure 1. Application partitions were implemented by VMMs, and inter-partition communication channels were provided by *ad-hoc* breaches of the isolation; e.g. some applications used shared virtual memory segments, others shared files.

Early virtualization lacked sufficiently strong partition (VM) separation/ isolation as illustrated by various penetration exercises [1]. Secure channels between partitions and user trusted paths were unavailable, and the association of VMs and applications with users was not completely under user control. For example, lack of trusted path implied that a user could not tell whether he was talking to his VM/application, since malware in a different VM could always spoof appropriate user interaction. Although, in principle, the VMM could support a reference monitor, in practice early VMMs were neither properly isolated nor small and simple enough to be formally verifiable. For example, VMMs had to

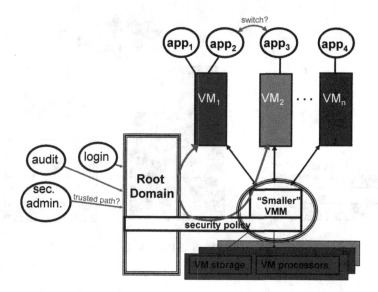

Fig. 2. Example of Modern Virtualization: Smaller and More Structured VMMs and Large Root Domains

implement full I/O device support since DMA transfers occurred in physical memory and hence VMs could not be trusted with device I/O. VM operating systems were also insufficiently layered to be amenable to formal verification.

The DEC VAX/VMM project [19] addressed most of the problems of early virtualization and achieved all the high-assurance security goals for TCBs, which remain beyond the reach of most systems today. For example, VAX/VMM implemented information-flow isolation between VM (partitions), secure channels between partitions, and dedicated trusted paths which enabled secure association of a VM with its users. The VMM supported all requirements of a reference monitor and a fully layered version of VMS operating system. Unfortunately, the development of VAX/VMM diverged from DEC's VMS commercial product, its time-to-market delay and opportunity cost were high, and hence development was canceled before it could become a niche or special-application product.[1]

Modern Virtualization. Present day commodity systems include Xen, VMware, and Hyper-V [16,34,35]. All are better structured than early commodity systems, and yet do not support the requirements for partition isolation, trustworthy communication, and high-assurance reference monitors. None provide layering of operating system VMs. For example, the Xen hypervisor does not include device drivers and virtually all I/O support is implemented in a separate trusted *root domain*; viz., Figure 2. This hypervisor supports inter VM communication in more structured ways than in early virtualization. It also provides full device virtualization.

---

[1] Note added in editing (2013): A recent enlightening assessment of the VAX/VMM project is provided by Lipner, Jaeger and Zurko [33].

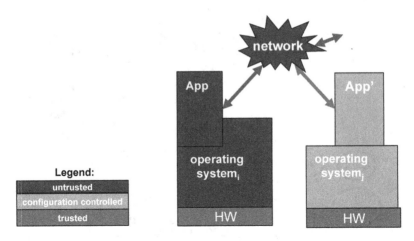

Fig. 3. Physical Partitions

However, users still cannot fully control their association with specific VMs and applications since trusted paths are not supported. The large VMM code sizes (e.g., between 200K and 650K SLoC) and Root Domain code size (over 10M SLoC) make it impossible to support a reference monitor (e.g., the VAX/VMM had approximately 50K SLoC) and trusted computing base (TCB) security.

All virtualization approaches have three common limitations of usable security. First, they are not designed to address specific application-oriented or network security policies, which is what users ultimately care about; viz., database management policies, message and mail system policies, separation of duty policies for enterprise insiders. Second, they are not designed to support trustworthy communication between partitions; at best, they only provide secure channels between partitions and only rarely trusted paths between users and their partitions. Third, are not designed to address specific client-side concerns of usable security; e,g., separate between security-sensitive and non-sensitive client transactions, feasible recourse in case of security breaches, support of simple application policies.

4.2 Physical and Logical Isolation

Physical Isolation. The fact that most users can distinguish between security sensitive transactions that access valuable assets and ordinary access to data and code assets of little value is illustrated by the common practice of using two physical computing or communication devices to access separate accounts and communication resources, and execute separate transactions. For example, most stock and bond traders use separate phones, laptops or desktops to separate trading activities from Internet browsing and document or program downloads. Military and other government personnel use different colored/labeled phones,

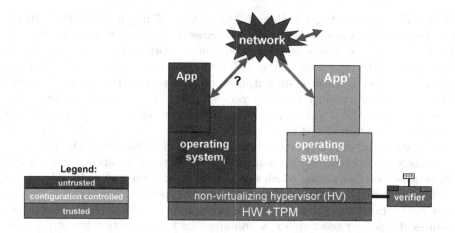

Fig. 4. Logical Partitions

laptops or desktops to communicate and process classified and unclassified information. Using physical separation of devices to partition and isolate execution environments (viz., Figure 3) has a number of advantages. Users are fully aware of having to take explicit action to (physically) switch processing environments, and the association between a user and a specific processing environment (e.g., trusted path) is implicitly provided and cannot be spoofed behind a users back by malicious software since it cannot possibly cause a physical device switch. The configuration of the device used for sensitive or classified data processing can be strictly controlled, and its maintenance (e.g., software patching) can be performed professionally under strict rules. Transactions these devices execute can be limited to those trusted by the user and allowed by his role.

The limitations of physical-device separation to partition and isolate execution environments are equally evident. The association of a strictly configured, professionally maintained device and execution of a limited set of trusted transactions does not imply that a client device is free of exploitable software vulnerabilities; nor that it is immune from attacks launched by malicious software inadvertently imported from a compromised server by an unsuspecting user. Communication security and trustworthiness are not assured even though a device owner could establish cryptographic channels between physically separate devices without relying on trusted third parties; e.g., by installing self-signed certificates, shared secret keys in his own devices. This is the case because the untrusted device may be compromised by malicious software and hence channel secrecy and authenticity cannot be guaranteed. Finally, form-factor inconvenience becomes particularly evident in mobile environments; e.g., a user needs to carry, recharge, and avoid loss or theft of more than one device.

Logical Isolation. Logical machine isolation can be achieved by a *non-virtualizing hypervisor* that partitions the resources of a single machine and eliminates the form-factor inconvenience of physical partitions. Logical isolation retains all the advantages and most limitations of physical isolation. In effect, such a hypervisor exceeds the requirements of *red-green* machine separation [20,22], namely the separation of an untrustworthy (red) machine from a less untrustworthy, carefully configured, maintained, and connected full-service (green) one. This is the case since it must support both a trusted boot [15] and trusted-switch operation using an *external verifier* device and a Trusted Platform Module (TPM) [14]; viz., Figure 4 . The former enables a user to determine whether the green machine (to the right of Figure 4) was booted in a correct configuration and provides attestation to this effect to the user. The latter enables users to determine which machine they talk to by observing whether the red or green verifier lights, which are located to the left and right side of the verifier, respectively, flicker (or hearing an appropriate buzzing sound for vision impaired users) upon performing a machine-switch operation. Neither operation requires the verifier to store any secret since its sole security-relevant function is signature verifications using public keys. As illustrated by the Lockdown system [8], this type of hypervisor can be very small (e.g., under 8.5K SLoC) and simple since it does not virtualize resources for a large number of VMs, and can create isolated execution environments for *unmodified* commodity operating systems; e.g., Linux or Windows (e.g., 2003 SP1). In this sense, the non-virtualizing hypervisor is an "add-on" component to existing commodity operating systems – and not a native foundation built at inception.

One might argue that such a add-on hypervisor implements a reference monitor for humans. It enforces a very simple all-or-nothing policy for mediating all accesses of the two subjects (i.e., the red and green partitions) of a human to system resources; it is isolated from external tampering by the two subjects; and it is small and simple enough to be formally verified. The correct partitioning of resources is much simpler to prove than correct virtualization. Although all insecurity axioms still hold for the two individual commodity operating systems, they do not hold for the commodity system as a whole.

The usability axioms hold for both physically and logically isolated machines. For example, the green machine's access to Internet services can be restricted to few services the user trusts; e.g., its connectivity can be limited to trusted web servers. Internet services whose security is uncertain (e.g., DNS services) can be avoided. Green machine configuration and maintenance (e.g., updates, patching) and recovery from security breaches can be performed by outside professional services. Finally, the security policy the user needs to learn is as simple as it gets: s/he only needs to switch to the green machine to access valuable assets and execute sensitive transactions. However, the usability axioms (e.g., feasible recourse) may still fail whenever the green machine accepts input from or provides sensitive output to the red machine since trustworthy red-green communication is *not* supported.

4.3   Developer-Selected Code Partitions

Red-green partitioning has two obvious limitations. First, as already mentioned above, they cannot support secure red-green channels, which means that

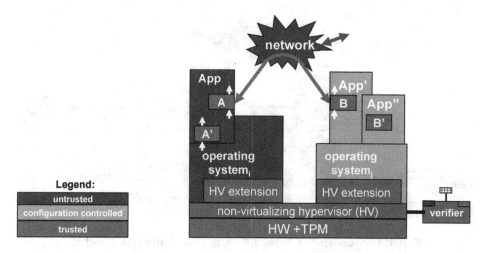

Fig. 5. User-Selected Code Partitions A and B for Isolated Execution

trustworthy communication is not possible. Second, they cannot isolate client-side code and data of different applications in the green machine, which must protect their sensitive data (e.g., private cryptographic keys) and credentials (e.g., unlinkable anonymous identifiers). For example, modules B and B' of applications App' and App" may trust operating system services of the green machine but not each other, and hence need to be isolated. Partitioning application-level code into fine-grain isolated execution environments by application developers can eliminate both these limitations.

Partitioning code and data to protect the secrecy and integrity of selected security-sensitive modules of an application can be achieved by a small *hypervisor extension*; i.e., about 7.6K SLoC [7]. This retains the ability to formally verify the hypervisor and demonstrate code-execution integrity and data isolation. It also preserves the "add-on" property of the underlying hypervisor since it does not require any operating system modification. The hypervisor extension also attests to the existence of security-sensitive modules A and A' in the red machine (at the left in Figure 5) and B, and B' in the green machine (at the right in Figure 5) to the external verifier. (As before, the verifier does not need to store any secret.) Thus, a selected security-sensitive module can be isolated from an untrusted commodity operating system (e.g., modules A and A') and from other applications of a trusted operating system (e.g., modules B of application App' and B' of application App" on the green machine) in execution environments created by the hypervisor extension.

A module selected for isolation by an application developer is registered with the hypervisor extension, which initializes the execution environment to a secure configuration state. The module is recompiled before registration and a special communication area is established by the hypervisor extension to marshal parameters, which are always passed by value between the untrusted portions of the

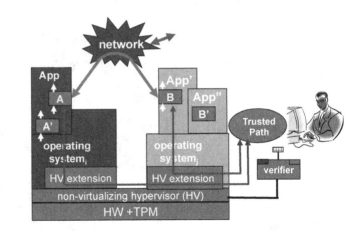

Fig. 6. User-Controlled Trusted Path to Code Partitions A and B

application and OS and the isolated module, before the isolated module begins execution. The hypervisor extension can use hardware virtualization support to provide memory isolation and DMA protection for each module. It also uses the TPM to implement attestation functions for the hypervisor itself, isolated modules, and sealed module storage. An example of a hypervisor extension that implements these security function is TrustVisor [7].

Modules which execute in isolated environments can protect secret keys and code needed for secure channel implementation as well as other private credentials of different clients executing on either the red or green machine. (Additional requirements for trustworthy communication are discussed in the next section.) For example, since isolated execution is available both on the untrustworthy (red) machine (e.g., module A) and the more trustworthy (green) one (e.g., module B), the confidentiality and authenticity of channel data can be protected while being transmitted by the isolated sender module over an untrusted network to the isolated receiver module; e.g., the channel between modules A and B in Figure 5. Similarly, two isolated client modules can execute on the same machine without being able to tamper with each other's code and data, or read each others sealed memory contents; e.g., modules A and A' in the red machine and B and B' of the green machine in Figure 5.

4.4   User-Verifiable Execution of Code Modules via Trusted Path

Isolated execution of application modules has an obvious limitation. That is, there is no secure channel, *aka* a *trusted path*, between that module and the user's I/O devices; e.g., a keyboard, video display, mouse. Building a trusted path is required by a variety of security-sensitive applications, including: (1) defining and maintaining security policy data (e,g., credentials, access control lists) encapsulated in isolated application code; (2) user I/O operations for accessing sensitive information (e.g., inputting account and password information, displaying account balances in financial applications); and (3) operator I/O for sending commands to physical devices that control critical processes, and displaying authentic device-status information.

Building a trusted path between users and isolated application modules is a non-trivial exercise considering that an adversary (e.g., malware, insiders) can control an untrusted operating system. For example, the operating system of the red (left) machine of Figure 6 can intercept any communication between the user keyboard/display and isolated module A. This could also happen if the adversary compromises the operating system of the green machine, though this would be less likely to happen than in the red machine. A compromised operating system can access and reconfigure any devices it controls; e.g., it can modify a devices memory mapped I/O regions, or induce the device to perform arbitrary operations (e.g., trigger interrupts, issue DMA write requests) using compromised I/O commands. In short, a compromised operating system can affect the confidentiality and integrity of trusted path transfers to/from isolated modules.

Unlike a traditional trusted path, which only includes activation of TCB commands [19,23,38], our non-virtualizing hypervisor can support commands of any isolated module. However, it can implement management functions for very few simple user-oriented devices, such as keyboards and video displays, without unduly increasing the hypervisor's size beyond the level that affords formal verification; viz., a USB subsystem. Most device management functions would have to be handled in the isolated execution environment for the application modules, and I/O transfers must take place directly in user space, instead of the hypervisor's.[2] A key requirement is to enable a user to verify the trusted-path state (e.g., correct configuration and activation) using the external verifier device illustrated in Figures 4–6.

The ability to isolate the execution environments for application modules on an untrusted operating system (e.g., modules A and A' of application App on the red machine, at the left of Figure 6), and to verify the activation of those modules and perform protected I/O operations via the trusted path raises the question of whether the green-machine operating system (at the right of Figure 6) is needed at all. Supporting a green machine is motivated by the different availability of trusted services that could be used by the isolated application modules on the two machines. For example, remote attestation can help enforce a policy that access to a corporate virtual private network and other security-sensitive (e.g., financial, health-care) services may be allowed only through green operating system applications, such as App' and App" and clients B and B'. The green machine would also be needed since its operating system could make user-trusted services available to isolated modules of the red machine, which would

---

[2] Note added in editing (2013): the challenges of implementing trusted path to isolated application-module space and a practical solution are described in detail by Zhou et al. [17]. The hypervisor extension including the trusted path for two simple user devices are implemented in less than 16K SLoC.

otherwise be inaccessible; e.g., I/O services for devices not supported by the trusted path of the red machine. We note again that while the services of the green operating system are *not* formally verified, they are more trustworthy than those of the red operating system.

5   Trustworthy Communication

In this section, we restrict our focus to the requirements of trustworthy communication over an above those of secure channels and trusted paths. The governing principle of trust, which also governs trustworthy communication, is that *all trust is local* [22]. This means that the receiver of a message, which may have arrived on a secure channel, is always empowered to decide whether to accept the message content and act upon it. Similarly, the sender can decide whether to output a message containing private data. This decision must be exercised at receipt of messages from an untrusted source and output of messages to an untrusted destination. For example, isolated modules A and A' of Figure 6 act as both senders and receivers (as denoted by the white arrows) when they use the file system services of the untrusted (red) machine. They can encrypt the content of their data in an authenticated encryption mode using their secret keys, which automatically protects them from confidentiality and authenticity compromise. That is, upon receipt of these files the isolated modules can attempt to decrypt the data with their secret key and if the decryption succeeds the confidentiality and authenticity of those data are assured with overwhelming probability. Similarly, these modules can use the untrusted protocol stack of the red operating system to send and receive encrypted messages over the untrusted network.

However, verifying the acceptability of one's input and protecting the privacy of one's output is not always practical or even possible.[3] For example, a module cannot always accept a *ppt, doc, xls* or *pdf* file since these file representations contain active code whose effects cannot always be verified; e.g., verification is undecidable, in general, or at least inefficient in some cases. Even the acceptability of *ascii* characters may be questionable in some cases (e.g., they may represent English *shellcode* [26]). In such cases, the receiver may decide to coerce its input to a verifiable format, if the loss of information can be tolerated; e.g., a *ppt* file is converted to ordinary *pdf* format, and the *pdf* to *clean pdf*. In short, the receiver can sometimes "make its input right" before acceptance. In other cases, when the receiver cannot verify the validity of its input, it may still accept the input provided that the sender is accountable. For authentication tickets or certificates received as inputs to authentication protocols, the acceptance policy is always based on some form of accountability [4]. In other cases, acceptability of these inputs is established based on social relations, such as friends' recommendations and evidence of past input use [39].

It is sometimes possible for a sender to determine that the recipient of its sensitive output is trusted not to misuse the received output, or at least

---

[3] Note added in editing (2013): A detailed account of trustworthy communication is given by Gligor and Wing at the 19th SPW [25].

accountable for it. This is the case when the recipient is a trusted "guard" or service provider that has a public commitment to safeguard a sender's private data. In such cases, output control policies, such as originator control (ORCON) and digital rights management, may be enforced. As in the case of a receiver, the sender can sometimes "make its output right" before sending it to a receiver it does not trust; e.g., the sender can anonymise private data and make them unlinkable to it.

6 Conclusions

High-assurance usable security will continue to elude commodity computers even when they employ new hardware for efficient virtualization. However, high-assurance usable security appears possible when using non-virtualizing hypervisors as *add-ons* to commodity operating systems to provide isolated code execution and trustworthy communication between isolated partitions and between users and partitions. These hypervisors are small (e.g., fewer than 25K SLoC), and have simple properties whose verification is well within the capabilities of today's formal methods. Usable security, application development, and system maintenance have modest requirements, and inconvenience is minimized. Users need to switch between a trusted and an untrusted partition of a single computer; developers need to figure out which application modules are security sensitive and isolate them; and special maintenance is required only for the trusted partition and a few isolated modules in the untrusted one. Trustworthy communication is more challenging since it requires trust decisions, not merely secure channels.

Acknowledgments. The author benefited from discussions with Jon McCune, Bryan Parno, Adrian Perrig, Amit Vasudevan, and Zongwei Zhou on several topics covered in this paper. Their insights are gratefully acknowledged. This work was supported in part by the National Science Foundation (NSF) under grants CNS083142 and CNS105224. The views and conclusions contained in this document are those of the author and should not be interpreted as representing the official policies, either expressed or implied, of any sponsoring institution, the U.S. government or any other entity.

References

1. Attanasio, C.R., Markstein, P.W., Phillips, R.J.: Penetrating an Operating System: A Study of VM/370 Integrity. IBM Systems Journal 15(1), 102–116 (1976)
2. Richard Attanasio, C.: Virtual Control Storage - Security Measures in VM/370. IBM Systems Journal 18(1), 93–110 (1979)
3. Anderson, J.P.: Computer security technology planning study. Volume 2. Technical Report ESD-TR-73-51, Air Force Electronic Systems Division (1972)
4. Gligor, V., Luan, S.-W., Pato, J.: Inter-Realm Authentication in Large Distributed Systems. In: Proc. of IEEE Symp. on Security and Privacy, Oakland, CA (1992); also in the Journal of Computer Security 1993

5. BAE Systems. Information Technology LLC. Security Target, Version 1.11 for XTS-400, Version 6 (2004)
6. Lampson, B.W.: Software components: Only the giants survive. In: Computer Systems: Theory, Technology, and Applications, vol. (9), pp. 137–145. Springer (2004)
7. McCune, J., Li, Y., Qu, N., Zhou, Z., Datta, A., Gligor, V., Perrig, A.: TrustVisor: Efficient TCB Reduction and Attestation. Technical Report, CMU-CyLab-09-003 (March 2009); also in Proc. of IEEE Symp. on Security and Privacy, Oakland, CA (May 2010)
8. Vasudevan, A., Parno, B., Qu, N., Gligor, V., Perrig, A.: Lockdown: A Safe and Practical Environment for Security Applications. Technical Report, CMU-CyLab-09-011 (July 14, 2009); Also in International Conference on Trust and Trustworthy Computing (TRUST), Vienna, Austria, (2012)
9. Rushby, J.M.: Design and verification of secure systems. Proc. of SOSP 15(5), 12–21 (1981)
10. Rushby, J.M.: Separation and Integration in MILS (The MILS Constitution). Technical Report, SRI-CSL-TR-08-XX (February 2008)
11. Boettcher, C., DeLong, R., Rushby, J., Sifre, W.: The MILS Component Integration Approach to Secure Information Sharing. In: 27th IEEE/AIAA Digital Avionics Systems Conference (DASC), St. Paul MN (October 2008)
12. Peinado, M., Chen, Y., Engl, P., Manferdelli, J.: NGSCB: A Trusted Open System. In: Proc. Australasian Conference on Information Security and Privacy (2004)
13. Schell, R., Tao, T., Heckman, M.: Designing the GEMSOS security kernel for security and performance. In: Proc. National Computer Security Conference, Baltimore, MD (1985)
14. Trusted Computing Group. Trusted platform module main specification, Part 1: Design principles, Part 2: TPM structures, Part 3: Commands. Version 1.2, Revision 103 (July 2007)
15. Parno, B., McCune, J.M., Perrig, A.: Bootstrapping Trust in Commodity Computers. In: Proc. of the IEEE Symposium on Security and Privacy (May 2010)
16. Fraser, K., Hand, S., Neugebauer, R., Pratt, I., Warfield, A., Williamson, M.: Safe hardware access with the Xen virtual machine monitor. In: Proc. Workshop on Operating System and Architectural Support for the on demand IT InfraStructure (OASIS) (2004)
17. Zhou, Z., Gligor, V.D., Newsome, J., McCune, J.M.: Building verifiable trusted path on commodity x86 computers. In: Proc. IEEE Symposium on Security and Privacy (2012)
18. Gold, B.D., Linde, R.R., Cudney, P.: KVM/370 in Retrospect. In: Proc. of IEEE Symp. on Security and Privacy, Oakland, CA (May 1984)
19. Karger, P.A., Zurko, M.E., Bonin, D.W., Mason, A.H.: A Retrospective on the VAX VMM Security Kernel. IEEE Transaction on Software Engineering 17(11) (November 1991)
20. Lampson, B.W.: Accountability and Freedom Slides., http://research.microsoft.com/en-us/um/people/blampson/slides/accountabilityAndFreedomAbstract.htm
21. Lucky, R.W.: When is Dumb Smart. IEEE Spectrum, 21 (November 1997)
22. Lampson, B.W.: Usable Security: How to Get It. Comm. ACM (November 2009)
23. Fraim, L.J.: SCOMP: A Solution to the Multilevel Security Problem. IEEE Computer 16(7), 26–34 (1983)
24. Gligor, V.D.: On the evolution of adversary models in security protocols (or know your friend and foe alike). In: Christianson, B., Crispo, B., Malcolm, J.A., Roe, M. (eds.) Security Protocols 2005. LNCS, vol. 4631, pp. 276–283. Springer, Heidelberg (2007)

25. Gligor, V., Wing, J.M.: Towards a Theory of Trust in Networks of Humans and Computers. In: Christianson, B., Crispo, B., Malcolm, J., Stajano, F. (eds.) Security Protocols 2011. LNCS, vol. 7114, pp. 223–242. Springer, Heidelberg (2011)
26. Mason, J., Small, S., McManus, G., Monrose, F.: English Shellcode. In: Proc. of the 16th ACM Conference on Computer and Communications Security (CCS), pp. 524–533 (November 2009)
27. Bell, D.E., LaPadula, L.J.: Secure Computer System: Unified Exposition and Multics Interpretation. In: Deputy for Command and Management Systems, HQ Electronic Systems Division (AFSC), ESD-TR-75-306 (March 1976)
28. Adleman, N., Gilson, J.R., Sestak, R.J., Ziller, R.J.: Security Kernel Evaluation for Multics and Secure Multics Design. Technical Report, Honeywell Information Systems Inc., Mclean Va Federal Systems Operations (August 1976); Available at NTIS AD-A038 261/4
29. Klein, G., Elphinstone, K., Heiser, G., Andronick, J., Cock, D., Derrin, P., Elkaduwe, D., Engelhardt, K., Kolanski, R., Norrish, M., Sewell, T., Tuch, H., Winwood, S.: seL4: formal verification of an OS kernel. In: Proc. of SOSP, pp. 207–220. ACM (2009)
30. Howard, M., Pincus, J., Wing, J.M.: Computer Security in the 21st Century. In: Lee, D.T., Shieh, S.P., Tygar, J.D. (eds.) Measuring Relative Attack Surfaces, pp. 109–137. Springer (March 2005)
31. Manadhata, P.K., Karabulut, Y., Wing, J.M.: Report: Measuring the Attack Surfaces of Enterprise Software. In: Massacci, F., Redwine Jr., S.T., Zannone, N. (eds.) ESSoS 2009. LNCS, vol. 5429, pp. 91–100. Springer, Heidelberg (2009)
32. Reeder, R.W., Maxion, R.A.: User Interface Dependability through Goal-Error Prevention. In: Proc. of International Conference on Dependable Systems and Networks, Yokohama, Japan, June 28 -July 01, pp. 60–69 (2005)
33. Lipner, S., Jaeger, T., Zurko, M.E.: Lessons from VAX/SVS for High Assurance VM Systems. IEEE Security and Privacy 10(6), 26–35 (2012)
34. VMware White paper. Understanding Full Virtualization, Paravirtualization and Hardware Assist, http://www.vmware.com/files/pdf/VMware_paravirtualization.pdf (accessed March 23, 2010)
35. De Clercq, J.: Windows Server 2008 Hyper-V Security, http://windowsitpro.com/virtualization/windows-server-2008-hyper-v-security (accessed March 23, 2010)
36. Schroeder, M.D., Clark, D.D., Saltzer, J.H.: The Multics Kernel Design Project. In: Proc. of SOSP, pp. 43–56. ACM (1977)
37. Neumann, P.G., Feiertag, R.J.: PSOS Revisited. In: Proc. of the 19th Annual Computer Security Applications Conference (2003)
38. Schell, R.R., Tao, T.F., Heckman, M.: Designing the GEMSOS security kernel for security and performance. In: Proc. of the 8th National Computer Security Conference, Gaithersburg, MD, pp. 108–119 (1985)
39. Wendlandt, D., Andersen, D., Perrig, A.: Perspectives: Improving SSH-style Host Authentication with Multi-Path Probing. In: Proceedings of USENIX Annual Technical Conference (June 2008)

Security Limitations of Virtualization and How to Overcome Them (Transcript of Discussion)

Virgil Gligor

Carnegie Mellon University

Many of the ideas I will present were developed in collaboration with Jonathan McCune, Bryan Parno, Adrian Perrig, Amit Vasudevan and Zongwei Zhou over the past couple of years. I will begin the presentation with my "axioms" of insecurity and usable security. These axioms are in fact observations that I believe will be true in the future. Then I will review virtualization for security and experiences that we have had with it practically since day one. I will also review the limitations of virtual-machine isolation for application-level code and usable security. And finally, the main proposition of this presentation is that we should switch our attention from virtualization and virtual-machine isolation, to *red-green* machine partitions, which is somewhat of a new area[1], and to *trustworthy communication*. I will argue that trustworthy communication requires more than secure-channel protocols.

Axioms of Insecurity. Let me start with the "axioms" of insecurity. A more detailed formulation and explanation of these axioms is given in the accompanying paper. The first axiom is that there will always be rapid innovation in information technology, and this will inevitably lead to use of low-assurance software components of diverse provenance in the supply chain. Most applications we will use will have components provided by different suppliers, and hence with diverse degrees of assurance. And all these components will be integrated into larger software systems and applications. For example, roughly half of the many thousands of device drivers in Microsoft's Windows are not written by Microsoft developers, and some fraction of those may not necessarily be written to meet all Microsoft's standards.

The second axiom is that there will always be large, complex software systems whose security is not fully understood by most users. In fact, Butler Lampson makes the stronger statement about the software components of various systems, namely that among software components only the giants survive.[2] For security-sensitive components, this is clearly not a very good thing.

The third axiom is that there will always be bugs, operator/user errors, that lead to security vulnerabilities, and there will always be adversaries (e.g., in malware, insiders) willing and able to exploit these security vulnerabilities. In these axioms, the qualifier "always" means 15+ years, which is essentially beyond

---

[1] B. W. Lampson. Usable Security: How to Get It. In *Comm. ACM*, Nov. (2009).

[2] B. W. Lampson. Software components: Only the Giants Survive. In *Computer Systems: Theory, Technology, and Applications.*, Springer Verlag, 2004:137–145.

B. Christianson and J. Malcolm (Eds.): Security Protocols 2010, LNCS 7061, pp. 252–265, 2014.
© Springer-Verlag Berlin Heidelberg 2014

our technology horizon and hopefully my retirement. So if these axioms will be proven false then, it will be hard to hold me accountable (laughter).

A key question is how do we reconcile these axioms of insecurity with what users want and need, which I will formulate as my three "axioms" of usable security.

Axioms of Usable Security. First, users typically need a high level of security for a few types of transactions, particularly those in which significant assets are at stake; e.g., transactions for financial assets, healthcare, defence and intelligence assets; assets of high-stake, multi-player interactive games, which eventually map back to handling financial assets; assets in physical systems and process control. At the same time, users want the freedom of choice for all other types of transactions. In other words, unrestricted Internet access is non-negotiable: it cannot be ruled out for the sake of security. For example, it doesn't matter how highly classified an intelligence environment might be, many people will still read papers online and browse the Internet. Ruling out use of the Internet would imply that people will be unable to do their daily work.

Second, users need to isolate and limit the effects of security breaches; e.g., isolate themselves from malicious insiders and malware actions, and recover from inevitable security breaches. And they want accountability and attribution: they actually need to punish an adversary for a security breach.

Third, users can always benefit from policy simplicity and uniformity. The simpler the policy the better. Complexity whenever necessary should be introduced incrementally. Typical users prefer to have uniform security interfaces, so that they don't have to learn new ways to interact with new applications, and need security tools and aids.

Virtualization for Security — A Brief History. Virtualization has been claimed to provide much of what users need. Reliance on virtualization for usable security is not new. However, it has not worked well in the past for commodity systems, and I argue that one should not have high expectations that it will work in the future.

The first to suggest virtualization for security were Stuart Madnick and John Donovan of the MIT Sloan School of Business[3] who argued that virtual machine isolation provides substantially better software security than conventional operating systems. Very shortly after that IBM and the System Development Corporation (SDC) began a study on the security of the VM/370.[4] And, of course, what they found was quite interesting at the time, namely that there is virtually no real security in these systems. Hence, about 1976, SDC started a project to secure VM/370 and produce the kernalised VM/370 (KVM) architecture, which supported multi-level security, whereby each isolated VM represented a separate

---

[3] S. E. Madnick and J. J. Donovan. Application and Analysis of the Virtual Machine Approach to Information System Security. In Proceedings of the *ACM SIGARCH-SIGOPS Workshop on Virtual Computer Systems,* pages 210–224, Harvard University, Cambridge, MA, USA, 26–27 March 1973.

[4] C. R. Attanasio, P. W. Markstein, R. J. Phillips. Penetrating an Operating System: A Study of VM/370 Integrity. In *IBM Systems Journal,* 15(1): 102–116, 1976.

security level. This project lasted until early '80s, and the approach taken was considered good enough for use in the military.

Between about 1982 and 1989, Digital Equipment Corporation (DEC) produced a VMM-based version of VAX VMS, which was eventually evaluated at the highest level of assurance available in the Orange Book, namely an A1 class system. It was a very interesting design, and I'll mention a few things about it as we go along. However, in early 1990s, the project was cancelled for obvious business reasons related to commodity systems, which I'll go into in a minute.

Between the early 1990s and early 2000s we entered the "dark age" of VM-based security. Essentially this idea disappeared, only to resurface in the mid 2000s. The reason it resurfaced is that virtual machine architectures got a lot of traction as commodity systems, for other significant reasons. For example, these architectures were motivated by server consolidation, load balancing, and later cloud computing. We start to find some of the first papers on virtual machine and security again around 2004. New interest in this area was fueled by the NSA who convinced defense-oriented companies to take a close look at virtualized architectures as the basis for high-assurance separation kernels.[5] Eventually, the effort to provide high-assurance separation kernels for commodity workstations was abandoned.[6]

How well did virtualization fare in commodity systems security? The initial idea was to implement a reference monitor within the virtual machine monitor (VMM), which is isolated from external tampering, always invoked on every object reference, and small enough to be verifiable. The reference monitor isolated virtual machines from each other. However, as more and more applications were developed, application developers experienced an increased need for application communications, which led to breaches of the isolation between virtual machines, in ad-hoc ways. For example, some applications started communicating through message pipes, others using network interfaces, yet others through shared files and shared segments. There were many ways in which applications breached isolation legitimately, but unfortunately many of those ways led to system penetration. An additional problem that caused security exposures was that none of the virtual machines (VMs) attached to users were under user control. For example, there could be unauthorized switches between VMs. As Ross[7] pointed out yesterday, a user could not tell what virtual machine was running at any time. There was no trusted path for either administrators or ordinary users. Figure 1 of the accompanying paper illustrates the initial approaches to virtualization. A user couldn't tell that one VM had switched to another unbeknownst to him, since a different VM running now could paint the same image as the original one

[5] R. W. Beckwith, W. M. Vanfleet, and L. MacLaren. High Assurance Security/Safety for Deeply Embedded, Real-time Systems. In Proc. of *Embedded Systems Conference*, 2004. pp. 247–267.

[6] National Security Agency. *Separation Kernels on Commodity Workstations*. In Systems and Network Analysis Center, Information Assurance Directorate, 11 March 2010. http://www.niap-ccevs.org/announcements/ Separation%20Kernels%20on%20 Commodity%20Workstations.pdf

[7] Anderson, these proceedings.

on the user's video display. Yet another problem was that the trusted computing base (TCB) was very large, and thus impractical for any degree of systematic, let alone formal, verification. And that wasn't all. While the DEC VAX VMM fixed these security problems, it had some significant usability problems typical of Orange Book evaluated systems. One of them was that the TCB configuration was so strict that an installation couldn't add more devices (i.e., drivers) than the ones which were evaluated, without losing its rating. Another was that the evaluated TCB diverged from and fell behind commodity VAX VMS development. The VAX VMM project had to be cancelled after it received its A1 rating, because it lacked paying customers.

An interesting development that followed was Xen, which produced a VMM of reasonable size for a commodity system; i.e., it started out with about 120K source lines of code (SLoC) and by 2008 grew to about 200K SLoC. Xen removed many services from the VMM and placed them into a large "root domain" of approximately the size of Linux, or 10–14M SLoC. Communication between VMs was done via virtualized devices and so it was much better structured than in the original VM/370 architectures. A simplified view of this approach to virtualization is illustrated in Figure 2 of the accompanying paper. Other commodity VMMs, like VMware and Hyper-V, had code bases between 200–650K SLoC, which places them beyond any practical approaches to formal verification.

Other security problems persisted; e.g., VMs were not under exclusive user control, trusted path for humans was still not supported, and the system TCB remained very large since the root domain size was essentially that of an entire operating system; i.e., millions of SLoC. In general, virtualized systems offered no mechanisms to isolate and protect security-sensitive code modules of an application, and modules of diverse provenance could not coexist securely within an application. Also, they offered no protection against insider attacks, and no protection against establishing unauthorized Internet connections behind a user's back.

Physical Red-Green Partitions. An approach to usable security was recently proposed by Lampson in the *Communications of the ACM*, in November 2009. Essentially he describes an architecture comprising two separate machines: an untrusted (red) machine and a trusted (green) one.[8] Imagine for the moment that these machines are physically distinct and share no resources (viz., Figure 3 of the accompanying paper). They can only communicate via secure channels over the Internet; e.g., via IPSEC protocols. Users have full control over which machines they use at any time, since they can log into one or the other machine. Trusted path to each of the two machines is provided by default: a user always knows with which machine s/he would interact. The configuration and connectivity of the green machine are strictly controlled. It could access very few trusted Internet websites and their IP addresses would be preconfigured, so DNS would not have to be used. And its code is carefully maintained, and arbitrary software could

---

[8] In this presentation, colors have special meaning: green denotes security-code and data that need configuration control, and protection. Dark green denotes trusted components. Red denotes those whose security matters less, or not at all. Red components can be assumed to be captured by an adversary and hence untrusted.

not be downloaded on it. However, the green machine is not necessarily free of exploitable security flaws nor highly assured. In short, the user environment of the green machine is a lot more secure, and more restricted at the same time, than that of the red machine, where one has the freedom of unrestricted access to the Internet.

The primary usability problem of such systems is the inconvenience created by the large device footprint in mobile systems. For example, in defence settings, soldiers would often complain about having to carry two laptops each in a crammed HumV: one for classified and the other for unclassified information and communication.

A key remaining problem of red-green separation is the trustworthy communication between red and green, of course. The first question is, how does green accept input from red? And under what conditions? Are secure network channels sufficient? The second question is how does green output confidential information to red, and how is the confidentiality of that information protected (again, even if secure network channels exist)? David Clark is reported to have remarked that red-green communication is akin to passing through Checkpoint Charlie between East and West Berlin during the Cold War.

Logical Red-Green Partitions. Given the usability characteristics of physical red-green separation, we decided to build a prototype of it on a single laptop to decrease inconvenience of use. I would like to emphasize that the red-green partitioning is *not* implemented by virtual machine isolation. There is no VM scheduling on a multiplexed hardware base. Instead, the separation between the two machines is implemented by resource partitioning at a low enough system level so that full object-code compatibility with commodity operating system code is preserved. Security is an "add-on" to an unmodified operating system, here.

Logical machine partitioning is performed using a very thin layer of code (i.e., under 8.5K SLoC), or *non-virtualizing hypervisor*, called Lockdown, which enables a user to switch between red and green. The switch is done using an external verifier device, which also runs an attestation protocol and allows the user to determine in which machine s/he is at any time. The external verifier has a red and green light and a button, and the switch between green and red, and red and green, cannot be done by the machine itself. Instead, it has to be done explicitly by the user with the help of the external verifier. Malware cannot perform the switch behind the user's back. If the user pushes the button and the laptop transitions from the green machine to the red one, s/he can work on the red one for however long s/he wants. Similarly, when the user wants to switch back to green for executing a sensitive transactions, s/he pushes the button, attestation is done to make sure that the transition to the green area is done correctly. Figure 4 of the accompanying paper illustrates the logical red-green machine separation.

This machine switching mode on the same hardware base is reminiscent of what used to be called "periods processing" of classified and unclassified information the early 1970s. For example, classified processing might be done in a six-hour period, after which the primary memory and disk would be scrubbed of all information, and classified tapes unmounted. A twelve-hour period of unclassified information processing would follow, and the cycle would start again. In our case, the green period of processing would begin on demand whenever the user would want to run a sensitive transaction. The red-green switch takes place on a time scale commensurate with a user's attention span.

Michael Roe: Are you using cryptography to protect the state of the green machine when you're swapping, so the red machine can't access its bits on the disk?

Reply: Yes. Cryptography is used to verify that the switch between the red and green machines was in fact performed correctly. However, if available, disk encryption is done separately by the operating system of each machine. By the way, all of this is described in a 2010 CMU Technical Report on *Lockdown*, which is available online.[9] The Lockdown project made no attempt to address problems of trustworthy communications.

Application-level code partitioning. Remember that the green machine is not fully trustworthy. For example, it may have exploitable software bugs. Hence, we decided to implement another thin-layer hypervisor that extends Lockdown, and can be configured to run on the bare hardware instead of Lockdown. This hypervisor isolates security-sensitive code blocks of applications of the green machine as well as the red one. A security-sensitive code block is completely isolated from the rest of the untrusted application and operating system, and vice versa. The isolated code block and the rest of the (untrusted) application or operating system code can communicate only through well defined interfaces.

For example, an isolated code block within an application could be the RSA libraries of SSL. Library code using the user's secret keys could be isolated so that no amount of malware or code of an unscrupulous insider could ever touch the crypto code and secret keys used.

The thin-layer hypervisor extension (i.e., less than 7.6K SLoC) is called TrustVisor and its design goals and implementation are described in a paper that will be presented at the IEEE Security and Privacy Symposium in May.[10] After a developer selects the application module that needs to be isolated, s/he recompiles it and the application registers the code with TrustVisor. Then, whenever the application invokes the module, it enters TrustVisor which executes the module code in an address space that is separated from the rest of the untrusted application and operating system. Upon termination the module exits via TrustVisor, which returns control back to the application. Transfer of control can take place only at specified module entry points, and return of control can be executed only at the particular application return point. Parameters are

[9] A. Vasudevan, B. Parno, N. Qu, V. Gligor and A. Perrig. Lockdown: A Safe and Practical Environment for Security Applications. Technical Report, CMU-CyLab-09-011, July 14, 2009.

[10] J. McCune, Y. Li, N. Qu, Z. Zhou, A. Datta, V. Gligor, and A. Perrig. TrustVisor: Efficient TCB Reduction and Attestation. Technical Report, CMU-CyLab-09-003, March, 2009 (also in Proc. of IEEE Symp. on Security and Privacy, Oakland, CA, May 2010).

copied to a memory area of the isolated a code block before their validity is verified. Again, we face the challenge of trustworthy communication between red (application code) and green (isolated module), in addition to trustworthy communication between isolated green modules. A simplified view of this architecture is illustrated in Figure 5 of the accompanying paper. The selection of sensitive code modules for isolated execution is no easy matter because most application code is not well modularised; e.g., it has lots of global variables, shared pointer structures. However, code re-modularizing tools may help in the future. Please note that, although we could verify the validity of the parameters exchanged between untrusted applications and isolated modules, we still haven't resolved this problem of trustworthy communications.

Trusted Path to Isolated Modules. One of the things that may happen is that the module a developer selects for isolation needs to communicate with the user. So the next design task that one has is to offer a "trusted path" between the user and an isolated application module, not just simply switching between red and green machines.

TrustVisor can support trusted path, in principle, since TrustVisor has access to the address space of the isolated application. If the trusted path needs only simple functions of simple I/O devices (e.g., a PS/2 keyboard and a video display), then TrustVisor will still have a small code base. Note that, unlike the traditional trusted path, which offers a user-communication channel only to a TCB, our notion of trusted path provides a user-communication channel to *any* isolated module of an application. Figure 6 of the accompanying paper illustrates our view of trusted path.

In summary, the two notions of isolation we have here can be implemented as "add-ons" to commodity operating systems. We have done that at CyLab, our prototypes are running, and we demonstrate them (although the trusted path function is not implemented yet). The only significant challenge appeared when we implemented the red-green machine switch using the ACPI sleep-state S1 to suspend and activate a machine. The switch is rather slow: we managed to get it down to about 22 per seconds. However, "freezing" an entire machine and switching to another machine is not a simple operation, but we suspect that future technologies will make that lot faster. Nevertheless, that's essentially one of the things one can do to operate two isolated machines — not virtual machines — on the same hardware platform and retain object-code compatibility with a commodity operating system.

I hope I convinced you that these two types of isolation are no longer a mystery, and that they can be implemented in practice reasonably efficiently. By the way, switching in and out of an isolated module in TrustVisor decreases performance by between about 4% and 7% on the average, so that's something that most applications can tolerate; viz., the published benchmark presented in the TrustVisor paper. In any case, the challenging research problems are not in the isolation of security-sensitive code blocks of an untrusted application. Instead, they are in the trustworthy communication between isolated partitions. I argue that trustworthy communication does not mean only that the recipient must validate its input. It also means that it must also validate that its output to the red machine is handled by an isolated (green) module of that machine. Secure-channel communication requires that the receiving side, namely an isolated module within the red machine, controls its end of the communication channel. In other words, to support trustworthy communication, one needs secure channels to untrusted domains. Application code partitioning enables us to support such secure channels.

That is the significant take-away from this discussion. The rest of my presentation focuses on trustworthy communication using secure channels.

Trustworthy Communication. It's been often said that *all trust is local*; viz., Lampson's recent *Comm. ACM* paper already mentioned. This means that a user, or a system component, can always make all its trust decisions; e.g., a receiver of input has the ability to verify that input, and the authority to accept or reject it. Similarly, a sender can decide whether to output a piece of sensitive information to a receiver. However, I argue that we need more than a receiver's local control over its input ; e.g., sometimes the remote sender also has to comply with a receiver's input policy. This implies that even if the sender operates in a totally untrusted (red) environment, it would still have to comply with the (green) receiver's input policies. It would be nice if trust would always imply complete local control over inputs; e.g., a receiver could also control the rate with which the sender sends the input. However, even if a receiver could always control its inputs, which is not the case, discharging that responsibility is not always simple.

We would also expect that the trustworthy communication would have completely symmetric considerations for sensitive output, namely that all trust is local when outputting sensitive information, and that the sender can always control what it sends to others; e.g., it can always censor its own output. Unfortunately, this is not always the case either. Sometimes a receiver (in red) has to comply with a (green) sender's output policy, if the sender itself cannot enforce it locally. In other words, a sender has to be able to exercise control over what the receiver does with its sensitive output. Both these additional types of *non-local* control raise significant challenges for trustworthy communication.

Bruce Christianson: When you say input and output, are you talking from the green perspective only?

Reply: Yes, my point of reference is the green. Thanks for the clarification.

A green input taker has to figure out whether the input received is acceptable, and that, of course, depends on application semantics. Input messages comprising *ascii* code, are often acceptable, but not always. For example, a paper published at ACM CCS last year, called English Shellcode,[11] shows that *ascii* English text could actually start malicious shells in one's computation, so blindly accepting *ascii* code text is not always safe. What about *pdf* input? Well, *pdf* may be acceptable, but only the receiver can filter it to produce a "clean" *pdf*

---

[11] J. Mason, S. Small, G. McManus and F. Monrose. English Shellcode. In Proc. of the 16th ACM Conference on Computer and Communications Security (CCS), pages 524–533, November, 2009.

by removing all the unsafe code embedded in it. What about Word document inputs (i.e., *doc* files)? Of course, all the macros would have to be removed in the process of cleaning it up of unsafe code. Similarly, one would have to clean up PowerPoint input, which would remove animation and other features, and Excel files. Unfortunately, input filtering is seldom acceptable to users since it removes useful features for many applications, and it is usually not done. Accepting *ppt* and *doc* inputs leads some to assert, facetiously, that the highest security clearance of the US (and probably British) government is held by PowerPoint and Word since they have access to *all* the levels of security. I certainly do not know anyone who has such a security clearance.

One has to do some serious thinking about what to do with code-carrying input. Java and other scripts are not acceptable without validation unless one is willing to take substantial risks. The verification of whether an input is acceptable sometimes leads to undecidable problems. In such cases, one may seek accountability evidence for the input provider; i.e., to make the input provider accountable for the input it provides. In some cases is not entirely obvious how this could be done. For instance, what if the input is a self-signed certificate? How is a receiver supposed to decide whether the signer is accountable? In other cases certificate signers are fully accountable; e.g., they would be trusted entities whose role is to notarise signatures across international boundaries. In this example, one would know exactly where the certificates originate. A protocol for accepting signed tickets and certificates, which is analogous to accepting notarized signatures across international boundaries, is described in a paper presented at the IEEE Symposium on Security and Privacy in 1992.[12]

However, even when the providers of certificates and other signed input messages are demonstrably accountable, and even trusted, they may provide conflicting evidence. For example, your vehicle may receive three messages alerting you that there is an accident at a particular location ahead of you on a highway. Two of these messages may come from ordinary vehicles and agree on the reported location. The third is from an ambulance but the reported location is different. Then you may get a message from a police car, which says that there is no accident. So now which input message do you believe? All the entities are accountable, and in fact two are trustworthy; e.g., the police car and ambulance. It may very well be that the less trustworthy entities, namely the ordinary vehicles, give you the correct information since they may have witnessed the accident. In essence one has to decide upon the accountability and trustworthiness of the entities providing conflicting inputs and resolve the conflicts using some decision procedure. In general, this is not a simple matter.

Signers of certificates and other inputs are sometimes accountable, but often this is not the case. For example, when one receives a self-signed certificate from some service, one can go to Facebook where one may find that a friend of a friend actually used this service and is quite pleased with it. One may decide

---

[12] V. D. Gligor, S.-W. Luan, and J. Pato. Inter-Realm Authentication in Large Distributed Systems. In Proc. of IEEE Symp. on Security and Privacy, Oakland, CA (1992) (also in the *Journal of Computer Security*, 1993).

that accepting the certificate should be OK because your friend doesn't lie, and if his friend lies, he loses a friendship.

Michael Roe: So friends of my friends do the most notorious malware distribution on Facebook, so this wouldn't work for me.

Reply: The operational word is "sometimes" accountable.

Bruce Christianson: And the enemy of my enemy is actually a social media friend...

Reply: Or for example, "sometimes" accountable also means that certificates can be evaluated by systems like *Perspectives*.[13] This system deploys a large number of trusted "notaries" around the Internet and gathers statistics about the use of (e.g., self-signed) certificates. Also, a example of a decision policy for accepting self-signed certificates was presented at SPW 2002.[14]

A more interesting case is when a sender has to comply with a receiver's input policies. The sender may operate in red and receiver in green, yet the untrusted sender would have to comply with the receiver's input policies. In our system this is possible because we can encapsulate the sender's code in an isolated module within the red application and since this code is penetration proof, we can ensure compliance. How to do this using isolated code modules in an otherwise untrusted commodity system is described in a recent CMU technical report on a system called Assayer.[15] This report shows that isolated code modules inside red can eliminate spam, protect against flooding attacks that choke servers, and even defend against worm spreading. One can think of these isolated modules as isolated "virtual network interface cards" in (untrusted) red network components, which can protect the network, collect network and host analytics, encapsulate network controllers, and choke off attack traffic originating in bot-infested hosts. Botnets would have a hard time circumventing the isolated code (green) modules, because bots would be unable to penetrate (green) modules inside a red machine. These examples point to the fact that the receiver cannot always "make the input right," so it has to rely on trusted code in an untrusted sender, and that unfortunately trust is not always local; i.e., sometimes one has to be able to trust isolated code inside an untrusted sender to comply with one's input policies.

One can imagine that a similar decision has to be made regarding whether to output sensitive data. However, here the decision may become more politically (i.e., policy) charged. The decision to allow output can be made by an isolated module inside green, which can act as a trusted guard, filter, or censor that decides what output is allowed. Furthermore, the green-output guard ensures

[13] D. Wendlandt, D. Andersen, and A. Perrig. Perspectives: Improving SSH-style Host Authentication with Multi-Path Probing. In Proc. of USENIX Annual Technical Conference, June (2008).

[14] L. Eschenauer, V. Gligor, and J. Baras. On Trust Establishment in Mobile Ad-Hoc Networks. In Proc. of Security Protocols Workshop, Cambridge, U.K. (2002) (also in Springer LNCS Volume 2845, 2003).

[15] B. Parno, Z. Zhou, A. Perrig. Help Me Help You: Using Trustworthy Host-Based Information in the Network. In Carnegie Mellon Technical Report CMU-CyLab-09-016, November 18, 2009.

that all its memory is scrubbed and cleaned out, so there is no *object reuse* problem. Of course, the receiver of the sender's sensitive output might not be trustworthy, but maybe accountable for mishandling the sensitive data received. However, more politically (in)correct is that the receiver of the sensitive data has to comply with the sender's output policies. Here one has policies like originator control (ORCON), whereby the sender "attaches strings" to the data sent to others. For example, the strings attached to an email account of the receiver may enforce the policy that only the receiver could read his email, but may not do anything else with it, and that in two days from now this email will disappear.

Digital rights management is another instance of "attaching strings" to sensitive green data inside red and stipulating conditions of data use; i.e., in compliance with the sender's policies. Traitor tracing schemes could, in principle, be implemented on the type of systems described here. Furthermore, there may be cases when the isolated green modules inside the red machine have to be memoryless, and to be confined so that nothing leaks in the (untrusted) red machine, which can only use the sensitive data received in some limited way specified by the policy of the green module. For instance, the data can only be used during a green-red session and it cannot be leaked to red afterwards. And, by the way, receiver compliance with senders' policies is a component of some corporate compliance regulations in the United States now. Corporations have to be able to determine where their data might be located. (This does not refer to information, which can always be leaked). If one cannot enforce a receiver's compliance with the sender's policy, it will be difficult to support such corporate regulations.

My basic message is that figuring out what trustworthy communication is and how to enforce it via security protocols is important. In fact, it seems to be a more important research topic than system and module isolation, which we already know how to do.

Jonathan Anderson: So this seems to be designed with a pretty specifically kind of rigid security policy in mind.

Reply: My first initial reaction is, no, we can offer machine partitions in the wild Internet world with no restrictions. Most of the time we will operate in red. So we only move to green on our platform, when we really need to do so.

Jonathan Anderson: Well I guess the question is just how much and what would it take to see widespread tech transfer of this into conventional systems.

Reply: Well, we'll find out next year...

Jonathan Anderson: But what are the barriers? Are they strictly technical things, like it taking 22 seconds to switch machines, or do you think there are other barriers?

Reply: The first barrier is that one has to sell the external-verifier component along with the platform, so somebody has to distribute them. And the second barrier, which is probably more challenging, is having users remember that they have to switch to green for sensitive transactions. By the way, this (external-verifier) component costs very little; its cost is negligible, so that's not an issue.

Sandy Clark: But this is about what Bruce was saying a while ago, about having to reconfigure users.

Reply: Talking about usability, notice that very minimal attention is required of the user here. All a user has to do is to remember that s/he has to switch to green when s/he has to run a sensitive transaction. The transition from green to red is easy. Because green is fairly constrained, if one tries to browse the Internet and where one wants to go is not on the list of allowed IP addresses, one would obviously get an error, so one would know that a switch to red is necessary. However, it's the other transition where users have to pay attention.

The question is, whether a 70 year old grandmother would know how to do it. The only evidence I have is actually that 70 year old grandmothers are becoming fairly sophisticated now; e.g., they know about viruses, they know that some protection is needed, they know they have to act. It is not always clear what to do, at this point, since they don't have feasible recourse if successfully attacked by malware. They can only operate in red. If we can give them only one thing they would need do, it would be to switch to green, and that presumably is not much, but we'll hopefully find out soon.

Su-Yang Yu: Would it be possible if you were running a server to be able to tell if the user is running in green or red, because then if you're running on a bank server, for instance, you could say, look you're running in red machine code, you might want to switch it green, because we don't want you to do this?

Reply: Exactly, the switch to green is both possible and verifiable by the end user. I don't even have to verify anything in some cases, I just have to switch, if I know exactly on which machine I'm running. So I can use reminders from servers, indeed. In particular, I can get a reminder from my bank, and I know this would be a green transaction, from my healthcare provider, or from my high-stake game partners.

Bruce Christianson: You can't rely on that.

Reply: You don't have to rely on that, because you can look at your device, by sticking your verifier into the machine.

Bruce Christianson: No, you can't rely on the message from your bank to get through unscathed.

Reply: But you don't have to, it's just a reminder, it's a hint, this is what I am suggesting. And if you don't believe it — and you shouldn't — just stick the verifier into your device and check. That doesn't take much. It takes only a few seconds to see if you are in the red or green machine.

Bruce Christianson: But I'm worried about malicious software stripping the hint out.

So instead of saying, you should switch to green, your bank says, it's OK to stay in red for this transaction. Because the bank server is allowed to lie. . .

Reply: Sure, so the idea is that it's not a safe input, so you would still have to switch. . .

Bruce Christianson: So you shouldn't train users to rely on hints.

Reply: Right, you have to train users to rely only on the information received from one's external verifier, but not on hints. Users would have to know that these inputs are only hints, not guarantees.

Jonathan Anderson: So outside of the use case of soldiers in the HumVs with red and green concerns and stuff, if you have the TrustVisor thing and you're able to provide strong guarantees of this bit of green code operating in the red, because it's really green code, do you think in a commodity system you'd ever actually switch into the green operating system? Or would you just say, yes, we're going to run this bit of green code?

Reply: TrustVisor does not necessarily run only in the green machines. It was implemented primarily to run these pieces of green code inside red applications, and there are lots of applications for it. I only mentioned a few applications. It's not just protecting encryption keys, by the way. Looking at the red machine, imagine that you have trusted channel (i.e., path) facilities for communicating with a green module, which encapsulates your signature key. For example, now one can implement undeniable signatures without special cryptographic protocols. You can no longer deny your signature; e.g., you can't say, my dog signed with my key, because it was only you who could have used the external device and logged in via the trusted path to the green module, and hence you are accountable now. Your signature key is protected from red, and you are the only one who can access it.

There are lots of applications in which TrustVisor protects sensitive code. The properties that this green module inside the red machine provides include data secrecy and integrity, and the integrity of code execution. For example, for a set of acceptable inputs one always gets the same valid outputs, regardless of how much malware there is in the red machine and what an unscrupulous system administrator might do. A system administrator could take your laptop apart, but this means that s/he would have to mess with your hardware. It's no longer the case that a system administrator can always get into your laptop remotely and misconfigure all your software. What he might still misconfigure would be the red part, but not necessarily the green.

Jonathan Anderson: So I guess my question is, if you have the availability of this system you could guarantee the integrity of the green code and its execution, so why not have the whole web browser run as a bit of this green code? Is it because you'd also have to put the Windows system in the server in this mode?

Reply: Yes, this would be a bit too much code for a green module. Remember that we are protecting sensitive application components, and these components have to be properly modularised. Putting a large piece of code into an isolated green module would defeat the purpose, because remember one has to make sure that all the component interfaces implement trustworthy communication, which could not be easily done in this case.

Jonathan Anderson: So running an entire Firefox system call, that would be a ridiculous thing to try to do?

Reply: Yes. You have to really be careful what you really wish to protect. One could do what you suggest, but then one's life is going to become quite complicated because one would have to implement all the additional communication controls. So one only selects green code for which one can assure trustworthy communication with the red code inside the red machine, not just across the red and green machines.

Recapitulation

Bruce Christianson

Those definitions again in full:

1. Virtual
    - (a) not real, merely apparent
    - (b) powerful, effective (vir-tus)
2. Perfect
    - (a) flawless, without blemish
    - (b) complete, lacking nothing[1]
3. Secure
    - (a) safe, unthreatened
    - (b) careless (se-cure)

---

[1] For more on this antithesis, see Jeanette Winterson, 1985, "Oranges are not the only fruit", Chapter 3.

B. Christianson and J. Malcolm (Eds.): Security Protocols 2010, LNCS 7061, p. 266, 2014.
© Springer-Verlag Berlin Heidelberg 2014

Author Index

Aloteibi, Saad   207, 214
Anderson, Jonathan   98, 107
Anderson, Ross   127, 131

Bella, Giampaolo   161
Blaze, Matt   12
Bonneau, Joseph   25, 34

Chowdhury, Partha Das   115
Christianson, Bruce   1, 45, 115, 120, 266
Clark, Sandy   12, 18
Conti, Mauro   82, 90
Crispo, Bruno   82

Danezis, George   74

Gligor, Virgil   233, 252
Gollmann, Dieter   3, 4

Hong, Theodore   54

Madhavapeddy, Anil   54
Mauw, Sjouke   175, 185

Meier, Jan   3
Mortier, Richard   54
Murray, Derek   54

Ortolani, Stefano   82

Radomirović, Saša   175
Roe, Michael   71, 191, 200
Ryan, Peter Y.A.   161, 167, 175

Schwarzkopf, Malte   54, 60
Shafarenko, Alex   45, 47
Smith, Jonathan   12
Stajano, Frank   45, 98, 127, 207

Teague, Vanessa   161

Verissimo, Paulo   217, 224

Wong, Ford Long   45

Yan, Jeff   142, 154
Yu, Su-Yang   142